Technology and Learning

Technology and Learning

Issues Vital to Address

By

Rosemary Sage and Riccarda Matteucci

BRILL

LEIDEN | BOSTON

Cover illustration: iStock.com/SeventyFour

All chapters in this book have undergone peer review.

The Library of Congress Cataloging-in-Publication Data is available online at https://catalog.loc.gov

Typeface for the Latin, Greek, and Cyrillic scripts: "Brill". See and download: brill.com/brill-typeface.

ISBN 978-90-04-68859-9 (paperback)
ISBN 978-90-04-68860-5 (hardback)
ISBN 978-90-04-68861-2 (e-book)
DOI 10.1163/9789004688612

Printed by Printforce, the Netherlands

Advance Praise for
Technology and Learning: Issues Vital to Address

"Recent events, including the COVID-19 pandemic, have sharply disclosed a need to introduce technological tools in learning to make it more efficient and user-friendly. This is becoming particularly important with the increasing use of the Internet and the proliferation of e-learning. Advancements in technology create both positive and negative effects. A good side is making our life easier and providing the teacher with effective tools for a better presentation of the discussed content. However, this poses the danger of overloading the student's mind with information, enhanced by using the Internet, iPods, and phones. Neuropsychological studies show that our brain resources are limited and we are prone to get distracted. The book aims to help teachers acquire knowledge and skills to integrate technology and teaching to make it effective for students, with content and wording tailored to the learner needs. The authors emphasise the role of creative thinking, language, and emotions in developing cognitive abilities. They also indicate that learning is an active rather than passive process and requires interaction between learners and teachers. It means not only creating a positive climate that encourages exploration but also sharing experience. Thus, training communication becomes essential here and presenting examples of how to do it is one of the book's merits. The reader can find information on how to apply robotics in learning to make this process enjoyable and teach students to interchange ideas, cope with difficulties and avoid misunderstandings. It is combining theory and practice that is the strength of the book, under four headings: Processes – Practices – Performance – Predictions."
– Bozydar Kaczmarek, Head of the Social Psychology and Neuropsychology Laboratory, University of Economics and Innovation (WSEI), Lublin

"This book is a valuable source for all those who are interested in promoting the acquisition of knowledge and skills necessary to meet real-world challenges beyond school in the era of increasing digitalisation of education. The authors draw upon cutting-edge science and contemporary research to inform the readers about the need for proper and balanced use of technology alongside tasks designed to enhance communication competence and stimulate dialogical thinking if school aims at enabling students to deal creatively and flexibly with the rapid technological and societal changes of our century."
– Tamas Rotschild, Special Education Needs Teacher, Linguist, Doctoral Researcher, Universität Bremen, Germany

To all the engineering and other students who are doing amazing things with technology to improve bone and brain surgery

Contents

PART 1
The Processes of Learning

General Perspective

What Helps or Hinders

This book is released in times of uncertainty and anxiety, regarding all activities at home, school and work, resulting from effects of the world-wide COVID-19 pandemic and the Russia-Ukraine war. Students experienced schools closing suddenly and suffered anxiety during lockdown periods, which affected motivation and learning progression. This mental disturbance still haunts them.

From the darkness, emerges this text, which answers many questions formulated during the pandemic and demonstrates the positive relationships that technology can cultivate when experts in education and engineering work together with a common objective (Yadav & Vyas, 2021).

The book reviews and analyses a tremendous educational experience with the Educational Robotics programme in Italy. This is promoted by Europole, with Stefano Cobello, heading up 4,000 agencies across the world to introduce technology in learning that uses technological advances with children and teenagers. It demonstrates how the proper use of technology promotes the development and improvement of abilities to communicate, write and discuss, in learners of all ages, at a time when many publications talk about the dramatic decrease of these capabilities – the effects produced by abuse of tablets and cell phones (Campbell, 2006; McCoy, 2013). La Scuola di Robotica in Genoa, connected with the Engineering Robotic Department of the University of Genos, is another agency leader in this field and it offers on-line courses for students, teachers and parents. It is the one who organises the Robotic competitions among schools all over Italy.

Personal and practical competencies and experiences are essential for people's social and integral growth – language, dialogue, reflection, analysis and action, in a world of increasing intelligent machines working alongside us in all aspects of life.

Language, both verbal and non-verbal, forms the basis of socialisation and the transfer of values and beliefs (Bekir et al., 2018) and before the pandemic and consequent lockdowns, there was a consensus about the negative impact of screens on the communication competencies of all ages (McCoy, 2013).

The Italian teachers maintain that it "is vital to facilitate oracy (speaking and listening) now that students communicate more by technology" (Sage, 2017). The wonderful experience of Italian schools, using robotics to promote integrated subject work, after completing a process of inter-personal dialogue and analysis, demonstrates that communication, reflection and review are essential parts of the learning process.

Present generations have more access to technology. The profile of users relates not only to the devices employed and age ranges, but also the socio-economic aspects. This aligns with a study of 64 university students at the University of Chile, regarding the use of cell phones for academic purposes, that shows an inverse relationship of financial incomes and the complex use of devices (Romero, 2022).

Presently, the pandemic has forced the widespread use of technology in education. Therefore, the effective integration of individual competencies, the use of technological devices and contributions to global knowledge are all fundamental. The book encourages responses to this new model of learning that is applied to different levels in education.

Juan Romero
University of Chile Medical School

References

Bekir, H., Bayraktar, V., & Aydin, R. (2018). Language development and support in children. In Ü. Deniz, T. Çetin, N. Obralic, V. Bayraktar, & Y. Yildirim (Eds.), *Currents trends in pre-school education – 2*. LAP Lambert Academic Publishing.

Campbell, S. (2006). Perceptions of mobile phone in college classrooms: Ringing, cheating and classroom policies. *Communication Education, 55*(3), 280–294.

McCoy, B. (2013). Digital distractions in the classroom: Student classroom use of digital devices for non class related purposes. *College of Journalism & Mass Communications: Faculty Publications, 71*. https://digitalcommons.unl.edu/journalismfacpub/71

Romero, J. (2022). *How the world is changing education*. Brill.

Sage, R. (2017). The educational context. In R. Sage (Ed.), *Paradoxes in education: Learning in a plural society* (pp. 1–9). Sense Publishers.

Yadav, S., & Vyas, C. (2021). Impact of digital technology on preschoolers: A review. *International Journal of Scientific Research in Science, 8*(2), 223–227.

Perspectives on the Complexities of Digital Innovation and Transformation

This book provides a unique and holistic view on the future of teaching, learning and assessment in a world where learning and communication technologies present ever-increasing and complex digital options for educators. Whilst these can help to enhance learning programmes in addressing the changing needs and preferences of students, educators and employers, educational institutions face numerous challenges. These apply both to *digital innovation* in curriculum design and in the *digital transformation* of the entire institution (such that "digital" is completely embedded in culture, processes, systems, capabilities and practices). Digital transformation of institutions is of course, a long and convoluted journey and some would argue that such journeys never end.

Much can be learnt about how to address challenges by reviewing and evaluating the "track records" of educational institutions. In the UK, there have been two key periods of note. The first, during the period 2000–2020, saw multi-million pounds investments by the UK Government in digital innovations and transformation of universities and further education colleges. The second was in the period of COVID lockdown, where universities had to rapidly adapt to online teaching. What happened in these two key periods is described and reviewed in Chatterton (2022).

An overarching lesson learnt from the UK Government's digital innovation and transformation programme is that universities can be highly effective at digital innovations in curriculum design, especially if programme teams are supported and resourced. However, they are overwhelmingly less effective at digital transformation i.e. institutionally embedding innovations and "digital" in processes, systems, culture, capabilities and practices. In the COVID lockdown period, when academics were forced to engage with digital learning, an overarching lesson was that significant numbers of them developed "belief" in blended learning approaches, if they were comprehensively supported in experiencing good practices in digital learning. However, this does require an "all in it together" support approach, involving academics, senior managers, professional support staff and students (see Specht et al., 2021).

Key challenges that curriculum teams face with digital innovation include the overwhelming vast range of learning and communications technologies, together with reservations (amongst some) about the changing roles and capabilities required for teaching with such tools. Workload planning, that does not recognise the time and effort needed to innovate, is another key barrier. Most importantly, curriculum teams need to develop future-proofed and flexible curricula designs so that content can be delivered in multiple, flexible ways e.g. fully online or adopting a blended format, allowing rapid and flexible responses to changing external environments and needs.

Whilst barriers exist for digital innovation, there are always a significant number of "early adopter" educators who will drive such innovations and "experiment" with emerging technologies. They typically have the motivation and wherewithal to overcome institutional challenges. However, the problems come with the "non-early adopters" (the majority) who are not so motivated nor willing to overcome organisational barriers. For instance, curriculum design and review and Quality Assurance (QA) processes and systems need to be updated to fully embrace digital innovation, ensuring that programme teams are effectively supported and resourced at critical periods of curriculum delivery. Co-ordinated and integrated approaches to data systems and management (incorporating e.g. student records, e-portfolio and virtual learning systems) need to be effected to provide tutors with real-time data for learner analytics (which can support student progression).

Institutions will, therefore, urgently need to address the deep-rooted cultural, structural, technical, management, capabilities, commercial and behavioural factors that constrain widespread adoption and innovative use of emerging technologies. This can be referred to as "digital transformation". Institutions should draw on lessons learnt from external sectors which are already well into their digital transformation journeys, as in the publishing sector. Key lessons include the need to co-align and co-evolve digital and ALL institutional strategies. We are already witnessing new business models, partnerships and services in the education sector (e.g. partnerships with private sector EdTech companies) and institutions will need to be open to such brave ideas. Ethics, values, safety and behaviours will also need to be addressed for digital learning, recognising that the digital world is an "open" one.

A significant "elephant in the room" when it comes to digital transformation is the motivation and capabilities of senior leaders. Many of these have minimal digital management and practical experience and this can make them insecure and stifle informed decision-making. Many aspiring leaders have perceived the digital agenda as a "poisoned chalice" for their career plans, due to the complexities involved, so have tended to side-step the issue. This of course, has to change and institutions need to recruit a new breed of digitally savvy leaders who have proven skills in complex environments. The role and capabilities of IT directors/CIOs (Chief Information Officers) will also need to evolve.

To-date, in the UK, digital learning has often been led and managed outside of the IT department, due to many reasons including the often poor communications and interdisciplinary working abilities of technical people. Although this is slowly changing, digital learning and IT will need to come under the same umbrella if a unified approach to learning/management systems and data and learner analytics is the goal (which it needs to be). It is not unlikely that the role of CIO will merge into a role of CCO (Chief Complexity Officer). Individuals who succeed in such a role would then be well-placed to lead the organisation.

Core to addressing the complexities of digital transformation will be to effect much improved communication and collaboration between the "generalists" and "specialists" (e.g. technical specialists and educators) and across departments. This will require new and novel approaches to professional development combined with developing an "all in it together" culture and working practices. This will all be essential to exploit emerging technologies fully and effectively as the digital world becomes increasingly pervasive. The aim should be for teaching with technology to be embedded throughout institutions (rather than just the preserve of the early adopters) and for it to become cost-effective, efficient and responsive to student, tutor and employer needs.

Peter Chatterton

References

Chatterton, P. (2022). The rise and rise of digital learning in higher education. In R. Sage & R. Matteucci (Eds.), *How world events are changing education* (pp. 177–196). Brill.

Sage, R., & Mattueccci, R. (Eds.). (2022). *How world events are changing education*. Brill.

Specht, D., Chatterton, P., Hartley, P., & Saunders, G. (2021). Developing belief in online teaching: Efficacy and digital transformation. *Journal of Perspectives in Applied Academic Practice*, 9(2), 68–76. https://doi.org/10.14297/jpaap.v9i2.486

An Educational Perspective

As far as human beings go, the tendency is to always exaggerate the importance of their own work. Conversely, we worry about claiming too much literary power. That said, this text, which expands on the book *How World Events are Changing Education* (Sage & Matteucci, 2022) is not just a set of nostrums and prejudices about how technology can sort out today's problems. The work described is underpinned by years of deep research by devoted authors with extraordinary insight and foresight into the mechanical age in which we live. The focal problem is to understand the complexities technologies pose to education and how humans and robots reach compromise. Like many others who engage with the social determinants of technology, our training in Robotics, Artificial Intelligence and Information Technology has revealed that the postmodern culture has become wholly reliant on new models and maps, so we have lost all contact with the world that preceded these changes. The term 'evidence-based technology' is used in this context to describe current efforts to ensure that technological enlightenment is based on the best scientific evidence on what does and does not work.

The research which underpins what the authors describe comes from a solid team of world renowned experts, such as those trained in Educational Robotics. The book delivers across a wide spectrum in 4 parts: Processes, Practices, Performance and Predictions, which provide an appropriate range of technology perspectives and how they influence education. Replicable methods have been used to study observable and objective outcomes. Focus is based on methods of those who have a keen eye for technology and its impact on the future. The book emphasis has come to be regarded as the quintessence of academic responsibility. In an enlightened postmodern era, technology is highly esteemed. It, therefore, could be argued that it is another 'species' of intellectual demand because the research endorses current fashionable social theories. Those who have read this text regard it as one of the most significant books of the twenty-first century and most assuredly a representation of the unique ways in which technology can question and disturb our presuppositions. The book takes a holistic approach not seen in other technology ones and readers may choose from the parts according to requirements. The four parts resonate with teachers who need more understanding of the context of technology and its universal use.

The rapid growth in technologies, particularly hand-held smart devices, means people now spend more time reading on a screen than through printed materials. Thus, scrutinising long texts is slower, more tiring and demanding than reading from paper. These negative aspects are caused by parameters like font type and size, resolution or display form, in three categories: *typographical, device-* and *user*-related factors. They produce digital vision problems, including eyes that itch, tear and are dry and red. People blink less when using a screen than when reading printed text to contribute to digital eye strain. Eyes will feel tired or uncomfortable to prevent normal focus. These problems have been increasing over the past decades. All children and adults have some symptoms if using a computer or digital device for long periods. Studies by The Nielsen Company (2012–2020), show *only* '23% of 0–17s read for pleasure', down from 26% in 2019 and 38% in 2012. The proportion of 3–4-year olds who read or look at books for fun 'daily or nearly every day' has almost halved since 2012, while reading 'rarely or never' has grown from 10% to 23% over the same time period. Technology brings flexibility but this text reminds us of the importance of understanding both the up and downsides of machines in our lives, so that we can employ them for the good of everyone. As a teacher, how technology is affecting reading habits is now disturbing. The authors have enabled the readers to gain a unique overview of the machine world, so we can use it with more awareness.

Elizabeth Negus (Dame)

Reference

The Nielsen Company. (2012–2020). *Understanding the UK children's book consumer.* Farshore (formerly Egmont UK).

A Business Perspective

Facing the Future

The COVID-19 pandemic catapulted educational institutions into using technology for student contacts and delivering teaching, to continue their studies. However, many learners found this a difficult move because they need personal, direct support of peers and tutors, with remote technology not always reliable and so frustrating users. Responses to educational experiences demonstrate that changes to the delivery of information are urgent. Today's students have been brought up in an era when general contact between people is mainly made via text or other messaging systems, so that they have learnt to process information visually better than verbally.

Teaching predominately relies on visual *and* verbal processing happening simultaneously. In face-to-face teaching, there is the possibility of constantly adjusting output to suit the audience ongoing requirements. Unlike face-to-face teaching, online webinars cannot monitor the non-verbal responses of students, such as their facial expressions, postures, and movements, so instructional presentations of information are often too fast for easy processing, although recordings make it possible to review content repeatedly. However, students complain of the many demands made of them, so in practice, reviewing recordings is not always a realistic possibility.

On-line assessments of students have become more common and are predominately the "tick-box" type for easy computer marking, but these present greater opportunities for cheating. This form of judging provides limited options from a small range of possibilities, so that superficial responses may not record the student's broader understanding of knowledge or demonstrate application in real circumstances. Tests and exams suit some participants better than others, so a broader assessment, as is available in personal portfolios of many different types of evidence, is likely to evaluate the student range more accurately and effectively. Some countries are using this method and finding that employers and universities are given a more useful idea of personal performance, by demonstrating personal and practical, as well as academic competencies.

It is for this latter reason that I developed, at the University of Buckingham, courses that were based on student ability to apply their knowledge and understanding in entrepreneurial situations. Students pitched for money and support to develop an idea for a product or service, which was an integral part of their degree. The course content sought to develop their abilities to perform in the workplace personally, practically as well as academically. In an age when experts continually discuss the disconnect between education and workplace goals and needs, these issues are of fundamental importance if we wish to progress society in a way that signals equality for the whole range of attributes demonstrated by everyone.

It is urgent that teachers, at all levels, receive initial and ongoing training that focuses not only on content but how it must be delivered to suit the array of student learning preferences and support needs. Educating others is a challenging job and has become more so within our plural societies, demonstrating different attitudes, values and ways of achieving things. We have to take account of these changes in society, which are positive in extending our thinking and experiences, but need more knowledge and comprehension of these intercultural circumstances. The Organisation for Economic Co-operation and Development (OECD), to which Britain belongs, in recent webinars has emphasised the importance of teachers researching their own context of operation, as studies indicate this is the best way to increase performance. The practitioner doctorate is an example of this practice, which is common in many countries but less so in Britain, which feels it compromises the traditional PhD qualification.

The curricula of teachers in training, as well as for students in primary, secondary, further and higher education, needs to be changed to fit the requirements of a world, where routines are more efficiently accomplished by machines and people require to be educated to think and operate at higher levels to solve the very real, complex problems of the planet, such as climate change. This means interdisciplinary teams are becoming the norm, so education must develop communication to the level that enables these networks to exchange and develop ideas together with understanding of all disciplines and their basic principles and knowledge. This requires a more general background to be cultivated in us all as well our specialist areas that are needed to provide detailed information for decision-making.

Change is always difficult and happens slowly, giving time for us all to appreciate the need to alter policy and practice and how this is best effected. The issue today is that society changes so rapidly, accelerated by technological developments and the global approach to living and working. Therefore, we must be freer, rather than fixed in our thinking, as flexibility and resilience are requirements of our modern existence. This is challenging, but worth grappling with to grasp new opportunities. This book opens up the debate and presents evidence that can help us all discuss the future and plan for it with

more confidence. It will help to stem the narrow thinking and resultant conflicts that are occurring at present. Thus, we can face the future knowing that
we are well prepared, because we have reflected on the many possibilities open
to us and are able to make the changes that are appropriate for the particular
circumstances we face.

Nigel Owen
Enterprise & Innovation Unit
University of Buckingham

Teaching for the New Industrial Age

The Europole System

This book presents effective use of new technology to assist learning. The background is given for teaching today and describes how this has developed in Italian schools, universities, robotic training courses and national competitions, where students present projects involving new technology in their educational experiences. Examining such a successful practice model is the best way to learn and improve practice. It provides inspiration and motivation.

Our new challenge is not to adapt education to technology for the industrial age but to find out how it can be suitably employed to prepare us for working with intelligent machines in the future. Also, technology enables personalised learning for those we called gifted and talented as well as others with specific learning needs. This enables improvement in the quality of education across the ability range, so that everyone can contribute their talents to the social and working needs of the society in which they live.

This is the real challenge for education today, which is one of the Nobody-less Community World Network's key strategies: How do we harmonize the industrial age needs with those of education?[1]

The European Pole of Knowledge Network[2] demonstrates an effective example of independent, free thinking in education, which helps children become future creative professionals in the most advanced technology fields, as well as promoting prosocial values. It also facilitates the learning processes suitable for the new industrial system. To achieve this goal, the Italian network provides teacher training in Educational Robotics to enhance awareness and introduce the approaches that will embed this new concept of education and fit it into a new "clean work" future strategy that is designed to improve the lives of all human beings in the world.

The robotics, in this context, provide a means of interaction within our institutional systems and act as facilitator of an harmonic collaboration between human life, individual needs, productive methods and nature. How is this possible? Educational robotics is a perfect tool to promote the integration of technology within a new concept of education with prosocial values. Any future scientific job, will be only possible if respecting natural resources and preserving them for the future. The natural environment is very important for human life, but, how do we consider the needs of technology along with the protection of the environment? How can robotics support the environment? The European Pole of Knowledge Network's work in schools has tackled this issue in three main ways:

1. Integrating three European projects with the aim of reducing the use of resources – energy and pollution.
2. Using robotics as a serious educational tool that can motivate learners to prepare effectively for the new scientific era when they must work with and alongside intelligent machines, in harmony with nature.
3. Demonstrating how robotics can help nature to regain importance and through activities with robots educate the new generation in "good technology". This respects nature, starting from an increased awareness of the origin and use of materials, like trees, and how best to employ them to enhance the world order.

Three projects, funded by the Erasmus+ European programme have formed a strategic partnership with adult education to support policy reform for social inclusion and have included a multi-discipline approach to reach this goal. An initiative, called the 3D Printer project has been promoted in primary schools with engineering support.[3] The 3D printers are using natural materials instead of plastic, which is now a serious polluter of land and sea. The Robotics versus Bullying project promotes the use of robotics to prevent an escalating social problem, as technology connections anonymize users to hugely increase mental abuse and cause emotional distress.[4] At the same time, this regular use of robotics enables programme coding to be acquired, with the prosocial values charter of the Nobodyless Network and School Plastic Free Movement project. The science in the primary schools is encouraging technology that can preserve our future life and enable time-consuming routines to be completed by machines to allow human beings to be involved in higher-level work.[5]

All these projects, that are widespread in schools across the Europole Network, are integrating the necessary technology for the industrial modern age with values preserving human identity and integrity. They enhance awareness that technology, without prosocial values, cannot facilitate the effective human transition towards a possible reasonable future for those living on our planet. Therefore, teaching cannot detach education from technology. Also, technology cannot be promoted outside of human values. The Italian experience is stimulating many countries in the world to believe in a better human future, preserving the natural environment and working for better communication and interaction between disciplines.

Stefano Cobello
National Network of Educational Institutions

Notes

1   www.nobodyless.org
2   www.europole.org
3   https://3dprint-training.com/
4   https://www.roboticavsbullismo.net
5   www.schoolplasticfreemovement.org

Preface

The COVID-19 pandemic has massively increased technology as a learning tool. Experts consider this will be a permanent change in a world of swelling populations, but increasing difficulty in supplying teachers trained to cope with diversity. Thus, the traditional face-to-face trans-missive learning approach, with a teacher in front of the class delivering information, will alter to become a "flipped" experience. Flipped learning helps teachers to prioritise active face-to-face experience by assigning materials and presentations to be viewed online by students at home or outside class. This is an exhilarating advancement, using technology to support learning in a more personal way. However, as the book indicates, online output must present information in ways that can be understood by a range of learning and linguistic styles. It must also give learners opportunities to talk and share knowledge and experiences to broaden thinking. Student surveys show that this is not yet happening. Riccarda Matteucci (author) has experienced flipped learning in America and Italy and when in Africa felt it would be a successful new way to learn when technology was more available. The psychology of cognition and communication must be understood to develop effective human information processing, with insufficient knowledge amongst users at present.

Technology refers to methods, systems and devices that result from scientific knowledge being employed for practical purposes. Terms used are robotics, referring to the intersection of science, engineering and technology that produces machines, called robots, replicating or substituting for human actions. Educational Robotics is an interdisciplinary learning environment based on the use of robots and electronic components to enhance the development of learner competencies. Artificial intelligence (AI) is another term leveraging computers and machines to mimic the problem-solving and decision-making activities of the human mind. It now produces course content, marks examinations and writes reports, as example of use in education.

There are texts that focus on technology issues. Examples are *Out of Our Minds* (Ken Robinson) – indicating that schools kill creativity and technology does not always counter this issue; *Teaching like a Pirate* (Matt Miller) making learning memorable using technology and *The Google Infused Classroom* (Holly Clark & Tanya Avrith), focusing on mental health issues from technology use. These volumes, like others, take a specific, specialist perspective and do not provide the complex context that surrounds technology use in learning, which this book presents in a generalist approach. Based on stakeholder discussions, the text considers the many ways that technology is changing

learning, to reveal issues needing attention – grouped under four parts, suggested by educators that they would like information about:

– *Processes*: defining thinking and expressive actions for learning, which must
  be understood to apply appropriate technology support successfully. Information processing is presented in general terms appropriate to audiences
  who may not have studied neurology or psychology, for considering how
  to present information effectively through computer technology. This is an
  aspect not always studied by educators or trainers.
– *Practices*: ways learning can be made effective using technology support
  (Education for Robotics programmes; Communication Opportunity Group
  Strategy). These assist thinking, communication and collaboration, which
  employers say must upgrade. Chapters show how the Polo Europa programmes provide personal and practical application of knowledge, using
  robots to solve problems and address the attributes lacking in employees.
– *Performance*: how learning is presented and experienced by students to
  grasp principles for transmitting information face-to-face or by remote
  learning technology. In order to understand learning needs, it is useful to
  reflect on teacher and student views have on the new computer way of
  learning. Surveys and interviews were conducted with these at primary, secondary and university levels to reinforce their views on present practices.
– *Predictions*: trends to integrate technology and teaching must be acknowledged to predict regulations and stan dards required for safety and accuracy. Machine intelligence for writing essays and theses, along with brain
  implants to enhance and track learning are discussed. The question of
  machine consciousness is explored. The microchip inventor has set up a
  foundation to research this, as technology could become taskmaster rather
  than human tool, if we do not develop better understanding along with
  monitoring impact.

These four parts develop technology and learning for reflective practice and
educators have intimated that this information structure would provide the
range of information needed. Processes consider information handling issues
that underpin learning and must be understood to present content through
technology modes for all learning styles. Practices look how this is working
in contexts that make educational robotics mandatory in the curriculum.
Performance targets principles behind transmitting knowledge that must be
accounted for in presentations employing technology, along with stakeholder
views. Predictions look at the future, which will demand international regulations to prevent unsuitable materials reaching users and how new technology
features will radically change the educational process.

The book progresses to provide a holistic (academic, personal & practical) picture of teaching, which acknowledges the positive power of technology to improve the world as in Education for Robotics. It takes a serious look at negative influences infiltrating learning, via technology platforms, that damage education as a force for moral progress. Aza Raskin, co-founder of the Center for Humane Technology, San Francisco, and of the Earth Species Project, has publicly apologised for social media, estimating in 2019 that it "wastes about 200,000 lifetimes per day". This figure will have escalated since. On a recent bus journey everyone was on their phone screens! Contributions from leading experts in health, education, business and politics, wish to support the book amongst contacts with their range of views and experiences for reflection.

Thus, the text is unique in providing an extensive picture of learning that now incorporates technology in both teaching, monitoring and performance assessments. The market will be policy makers and practitioners and other interested stakeholders, who acknowledge that education has reached a watershed and change is urgent and inevitable. The content presents a range of relevant background issues when considering what must be reviewed, refined, planned and implemented. There are areas, such as technology management and devices for special educational needs, mental health issues, creativity and personal learning networks, which are only briefly mentioned in the book. These are regarded as specialist topics and would benefit from detailed treatment in a text focusing just on these areas. Although primarily directed at educators and policy makers, it is valuable reading for anyone wishing to acquaint themselves with issues that technology presents for learning.

Both authors have interdisciplinary qualifications and wide experience of schools, universities and training institutes nationally and internationally, with world research and government advisory roles, focusing on improving education, language and employment performance. The text supports a multidiscipline approach to training and workplace engagement, as the Education for Robotics and Communication Opportunity Group Strategy demonstrate. Trained in these approaches to use technology effectively for learning, the authors pursue these in international projects.

The central question addressed is how we can employ technology safely and successfully to improve learning for everyone. Reports suggest a mismatch between education and work-place requirements (Sage & Matteucci, 2022). There is a lack of full understanding, which results from the way we educate people in a specialist rather than a generalist way, particularly in the UK. Chapters look at this problem in relation to technology and learning. This disconnection is of concern and the book produces a picture of reality and defines issues to be negotiated. Research evidence focuses on student and teacher responses, at all education and training levels, outlining changes envisaged for future learning. These support specific case studies in a general way. The text extends the debate in the book: *How World Events Are Changing Education* (2022) published by Brill.

Academic knowledge and practical experience enhance the experience of learning with technology, but aim to present information in a way that is understandable for those not having advanced qualifications in the neurological and psychological sciences. The goal is a holistic approach that looks at relevant cross-discipline perspectives, but not in the detail expected in a text on specific academic areas. Education is presently criticised for not focusing on applying knowledge and the personal abilities (like communication) important for the team approaches needed to solve complex world problems. A range of information enables broad reflection and aligns this with practical examples of teaching and learning to illustrate what is possible with technology assistance. This information is essential if we are to make the most of technology for developing knowledge and competencies at a higher level. Now that routines are completed by machines this frees people to work on the world's complex problems, such as climate change, environmental degradation and over population.

References

Clark, H., & Avrith, T. (2017). *The Google infused classroom*. Elevate Books.

Miller, M. (2020). *Teaching like a pirate*. Dave Burgess Consulting.

Robinson, K. (2021). *Out of our minds* (3rd ed.). Capstone Publishing.

Sage, R., & Matteucci, R. (2022). *How world events are changing education: Politics, education, social, technology*. Brill.

Background Perspectives

Technology changes education, not only because it enables remote learning, but now accomplishes routine tasks quicker and more accurately than humans. Daniel Susskind, author of *A World without Work* (2020), shows how machines are taking on tasks thought only humans could do. Moravec's Paradox (1976) observes that many things that are hard to do with our heads are easy to automate. This is why we can use machine systems to make medical diagnoses and analyse criminal evidence, but do not have robot hairdressers or gardeners. Reasoning requires little computation, but sensorimotor and perception need huge calculating resources. This idea has been explained by Hans Moravec as well as Rodney Brooks (1986, 2022), Marvin Minsky (1986), and others. Moravec (1988, p. 15) wrote: "it is comparatively easy to make computers exhibit adult level performance on intelligence tests or playing checkers and difficult or impossible to give them the skills of a one-year-old when it comes to perception and mobility". Minsky (1986) stated that the most problematic human skills to reverse engineer are below conscious awareness. "In general, we're least aware of what our minds do best. We're more aware of simple processes that don't work well than of complex ones that work flawlessly" (p. 2). Steven Pinker (1994/2007) said: "the main lesson of thirty-five years of AI research is that the hard problems are easy and the easy problems are hard" (p. 190).

Computers are now so much faster than 50 years ago and now able to handle perception and sensory skills. Moravec predicted this in 1976 and now GPT-3 creates poetry, stories and even pastiche. GPT stands for Generative Pre-trained Transformer 3 (GPT-3) and is an autoregressive language model released in 2020 that uses deep learning to produce human-like text. As routines take up to 75% of job time, employees like teachers now need more flexible abilities for new work opportunities. Intelligent machines (robots) are doing basic thinking and actions for us, so there is unease that education is not addressing the higher thought processes required for smarter roles.

The World Thinking Project, initiated by Bozydar Kaczmarek, Head of the Social Psychology and Neuropsychology Laboratory at the Lublin University of Economics and Innovation (WSEI), is collecting data across countries. In Britain, this is showing limited responses to thinking tasks, so supporting concerns (Sage & Sage, 2022). This highlights a need for more attention to thinking for better judgement and decision-making, with a world in turmoil and people unable to connect with others peacefully. Prescriptive teaching for tests focuses on fixed thinking at the expense of a free approach (Sage, 2020). The latter is what develops working values and considers possibilities to solve complex problems effectively. Thus, a book that discusses issues that help or hinder learning, in an age where technology has an increasing role, is timely. It provides knowledge and awareness to evolve strategies that encourage thinking and how it is communicated for effective learning and decisions. Face-to-face as well as remote technology teaching methods need to grabble with implementing transferable competencies with greater flexibility and resilience for tackling changing demands. This must be within a moral framework that supports safe collaboration and cooperation, which technology must develop. However, regulation is not yet keeping up with rapid developments.

Web3 is a new, open 3D-immersive internet. Built on top of the block chain, applications are augmented by decentralised products and NFTs (digital tokens), bringing new ways of how to connect, interact, work and play within a transparent, open ecosystem. We cannot escape NFTs, the Metaverse (digital interaction) and now Web3. The internet must evolve beyond the platform-based ecosystem, as we develop new technology, user privacy standards and immersive content experiences. We can predict new development impacts and understand basic functions for using them in education programmes.

NFTs are unique, irreplaceable non-fungible tokens and are part of the ethereum blockchain – a type of cryptocurrency storing extra information in the form of graphics, drawings, music or videos. The Canadian musician, Grimes, sold a 50 second NFT video for $390,000, showing how digital content can be valued like fine art. NFTs could change the game for digital content creators, who are presently undervalued, as everything belongs to platforms. Pearson (the academic book company) is turning digital texts into NFTs. Thus, the Web3 vision is positive, bringing power back to people, in a digital space available to all. People can communicate and create without limitations, censorship or corporation interference. Web1.0 was "read-only", featuring webpage-focused content and cookie-based user tracking. The interactive, application-based Web 2.0 had content focused on logged-user IDs – evolving into social media and e-commerce. Web3 is personalised experience, giving users data ownership, employing blockchain technology and identifiers for control. Apple's Siri has Web3 technology, voice-recognition software.

A meme posted by an artist, "Love in The Time of Web3" – depicted a cartoon couple in bed gazing at Bitcoin and Ethereum prices. Elon Musk (the technology business magnate) reposted it on Twitter, gaining thousands of likes, enabling the artist to turn the meme into an NFT and sell it for $20,000. Thus, the Metaverse is the future of digital interaction, merging virtual and physical worlds. It is already impacting on education, providing virtual training opportunities for medics, educators and other professionals, so that they can observe what is happening in operating theatres, clinics and classrooms, etc. Presently,

Metaverse is owned by big platforms like Meta, Google and large gaming companies, but hopefully will be supported soon by Web3. As we adopt virtual and physical experiences, our education, leisure pursuits, live selling events and virtual product tries will be the way we operate. We can never be sure what the future holds, but are excited by evolving creativity, communication and technology. An open mind is the only way for new things to evolve, with education hopefully giving us judgement to implement them safely and wisely!

How technology can integrate into content teaching has been described in a model structure – the Technological Pedagogical Content Knowledge (TPACK).[1] The knowledge domains include: technology (TK), content (CK), pedagogical (PK), pedagogical content (PCK), technological content (TCK), technological pedagogical (TPK) and technological pedagogical content (TPCK. This model attempts to identify the nature of knowledge needed by educators for using technology in teaching, as well as addressing the complex, multifaceted nature of understanding. It is based on work of Shulman, Professor of Psychology at Stanford, USA – emphasising communication, comprehension & reasoning as learning priority (1986).

TPACK has been criticised for an imprecise definition of the structure. Other variations are proposed (TPACK-W for web technologies, G-TPACK for geospatial, TPACK-CT for computational thinking, TPAACK-P for practical, etc.). Practically, it is difficult to implement and assess adequately – lacking the exact strategies of how to develop this in teaching. It must be understood there is no coherent theory of technology and learning, as different cultures and educational systems operate in varying national contexts to evolve many modes of learning. Therefore, the book does not suggest a suitable model, in line with this situation. It hopes to provide a range of relevant ideas that are adaptable to all teaching/training contexts rather than an ideal pedagogy only of use in certain settings.

Peter Chatterton (2022), a world expert on technology and education, provides evidence to show that teachers and lecturers do not have the knowledge or experience to use technology in the most effective way. He advocates more attention to this process in initial training and professional development and provides ideas in this book. The text is a response to this situation and provides the range of necessary information in parts that cover relevant material.

Note

1   Available from http://matt-koehler.com/tpack2/hello-world/

References

Brooks, R. (1986). *Intelligence without representation.* MIT Artificial Intelligence Laboratory.

Brooks, R. (2002). *Flesh and machines.* Pantheon Books.

Chatterton, P. (2022). The rise and rise of digital learning in higher education. In R. Sage & R. Matteucci (Eds.), *How the world is changing education* (pp. 177–196). Brill.

Minsky, M. (1986). *The society of mind.* Simon & Schuster.

Moravac, H. (1976). *The role of raw power in intelligence.* exhibits.stanford.edu/ai/catalog/ws563scl6050

Moravec, H. (1988). *Mind children.* Harvard University Press.

Pinker, S. (2007). *The language instinct.* Harper. (Original work published 1994)

Shulman, L. (1986). Those who understand: Knowledge growth in teaching. *Educational Researcher, 15*(2), 4–14. http://www.jstor.org/stable/1175860

Sage, R. (2020). *Speechless: Issues for education.* University of Buckingham Press.

Sage, R., & Sage, L. (2020). *A thinking and language analysis of primary age children in four schools* [Report]. The Learning for Life Trust.

Susskind, D. (2020). *A world without work: Technology, automation and how we should respond.* Allen Lane.

Figures and Tables

Figures

Tables

Prologue

Rosemary Sage and Riccarda Matteucci

The book unpicks matters emerging from increased technology uses in learning, which have major impact on thinking and expression. Technology refers to tools and machines for solving real-world problems and assists more flexible learning. Discussions with educators indicate that issues may be grouped under four parts, providing a simple structure for chapter content:

- *Processes*: defining thinking and expression for learning, which must be understood to apply appropriate technology tools successfully to improve performance.
- *Practices*: ways learning can be made effective using technology support, as in the international Education for Robotics programmes in schools and colleges. These assist thinking, communication and collaboration, which employers say must upgrade.
- *Performance*: how learning is presented and students experience this to grasp principles for transmitting information face-to-face or by remote learning technology.
- *Predictions*: present trends to integrate technology and teaching and must be reckoned with to compile regulations and standards required for safety and accuracy.

Do you feel zoomed out from on-line lectures, webinars and meetings that have become practice in the COVID-19 pandemic? These are likely to become a permanent feature of interaction although face-to-face exchanges, with more non-verbal context to support meaning, are vital for full understanding. Direct contact allows educators to alter presentations to audience needs from immediate feedback to what is said or seen. Research indicates that 93% of affective meaning comes from non-verbal communication (vocal dynamics, facial expressions, postures, movements, manner, content, etc.) with online voice delivery lacking the range of direct communication because of less personal stimulus over distance (Sage, 2020). This needs more acknowledgement.

Have you been confused over which buttons to press and exasperated when sound fades and the screen picture wobbles and disappears? Maybe you have been distracted by the amazing backgrounds behind presenters? It is good to see how many bookcases abound, but frightening to see our own faces grin and grimace back at us!

© ROSEMARY SAGE AND RICCARDA MATTEUCCI, 2024 | DOI:10.1163/9789004688612_001

Learning is the process of acquiring new knowledge and abilities, with education as the organising system in a traditional face-to-face-mode with teachers mainly delivering content in monologue style and students listening and absorbing it (trans-missive learning). This has been turned upside down by the pandemic, with technology delivering learning remotely, through visual and auditory sense channels and non-verbal communication much reduced on screens (Sage, 2020). Digital networking is radically changing education with audio-visual inputs the main sensory routes transmitting knowledge. This mode enables flexible, scalable media systems controllable from custom interfaces. Networked designs, designed by technology experts at a UK university, were the first to use an early "flipped learning approach" called dual teaching (Sage, 2003). This could comprise many physical locations, whilst providing web-based, multi-site control and monitoring to any part.

Education has been put under the microscope. It is the means of gaining a good job, which now requires technical know-how, but is more than this, as it should expand not only capabilities, like communicating thinking, but also consciousness, cultural understanding, sensitivities and values determining actions. This personal, social education role is vital to prepare for collaborative higher-level work now intelligent machines take care of routines. Employer reports stress urgent attention to these issues, which are often lacking in staff. Steven Pinker (2021), in his book on rationality, explains why this is scarce. As it is not part of our educational curricula, we have a "pandemic of poppycock". Educational Robotics, as the chapters show, aim to bridge the education-work divide.

Pursuit of self-interest and sectarian solidarity cripple rationality. Responding to this, The California Healthy Minds Thriving Kids Project has made a video: Understanding Thoughts, linking these with values, feelings and behaviour. Thinking depends on values and feelings, but what do these mean? Value-graphics, the global research company, from 500,000 surveys across 152 languages, revealed what people thought and felt about values (2022). Financial security, freedom of speech and leisure were top responses. These are not values but things we care and have strong feelings about, which alter according to circumstances. As example, while writing this, a dog is barking madly, so peace and quiet is what is valued (cared about)! Values are more progressive attributes than simply reactions to immediacy. They are what a person wants to be, but if removable is not your value.

Freedom of speech is valuable, but under an oppressive government, workplace or technology provider it can be taken away. Thus, freedom of speech is not a value, but a thing valued. Honesty, in contrast, is something owned and a cross-cultural core value. One can choose to be truthful or lie to people. If frank, one is living according to the value of honesty. Why is this distinction

important? Values are central to human success. We need to define and understand them to live with integrity, using technology tools ethically for learning,
which is not happening because of no proper regulation over dangerous content. In monocultures, there are more shared values than in plural ones, where
conflicting ones exist. These must be acknowledged, as they bring moral problems when employing technology – demonstrated in the book chapters.

When defining values as attributes of the people we want to be, steps for
moving forward are clearer. Care about learners is a feeling not an action.
What is actionable is determination to teach them well. We can consider what
it means and strive to live up to the ideal by taking measures. This might be
studying the psychology of learning, which technology enables us to do flexibly
and remotely to suit circumstances. Thus, there is a difference between things
you value and your actual values upheld by actions. Technology for education
must develop core agreed values in both policy and practice regulations. This
is not happening presently, to cause problems for learning. Below are 20 values
a psychology group came up with to consider misunderstanding of values as
things rather than attributes, with social media supporting confusions:

1.   altruism
2.   appreciation
3.   attentiveness
4.   compassion
5.   courage
6.   determination
7.   empathy
8.   equanimity
9.   generosity
10. honesty
11. humility
12. integrity
13. kindness
14. loyalty
15. resilience
16. self-determination
17. selflessness
18. spirituality
19. tolerance
20. trustworthiness

Technology platforms commonly attack others with different values to ones
you hold. In remote mode, it is easy to strengthen the zeal of your base by using
more aggressive, divisive language than would occur in a face-to-face context.

Ofcom figures show 95% of British teenagers are on social media platforms, which Harry de Quetteville (2021) says "produces a blanket of camaraderie that smothers clear thinking". This is like the dystopian "double-think" of George Orwell's 1984. To know and not to know is to be conscious of truth, whilst telling carefully constructed lies which social media encourages to sell social justice. This virtue-signalling is not only wrong but evil and alienating. The action or practice of publicly expressing opinions or sentiments to demonstrate the moral correctness of one's position on an issue is now consisting of hate things, which technology spreads world-wide with no effective barrier to prevent abuse.

Impartiality is a concept people do not understand. Bullying is conducted consistently on emails, texts and social media to cost England £18 billion annually in reduced productivity, according to the Advisory, Conciliation and Arbitration Service (ACAS). Also, hours spent online isolate people, with 72% of the population now feeling lonely according to the Centre for Social Justice, with 85% of young people judging this as relevant for their future in education and training. Values guide learning, to provide a measure of progress. Failure is not living by moral values and success is taking daily action to personify them. We are constantly subverted by media sources to prevent rationality and social justice. The book opens with a discussion of consciousness and why thinking is warped and how to deal with it, before examining practice and performance and ending with predicted operations to meet changes.

References

de Quetteville, H. (2021, October 12). Blinded by groupthink – Why does it keep happening? *The Telegraph.* https://www.telegraph.co.uk/news/2021/10/12/blinded-groupthink-does-keep-happening-anything-can-do-stop/

Pinker, S. (2021). *Rationality: What it is, why it seems scare, why it matters.* Penguin Books.

Sage, R. (2003). *Lend us your ears: Listen & learn.* Bloomsbury.

Sage, R. (2020). *Speechless: Issues for education.* University of Buckingham Press.

Value Graphics Research Company. (2022). *Human values are now a predictive business insight.* https://valuegraphics.com

1   Technology Issues

The recent pandemic pushed us all to play with screens and keep teaching and learning going during lockdowns. According to American, Canadian and

British surveys, only 8% of students feel that online learning is effective for them (Sage & Matteucci, 2022; Siemens et al., 2015, Chapter 9). Not only are there issues about equality of access to suitable, reliable online resources, but also many students find the largely visual and verbal screen input insufficient for easy comprehension. Around 40% of us really only understand well when learning happens actively face-to-face, providing immediate non-verbal support and help as required We rely on class-mates to talk through learning matters and perhaps clarify muddles. Without this backup it is easy to lose motivation and get distracted by other events around us (Sage, 2003).

Nevertheless, on-line learning offers flexibility regarding time and space. Recordings allow students to plough through content at leisure and repeat it until confident about understanding and retaining information. This independent learning requires self-talk that comes from narrative speaking ability. Those with specific needs can have input designed by specialists to address them. Technology has been especially useful for teaching languages and for supporting learners with communication difficulties. There are strong calls for using e-portfolio evidence of student personal, practical as well as academic experiences, rather than just examination results or research reports, which give a limited picture of performance. Employers find numbers and grades unreliable for assessing work potential, as they fail to reflect conduct in real situations. Sophisticated cheating, increasing world-wide, employs technical devices, with bosses commenting that many graduates do not perform at degree level. This supports the personal e-portfolio record as the most dependable assessment (Sage, 2020). Technology enables it to be presented for various purposes, like a qualification or job interview. Thus technology tools provide means for storing and sharing broader audio-visual, graphic and written personal evidence for nations and institutions valuing this assessment mode.

2   Technology Warnings

Billions of pounds are poured into technology worldwide, with warnings that a third of existing work roles will be automated by 2030 and all human jobs automated in the next 120 years. A World Economic Forum report (2021) said that 85 million jobs will be replaced by artificial intelligence (AI) by 2025. Thus, people must be retooled with higher-level competencies, particularly processing, thinking and expression. This is needed to communicate more widely and deeply with colleagues for the greater inter-disciplinary engagement envisaged for tackling complex world problems.

Education is key to confronting the resignation felt by everyone left to languish underinvested, without the flexible competencies needed for present work. Inventions, like the robot Flippy, which makes meals for the American White Castle chain, have slashed staff costs dramatically now that machines control kitchens to reduce need for human labour. A new artificial intelligence machine tool detects heart disease in 20 seconds, providing more knowledge and greater accuracy in a fraction of the time it takes a doctor, to reduce reliance on human expertise.

Big tech giants should take responsibility and acknowledge the impact their creations are having on life. FACEBOOK must find its moral compass and protect the young in its new "METAVERSE", which allows entry to a virtual world. The Children's Commissioner for England has reported that 13 year-olds now enter virtual strip clubs, where they are encouraged to get naked and do erotic role play. METAVERSE is not secure by design in spite of first-class engineers existing with ability to create safe spaces.

The late Professor Stephen Hawking, speaking at The Royal Society in London ahead of the Starmus IV Festival (2017), said humanity may have created its own nemesis. Computer power doubles annually and technologists talk about Singularity - the point at which the combined networked computing power of world AI systems begins a massive increase in capability – an explosion of machine intelligence. We will then have handed over control of vital systems, from food distribution networks to power plants, sewage and water treatment works, as well as global banking. Could these machines bring us to our knees? Sceptics point out that the cleverest computers are no more intelligent than a cockroach and will not want to destroy the planet. However, the man versus machine battle, as in the Terminator films, could be a distinct probability.

3   **The Wider Context**

> It is in truth not for glory, nor riches, nor honours that we are fighting, but for freedom, for that alone, which no honest man gives up but with his life. (The 1320 Arbroath Declaration)

We are told the arc of history bends towards justice, but the 2022 Russian invasion of Ukraine shows civilisation is on shifting sands. Progress is powerful, but is it a delusion? The German word "verschlimmbesserung", meaning improvement that makes things worse, is quoted in relation to technology effects on learning and behaviour. We are stung by our complacency. The traditional truths – that security relies on strength and freedom on force, with laws and power to uphold them – are ignored. Whatever progress has been made with technology, human knowledge and commerce, the views, values and interests clashing between national, ethnic, religious and specific interest groups, seem unavoidable. Events show the domination of technology that makes conflicts more dangerous and violent, by discouraging multiple thinking. Consider how internet technologies control populations, persecute people and steal industrial and security secrets. We have faced the consequences of what social media allows to happen in terms of radicalisation and recruitment of young people by organisations aiming to destabilise societies.

Economists, sociologists, writers, researchers and journalists have recognised that global technological interconnectedness was supposed to make the world safer, presuming that nations trading with one another would not fight together. However, they highlight that open societies and economies are presently being exploited by more closed ones, to corrupt and weaken them, whilst empowering and enriching those behind such movements. The media show that criminals committing sophisticated cyber-crimes and organising child abuse undermine democratic processes to result in demonic ones. Politicians, officials, lawyers, accountants and other leading professionals are scrutinised, because they facilitate these activities, even if unwittingly. Freedom of speech, property rights and rule of law, essential for effective learning and advancement, have been exploited and because of revenues raised we have turned a blind eye.

Universities have been economically supported by powers that now have vital data from our knowledge base and infrastructure. Elites play identity politics, manipulate the press and hire expensive lawyers to shut down scrutiny. It is common to read that pliable idiots and naive politicians do the extremists' work for them. Therefore, it is vital to stop those using free societies to divide against themselves. Leaders are encountered, who do not show enough strength when needed, so causing division and destabilisation. There is a view that the West prefers tweeting rather than fighting for what matters and that we have taken freedom for granted and indulged in meaningless identity politics that only serve to polarise communities and embolden enemies. Globalism – the masterminding of interdependence between nations of different historical traditions and development stages – was thought to bring an end to historical enmities and produce civilisation. Winston Churchill, in a Bristol University lecture (1938) defined this as society based upon resident opinions. Thus, despotic rule gives way to parliamentary laws and courts of justice to maintain order and dispel riots and tyranny. Today, democratic dreams give way to unchecked technology platform dictatorship. Democracy is retreating, along with neighbourliness and people respect, to restrict learning needs, like a broad, balanced curriculum offering multiplicity of thought. Democracy Index, Freedom House and the Economist Intelligence Unit tell this same story.

Among technology issues, there is urgent need to educate for a greater range of personal and practical competencies. People must be appraised about reality and dangers of unregulated fake news promoted by technology outlets. Sociologists affirm that for society wellbeing, leaders will need to re-programme themselves psychologically and economically to keep people safe, along with encouraging flexible knowledge and competencies to cope with world changes. Also, experts maintain that people require clear thinking, good manners, respect, accurate use of communication and loyalty to communities, plus knowledge to survive successfully. Are social media technology platforms promoting these qualities? It appears not enough, so the education role is more than ever fundamental.

Agreement is needed about technology regulations and standards, reflecting core moral values, to mitigate against present community tensions arising from global connectivity. History is our best teacher and we need to become more determined and resilient to plan for the future. The book heightens awareness of issues seldom properly regarded and addresses these for a safer future in which technology can successfully promote accurate learning. This must encourages and respects different viewpoints.

4 Content

The book begins by breaking news that introduces the new Chat facility that uses language models to quickly produce information that not only provides ideas but writes reports and puts together information in seconds from user instructions. It then looks at consciousness, thinking, language and technology, as now machines undertake routines there is need to develop higher mental processes and the words expressing thoughts. A programme of Educational Robotics, taught in countries like Italy, prepares students for life and work, using technology to learn necessary knowledge and personal-practical competencies for solving community problems. Increasingly, technology is taking over time consuming activities, like crime analysis, medical diagnostics and examination marking. Thus, using it in schools and colleges, in the way expected for workplaces, means students can hit the ground running when starting jobs. Chapters investigate teaching and technology issues, like information processing styles and preferences, along with our responses to machines and downsides of on-line connections leading to fake news, bullying behaviour and distorted values. Ways to give effective performances, using technology and how people can be supported in times of change are discussed. The final section and epilogue assesses the future with the brain machine interface (BMI) that plugs into the cortex (brain grey matter) and connects to the digital world. It enables humans to control devices, tap into global knowledge and communicate with each other by thoughts alone. This gives an opportunity to change the world, but with everything new there are downsides which the book spells out clearly. The idea is that readers, having gained awareness and understanding, can go away with a positive feeling about the future of intelligent machines in their lives.

The following need to be considered when using technology to assist learning:

1. Language for presenting online materials, as programmes introduced from other countries may use words to mean differently. Digital simulations and models may be difficult for students to understand the concepts.

2. There is more interpersonal collaboration and communication expected in models, such as flipped learning, which demand effective narrative levels of communication.

3. Technology changes very rapidly so continual training is necessary for both students and their educators to understand clearly the positive and negative aspects of developments.

4. Education is opened up with a chance to be more flexible with learning and proceed at one's own pace. However, this needs close monitoring by staff to make sure everyone is coping successfully.

5. Assessment needs to change for greater accuracy of performance, with online personal portfolios now enabling a wide range of assessment possibilities that can suit the diversity of students.

6. Learning can be more fun and realistic especially now 3D technology allows this, but it is expensive and adds to economic pressures on institutions. Presently, many online assessments include various statements to choose for a tick box answer, but these need a face-to-face follow up to achieve real understanding by sharing perspectives. Flipped learning models can achieve this.

To Clarify – This Book Has a Generalist Rather Than a Specialist Approach...

– Selects pertinent issues for learning with technology (e.g. information processing)
– 8 contributors from diverse backgrounds focus on various perspectives to provide reflection

- Uses a structure educators have suggested- processes, practices, performances, prediction
- Gives examples of effective teaching with technology, such as Educational Robotics
- Wide knowledge not a theory of technology & learning is needed for plural societies
- Aims for reflection to review and refine practice relevant to specific working context

The book is suitable for a range of readers. Chapter 1 shows how technology is requiring us to think and communicate better. Chapter 2 gives a general view of learning and remote input using technology. Chapter 3 helps parents and teachers to become aware of what is needed to achieve successful learning for those who find limited technology input problematic. Chapter 4 describes the education for robotics international programme and 5 gives a description of complex systems. Chapter 6 considers technology errors and consequences, whilst Chapter 7 looks further at how technology can be used for effective performances. Chapter 8 reviews experiences of teachers and students regarding new approaches to processing information. Changes in communication from using technology is Chapter 9 content, while Chapter 10 predicts that teaching must focus on a more generalist approach to cope with a need for flexibility in a machine dominated world. Chapter 11 considers how humans and machines will evolve. Chapter 12 discusses how to cope with the new technology and the changes envisaged while chapter on ChatGPT gives an example with the ChatGPT language models. Finally the book summarises the main book messages and looks into the future of human brains connecting with computers for greater performance. The content should appeal to a wide range of education stakeholders, who are dedicated to making technology experiences valuable for everyone.

References

Sage, R. (2004). *Inclusion in Schools*. Bloomsbury.

Sage, R. (2020). The role of higher education in developing policy and practice for the development of the new industrial age. *Journal of Higher Education Policy and Leadership Studies, 1*(1), 64–76.

Sage, R., & Matteucci, R. (2022). *How world events are changing education*. Brill.

Siemens, G., Gašević, D., & Dawson, S. (2015). *Preparing for the digital university: A review of the history and current state of distance, blended, and online learning*. Athabasca University. http://linkresearchlab.org/PreparingDigitalUniversity.pdf

Laying the Groundwork
The Issue of Consciousness

Riccarda Matteucci

Abstract

This chapter results from present study on consciousness. Federico Faggin, the inventor of the microchip, wrote a section on this in the book I co-edited, *The Robots Are Here* (Sage & Matteucci, 2019). He believes that, according to present scientific knowledge, it is impossible to use robots in all human roles. In his latest book, *Irriducibile: La coscienza, la vita, i computer e la nostra natura* (2022), Faggin presents the technological and natural world along with human beings, employing scientific rigour and his vision of new possible connections from our increased knowledge of mental functioning. Faggin's views result from more than 30 years of research. He explains humans as *irriducibile* (incapable of being reduced or of being diminished or simplified further) as no machine will be able to substitute for all their abilities, such as what has been endowed from genetic inheritance. His explanations make sense to my humanistic mind and allow us to consider what is beyond our physical human bodies.

An opposite view is offered by Antonio Damasio's latest publication, *Feeling & Knowing: Making Minds Conscious* (2021). Damasio sheds light on the many aspects of consciousness to help us understand the relation between mind, intelligence and consciousness. Reviews consider it an authoritative text, based on scientific discoveries that explain a variety of views. Many philosophers, cognitive scientists, engineers and other investigators have been convinced that the question of consciousness was impossible to answer. Along with other prominent scientists, including Stuart Hameroff, David Chalmers, Christof Koch, Bernard Baars, Roger Penrose and Benjamin Libet, Damasio is convinced that recent biology, neuroscience, psychology and artificial intelligence (AI) findings are illuminating intelligence.[1] His research has transformed brain understanding and human behaviour regarding the development of consciousness. Being conscious is neither being awake nor sensing. *Feeling* and *knowing* explain human capacity for informing and transforming experience and perceiving the world. His thesis is of an evolved unified body and mind, but scientific explanations differ. These views are examined as a prerequisite for considering technology.

∙ ∙ ∙

Is It a Long Way to Go or Has It Been There Since the Beginning?

∵

Hoc erat in principio apud Deum. Omnia per ipsum facta sunt: sine ipso factum est nihil, quod factum est: in ipso vita erat, et via erat lux hominum: et lux in tenebris lucet, et tenebrae eam non comprehenderunt.

In the beginning was the Word, and the Word was with God, and the Word was God. He was with God in the beginning. Through him all things were made; without him nothing was made that has been made. In him was life, and life was the light of all mankind. The light shines in the darkness, and the darkness has not overcome it.

Gv1,1Ἐν ἀρχῇ ἦν ὁ λόγος, καὶ ὁ λόγος ἦν πρὸς τὸν θεόν, καὶ θεὸς ἦν ὁ λόγος. Gv1,2οὗτος ἦν ἐν ἀρχῇ πρὸς τὸν θεόν. Gv1,3πάντα δι' αὐτοῦ ἐγένετο, καὶ χωρὶς αὐτοῦ ἐγένετο οὐδὲ ἕν. ὃ γέγονεν.

Gv1,4ἐν αὐτῷ ζωὴ ἦν, καὶ ἡ ζωὴ ἦν τὸ φῶς τῶν ἀνθρώπων·

Gv1,5καὶ τὸ φῶς ἐν τῇ σκοτίᾳ φαίνει, καὶ ἡ σκοτία αὐτὸ οὐ κατέλαβεν. (John 1:1–5 NIV)

1   Introduction

Damasio (2021) says it is impossible to understand consciousness and its development without reference to biology, psychology and neuroscience, which address questions on intelligence and mind. Researchers from many fields approach the phenomenon with varying methods and explain it differently. For most of them, consciousness is a mental experience, when contents are felt from a singular perspective. Further analysis shows that self, subject and organism lead to the reality of "ownership", meaning that any organism possesses a particular mind. To understand this, we need to possess a clear meaning of mind, perspective and feeling, which the book explains.

Starting with bacteria, these numerous, living, earth organisms are unicellular. Are they intelligent? Yes. Have they a mind? No. Nor do they have consciousness, though demonstrating cognition in relation to their environment. They rely on "non-explicit competencies" based on molecular and sub-molecular processes (Damasio, 2021, p. 5). Their lives are governed by rules of homeostasis.[2]

Addressing the same questions to humans: "Do we have minds and only these?" No, Damasio affirms. Humans have minds where sensory representations, called images, are generated, but they also possess non-explicit competencies that simpler organisms employ. We are governed by two kinds of intelligence and cognition types. One, studied and investigated for longer, is based on reasoning and creativity – depending on using explicit patterns of information, recognised as images. The other non-explicit competence, present in bacteria, is considered an intelligence type. Living organisms rely on this competence – hidden to mental inspection.

The other issue to consider is ability to feel. How can we feel pleasure and pain, sickness, well-being, happiness or sadness? It is proposed that our brain allows us to feel, implying mechanisms that exist behind given feelings. Damasio wants to investigate these mechanisms, not from a chemical and neural viewpoint, but to shed light on how we "experience in the mind", a process in the "physical realm of the body" (2021, p. 6). He believes that the nervous system, through neuron activity, is not the only one achieving this remarkable transition. Two observations are made. One, based on the activity of the interoceptive nervous system, is responsible for signalling from body to brain. This explains the combination of body and neuro signals that contribute to experiencing physique. The other concerns the relationship and interaction between the body, the nervous system and the brain.

The external world is transmitted to our nervous systems, with feelings that not only convey conventional perceptions of the physique, but also body and brain hybrids. This may explain the distinction, but not the opposition between feeling and reason, that humans are "feeling creatures who think and thinking creatures who feel". They possess explicit and non-explicit intelligences and use feelings and reason, separately or combined. Damasio questions how the brain provides us with mental experiences that are clearly related to our beings and ourselves. He uses introspection for a direct view into the phenomena and reports on the observation. Nowadays, results are backed up and enriched with other methods that investigate mental phenomena from other viewpoints, such as focusing on behavioural displays and psychochemical, biological, neurophysiological and social aspects.

There is no other way of proceeding, though experts complain about the flaws inherent in self-observation with its obvious limits. Damasio advises that facts analysed in this way need cautious interpretation, as they present varied aspects that can fit different theories. Complex mental phenomena require space to be located in a specific area, as they have no consistent scientific recognition and must be considered as hypothesis.

Faggin presents an alternative viewpoint, referring to his latest publication, *Irriducibile* (2022), with a different explanation. This Italian physicist, the inventor of Intel 4004, a 4-bit central processing unit (CPU), the core device of all computer technology, has revolutionised life. In *Irriducibile*, he values our interior world and spirituality that enables collaboration and cooperation for life progression. Such attributes counter today's materialistic goals, leading to competition, aggression and rationalism that divide humans and make them unhappy. Faggin is a unique character, with such a life experience and so admired by everyone that it is difficult to find people who do not share such feelings towards him.

His interest in consciousness started when developing artificial neural networks, in his company, to create systems that could learn by themselves. Nobody believed in such a novelty that would prove fundamental for future applications such as the iPad, the touchscreen, etc. In 2011, with his wife, he founded the Federico and Elvia Faggin Foundation, dedicated to supporting research into the nature of consciousness and its origin.

Neuroscience and biology rarely mention consciousness. Faggin felt that it cannot be the same as electrical or biochemical signals, questioning: "How can we go from electrical signals to feelings? What would it take to make a conscious computer?"

Although successful, rich and famous, sustained by a healthy family, Faggin was unhappy for no reason. While trying to understand the nature of consciousness, he faced two problems: one scientific and the other how to deal with a deep inner feeling. At his home, on Lake Tahoe, he experienced love and unity. Waking one night, he was overwhelmed by a strong, powerful love, an energy both dazzling white and self-knowing, and coming from inside himself. Faggin felt an explosion of energy, believing that everything is "made" of that same love. It was mind-blowing because he had viewed himself as separate from the objects of observations. He relates this experience as being both the observer and the observed. This changed his life and he came to think that there is more to reality and that he wanted to understand consciousness, which can only be done by actually experiencing it.

In recent decades, Faggin has undertaken many experiences trying to give shape and boundaries to consciousness that must be fundamental, but cannot happen inside the brain. It is what creates brains, which is now the crux of his research. The result is that, along with the Italian quantum physicist Giacomo

Mauro D'Ariano, Faggin has developed a new physical model of reality in which consciousness, not matter, is seen as the basic principle of existence.

The book records his journey from basic, practical activities to advanced scientific practice and now to investigating the spiritual sphere. He describes consciousness as a quantum phenomenon that is an alternative to classic physics, one that opens perspectives to be explored and researched in more holistic, deeper ways. He believes that consciousness moves everything in the universe and is the inner force making our reality unique, exceptional and singular.

The description of his theory unfolds along the way in a journey that helps us to understand what makes us human: how to trust our intuition, to use free will and human agency and to move beyond a materialist vision of life. Faggin calls our creator the "One" who has shaped the world for better knowledge of "self". We need to be careful, though, because we cannot confuse the uniqueness of human life when compared to artificial intelligence (AI), epitomised in robots. We are different from machines because our genetic history and lived experience in comparison to AI are products of our intelligence and creativity and controlled by us.

Faggin affirms that if we want to unify physics it is necessary to abandon the status quo and present a fresh vision. New concepts arise from a "field and law" very different from the materialistic one. From a logical point of view, how can free will, consciousness and life be viewed as subsets in "no-animated" matter? How can freedom derive from a "no-freedom" state? The same happens for consciousness: How can it generate from "no-basis"? Life from "no-life"? There is no logic to thinking that a more general property could emerge from one that does not contain it. We need to consider the emergence of a much more profound reality, ignored until recently, from the physical one we acknowledge.

In *Irriducibile*, Faggin speaks of "bit", "qubit", "seity", "QIP", "One", "entanglement", "qualia", "panpsychism", "human agency" and many other concepts to make readers understand how his journey has developed. These ideas are defined in the second part of the chapter. Once again, Faggin astonishes the readers with this book addressed to people who want to be compassionate, ethical and responsible.

2 When Did This Start and How?

> "In the beginning was not the word; that much is clear…. Life sailed forth without words or thoughts, without feelings and reason, devoid of minds or consciousness", announces Damasio to explain creation (referring to John 1:1–5). (2021, p. 31, Figure 1)

Protocells	4 billion years
First cells (prokaryotes – like bacteria without nucleus)	3.8 billion years
Photosynthesis	3.5 billion years
First single cells with a nucleus (eukaryotes)	2 billion years
First multicellular organisms	7–600 million years
First nervous cells	500 million years
Fish	5–400 million years
Plants	470 million years
Mammals	200 million years
Primates	75 million years
Birds	60 million years
Hominids	14–12 million years
Homo sapiens	300 thousand years

FIGURE 1   A calendar of life (Source: Damasio, 2021, p. 31)

Living organisms began four billion years ago. Damasio imagines development in three distinct consecutive stages: *being*, *feeling* and *knowing*, but he does not say how protocells originated. Furthermore, these steps must be based on evaluations of parameters needing precise calculi (we have faith they are so).

The simplest living organisms, formed by one or few cells, are born and live till death from old age, disease or destruction by other creatures. They do not have a nervous system and lack premeditation, reflection and a mind illuminated by consciousness. They survive because of efficient chemical and physical processes, guided by hidden competencies in tune with homeostatic rules. The process has elementary cognition, manifested by "sensing" obstacles or estimating other organisms in their environment. They are able to live a good life, capable of surviving threats, while respecting reality. Such pseudo-simple creatures, identified as bacteria, can live as a social group in the wild. All living organisms possess the ability to sense and detect sensory stimuli: light, heat, cold, vibrations or a stab. Organisms can respond to their context or their body's interior, as defined by the cellular membrane containing it.

Living organisms "sense" others like them and their environments. The word "sense" means detecting a presence of another organism, or molecules produced by them. This represents the most elementary form of recognition. Damasio states that *sensing* is different from *perceiving*. It does not construct a model, based on something else, to create a representation for producing an image in mind. Sensing, contrary to being conscious, does not require a mind.

Living organisms react "with intelligence" to what they sense, with their response helping the continuation of life. Intelligence means that if they sense a problem they aim to solve it. They do not rely on explicit knowledge, based on images and representations, but on a hidden competence with the goal to maintain life. This non-explicit intelligence takes care of living, conforming to the rules of homeostasis. Parameters on which life depends, like presence of nutrients, certain temperature levels, or pH, are maintained.

2.1 *Purpose of Life: Its Own Maintenance*

The purpose of life brings problems of a different nature from the viewpoint of a simple organism, as the main goal is preservation until death comes, following the rules of homeostasis. When multicellular and -system organisms developed 3.5 million years later, homeostasis relied on a newly coordinated device, called the nervous system. It functioned to direct actions, but also to produce patterns in the form of images and maps. This process led to having *mind* as the result of feeling, which the nervous system made possible with the conscious mind.

Damasio explains that after millions of years homeostasis was governed by minds, to some extent. At this stage, creative reasoning was needed, based on memorised knowledge, managed and developed to extend the purpose of life. Survival was coupled with well-being, derived from the experience of its own intelligent creations. As mentioned, survival and the rules of homeostasis are still in use today, both in bacteria and in humans. Mindless organisms have non-explicit, non-conscious intelligence, but humans enjoy both non-explicit intelligence and the abundance and power of open representations.

2.2 *Bacteria, Viruses and Plants*

Scientific research has made great progress in understanding the role and evolution of bacteria and their largely beneficial interaction with humans. The microbiome is recognised as basic to understanding ourselves. Problems arise when we analyse viruses to understand their role in life. Bacteria, like plants, are capable of sensing, but neither are conscious. They sense and respond, as cellular membrane detect temperature, acidity, a micro push or shove and the result is to move away from such stimuli. Bacteria and plants have a form of cognition, an intelligence that is not explicit – lacking knowledge of what they do and why. They do not have a nervous system and sensing alone does not allow an organism to have a mind or consciousness. Bacteria and plants operate to the dictates of homeostasis without knowing why and how they behave as they do. Damasio explains their actions are not represented in other organism parts, with no possibility of disclosure, because of explicit knowledge (2021, p. 43). Another characteristic is that bacteria and plants respond to numerous anaesthetics, suspending activities in a kind of hibernation when ability to sense disappears.

Viruses are not living organisms and there is a paradox when speaking of "killing viruses", as in managing polio, measles, HIV, seasonal flu and the

SARS-CoV-2 virus that causes Covid-19. We are not prepared for viral epidemics and are ignorant of the necessary knowledge for speaking clearly about them and dealing with consequences, declares Damasio. Biologically speaking, what is the status of viruses? Where do they fit in evolution? Why and how do they "wreak havoc" amongst real living things? These questions receive tentative, ambiguous answers.

Compared to bacteria, viruses do not have metabolism, produce energy or waste and cannot initiate movement. They do have nuclei acid – DNA or RNA and some assorted proteins. Viruses cannot reproduce, but invade living organisms, attack their life systems, multiply and becoming parasitic, thereby destroying the host. Though they have a non-living status, they contain a non-explicit type of intelligence – a hidden competence disclosed only when they reach a suitable environment. They act intelligently from the viewpoint of their permanence. Although not living creatures, they possess the ability to expand, producing the nucleic acids that maintain them.

In the mid-19th century, Claude Bernard, a French physiologist, wrote that "the stability of internal environment – *the milieu intérieur* – is the condition for free and independent life".[3] This is the underlying principle of what later was called "homeostasis", a term coined by Walter Cannon. He was inspired by plant life and described the phenomenon of homeostasis and its importance. He noticed that plants were equipped with many cells and different tissues and could perform non-obvious, cautious movements with underground web-roots. In a knowledgeable way, they could grow at their pace, provided with water to produce leaves and flowers from their underground reservoirs. The distribution of water was made possible through a hydraulic system. Research discovered that the roots of forest trees form vast networks that contribute to a collective homeostasis. All this is performed in the absence of a nervous system, but with the aid of sensing and non-minded intelligence.

I belong to the group of people who talk to plants, especially in the spring, when on my balconies they explode with scents and colours. I thank them every morning for giving me such pleasure. Apparently, England's King Charles III does the same thing! There are many reasons to respect and love plants and poetic monologues make a difference to the lives of non-human organisms: their flowering time and scents last longer, I have noticed!

2.3   *Nervous System*

In the history of life, the nervous system appeared late, only when the complexity of organisms required high levels of functional coordination. This made it possible to generate remarkable phenomena with functions like feelings, minds, consciousness, explicit reasoning, verbal languages and mathematics, which were not present before. These "neuro-authorized novelties", as Damasio defines them, improved achievements of the non-explicit biological intelligences and cognitive abilities already there and serving the goal of maintaining life. It was optimising homeostatic rules for a more secure life, delivering the high level of functional coordination necessary for complex multicellular and -system organisms.

Minds, consciousness and creative thinking are possible only from nervous system contribution. Damasio asserts that theory based exclusively on the nervous system is invalid and the reason why attempts to explain consciousness have failed, because it is difficult to analyse a mystery.

Knowledge of consciousness is that it emerges in organisms with a nervous system, requiring copious interactions between the central part – the brain – and various body sections. Body and nervous system together generate basic biological intelligence. "[I]t meets homeostatic demands and that eventually is expressed in the form of feeling" (Damasio, 2021, p. 22). The nervous system, combined with the body, brings to this marriage the possibility of making knowledge explicit and constructing spatial patterns that constitute images. It is also responsible for memorising knowledge in images and opens up the possibility of manipulating them. This activity enables reflection, planning and reasoning, giving birth to the generation of symbols and the creation of new responses, art, crafts and ideas.

3 Being, Feeling and Knowing

The first stage, *being*, does not include explicit feeling or knowledge, although performing a type of good life without which survival would have been impossible or not started. Damasio, when describing the early steps of life, lists *feeling* as the second stage. At this point creatures, able to feel, had to be multicellular, with differentiated organs and a nervous system, considered a natural coordinator of internal life processes to deal with the environment. Scientific research has disclosed how neurons create movement in steps: bioelectrical phenomena ignite these processes in the muscle cell, followed by muscular contraction. The result is that movement happens in the muscles and bones. Less clear is how the chemical-electrical processes lead to mental states, though following the same logic. The neural activity concerning mental states is spread spatially over a set of neurons that constitute patterns naturally. Examples are in the sensory investigation of vision, hearing and touch, as well as probing our visceral interior. In spatial terms the patterns correspond to object, facts and qualities that generate neural activity. They delineate objects and facts in terms of generating maps according to time. As a result the "mapped patterns" are designed in reference to the physical details of objects and actions present in the outside world surrounding our nervous system, more specifically to ears and eyes. The images that form in the mind are the results of well-organised neural activity that transmits such patterns to the brain. Thus, neurobiological mapped patterns turn into imaginative mental events. Only when events are part of a context that includes feelings and self-perspective do they become conscious mental experiences. This process can be viewed as magic or a natural phenomenon, depending on our beliefs. This observation is not enough to explain it because the "deep fabric of mind", as Damasio calls it, is the structure of maps and images, which classical physics[4] cannot clarify, requiring more research.

The nervous system permits complex movements and the beginning of novelty (mind). We need to consider feelings as the first examples of mind phenomena that allow creatures to represent the state of their body in relation to their environment, previously preoccupied in regulating the internal organ functions required to survive. Thus, feelings provide organisms with experience of their own life in terms of quality "good living" – pleasant or unpleasant. This information was not in the organisms confined within the first stage, *being*. Feelings are excellent contributors to the origin of a mental process of the "self", animated by the organism's state. These are located in the body frame and oriented by sensory channels like vision and hearing.

Once being and feeling are structured and functional, they are ready to support and expand the third stage, *knowing*. The maps and images formed by the sensory information constitute a mind, with abundant images. Once experiences are memorised, feeling and conscious organisms can maintain a history of their lives, their interactions with others and the environment. Thus, the history of each individual life is lived inside each organism. This is how Damasio explains the frame of personhood.

4   Intelligence, Mind-Perspective and Feelings

It is difficult to assess definitions, especially for abstract concepts, to clarify what they represent. *Intelligence* is considered the ability to resolve problems of life and attributed to all living organisms. Naturally, there is a difference between the intelligence of bacteria and humans, in terms of time, millions of years and achievements. Damasio (2021, p. 39) proposes the following scheme.

4.1   *Intelligence*
The term "intelligence" refers to the ability to solve problems encountered in life. This extends from available energy sources (nutrients and oxygen) to

Covert	Overt
Hidden, concealed	Manifest
Non-explicit	Explicit
Based on chemical/ bioelectrical processes in organelles and cells membranes	Based on partially mapped neural patterns which "represent and resemble" objects and actions; imagetic

FIGURE 2   Covert and overt intelligence (Source: Damasio, 2021, p. 39)

territory control, defence from predatory behaviour, along with strategies for addressing difficulties – involving confrontation and social cooperation.

Damasio states that human intelligences are not simple or limited. They are explicit and require a mind and outcome support, such as *feelings* and *consciousness* employing perception, memory and reasoning. The contents of mind produce spatial mapped patterns that present objects and actions that we perceive inside ourselves and from the world outside us. As we build our patterns, we can review their structures and reflect on specific objects. Content can be manipulated, as we are the owners and can organise it in various ways.

The same happens with reasoning, when attempting to sort out problems (Figure 2). Normally, we are engaged until a solution is found. When we speak of mind mental patterns, we account for "images" that are not only visual, but generated by any sensory channel: auditory, kinesthetic, smell, taste or visual. This happens in creative mode, when we use imagination to extend thinking.

Intelligence in bacteria acts differently. It is hidden and non-explicit, with non-transparent functioning. As far as knowledge goes, there is nothing in the interior of bacterium or unicellular creatures that could give birth to images and reasoning. Their intelligence is based on bioelectrical computation that operates in a small space and sits at a molecular level. Bacteria have benefited from unique non-explicit intelligence. Humans have both explicit and non-explicit abilities for use, according to the situation. We do not have to decide which to choose as our mental habits do it for us. The two intelligences came into existence for the same purpose: to solve problems encountered during living time in order to survive.

4.2   *Mind and Perspective*

The meaning we give to non-explicit and explicit intelligences may produce misunderstandings, suggests Damasio. The former does not imply magic, though there is biological mystery about how this happens. Mechanisms that operate in this case are not transparent and capable of being inspected without microscopes and sophisticated biochemical theories to make sense of facts. Explicit mechanisms can be examined through an imagetic pattern mode, analysing actions and relationships. These processes need the formation, presence and storage of imagetic patterns by the organism inside itself. Also, the organism needs to control and analyse the patterns internally, without technological support, in order to organise suitable behaviour. This does not mean that explicit intelligence can be fully explained, either.

Mind is one way to address the production and exhibition of images derived from perception, memory or both in continual procession. These are natural means to convey knowledge of any type, using senses singularly or combined.

Perspective refers not only to what we see, hear, touch, feel, smell and taste, but also to what our body perceives concerning the conscious mind. Images of a living organism flow within their own mind. Research on the origin of perspective assigns it to the head of organisms, as sensory tools and brains are positioned at the top of the body together with our organs affecting our balance.

4.3   *Feelings*

Damasio mentions Stuart Hameroff, an American anesthesiology professor at the University of Arizona, known for research on consciousness and influenced by the study of the English mathematical physicist Roger Penrose.

Among scientists, Hameroff states that organisms could have had feelings before the nervous system appeared. Damasio explains that the source of this idea is that certain configurations are likely to be associated with stable and viable life states (2021, p. 204). This does not explain clearly the presence of mental states concerning the current condition of the organism. Mental states require the presence of elaborate nervous systems and depend on the representation of the organism's states in neural maps. These are the foundations of consciousness and, if we dare list evolutionary events, they appear just before consciousness. Feelings help manage life following homeostatic requirements, residing in the organism's mind.

Feelings are hybrids of mind and body and move between them to make cognition work. We feel because our mind is conscious and are aware because of our feelings. This could be a paradox, but feelings are the beginning of "an adventure called consciousness" (Damasio, 2021, pp. 109–110).

4.4   *What Do They Stand For?*

Feelings protect our lives by informing us of dangers and opportunities. Furthermore, they provide the mind with facts and allow us to experience what is happening to us. In this way we become conscious and able to unify our thinking for effective results.

"Homeostatic feelings are the first enablers of consciousness". The process of interaction that takes place in a mind enables homeostatic adjustments to happen. Feelings inside organisms provide perspective and allow the mind to know how to act appropriately. They permit self-reference and are the basic component of standard consciousness.

Emotional states are displayed continuously in a mind, mirroring the life state within the body, whether spontaneous or modified by emotion. Participating in the process of generating consciousness, two sources are identified. One is the "never-ending" process of running life within the body, in terms of ups and downs – the need for air, the hunger for food, the feelings of thirst or pain, the sense of desire, pleasure, malaise, well-being – as examples of homeostatic feelings. The other is a collection of variable emotive reactions to states of fear, joy or discomfort we experience daily, as examples of feelings. These form internal narratives for forming consciousness. The discovery of ownership results from the mutual, clear influences of the organism's state and the images generated. Happenings in the surrounding exterior are constructed by adopting the organism's perspective.

5   Consciousness

Attempts to define "consciousness" could reduce its function. According to Damasio, we should consider it a new idea as it did not exist in Shakespeare's time.[5] In 1690, the word appeared in the writings of John Locke, who defined it as "the perception of what passes in a man's mind". This does not describe the thinking of today.

Consciousness is now prominent in scientific literature by philosophers, psychologists and sociologists, who investigate it from different viewpoints. The meaning of consciousness derives from what it dispenses to the human mind and is discovered through this process. All mental experiences, ranging from pleasure to pain and perception, memory, recall and manipulation explain the surrounding world, made possible because of consciousness. Without it we would still have images flowing in our minds, but not tied to us as individuals and owned by nobody.

Consciousness has been central for human cultures and permitted historical changes. The experience of human pain and suffering has enhanced creativity, invention of skills and the means to oppose negative feelings. This has led to better solutions to pain, suffering and death

The experience of well-being and pleasure has helped humans to develop more favourable conditions for a better life both as individuals or groups.

Non-humans, too, have succeeded in avoiding or softening possible causes of discomfort, but this did not allow them to modify their initial stage. Damasio's view is that consciousness is not realised differently in humans compared with non-humans. The difference depends on the intellectual resources of humans, which are broader and more sophisticated. These create objects and give birth to actions to progress cultures.

The characteristics of consciousness are as follows:

– It helps organisms govern their lives as far as observing its requirements regulation.
– It acts as an indispensable strength/means for solving difficulties encountered to govern life.
– It connects the mind to a specific organism for good.
– It helps the mind to act as pressing case for certain needs of that organism to survive.

Organisms with broad mental capacities can cope in various settings, as consciousness expands their sphere of influence to overcome difficulties. Damasio considers consciousness as an "enriched" state of mind that consists in "inserting additional elements of mind within the ongoing mind process" (2021, p. 136). Research is needed to understand "an initiation rite" that is the identification of an owner's mind in the setting of their body. Consciousness is a particular state of mind resulting from a biological process when multiple mental events make a contribution.

6   Artificial Intelligence (AI) towards Conscious Machines

The inventors, engineers and constructors who seek to make AI and robotics possible are inspired by living natural organisms, observing results of their movements in terms of efficiency and economy, along with capacities to solve problems. We may argue that there is nothing natural about this type of intelligence and its devices that help us to live more comfortably. Pioneers tried to imitate what they thought was the most essential and useful, leaving out what they regarded as less important and superfluous: such as the *feeling* aspect. Damasio's view is that what they left out did not take into consideration human evolution. Thus, the scope of AI is limited regarding creative potential and ultimate intelligence level. A prior historical manifestation of intelligence – the universe of affect – was neglected, which is key to the development of creativity.

Present researchers aim to develop machines that operate in terms of homeostatic feelings. They are trying to equip robots with a body that requires rules and modifications to continue. Paradoxically speaking, they are furnishing these machines with a degree of vulnerability and less precision, qualities that are the opposite to those present in the rigid structures of typical robotics.

The novel technologies of "soft robotics" aim to equip robots with more flexibility and adjustable capacities, transferring sensing characteristics into machines. Thus, robots could process and respond to conditions around them, offering appropriate, effective, intelligent responses. They are working to construct machines that can feel in their body and give qualified, efficacious responses. No longer do feeling machines belong to science fiction. Will they become conscious? Damasio and other scientists believe they will, but not immediately, and their feelings will not be the same as those of humans. The level of consciousness will depend on the amount and complexity of internal representations of both machine interiors and surrounds. They could become "efficacious assistants to really feeling humans", as hybrids of natural and artificial creatures.

7   Federico Faggin's View on Consciousness

Presenting his latest book *Irriducibile* (2022) at various universities, conferences and interviews, on 20th October, 2022 Faggin explained Maria Paola Scaramuccia, (journalist at Corriere Della Sera, Veneto edition) that the analysis of the world materialistically ignores our interior one. This is why this microchip inventor began researching what makes us human. His book refers to human parts, one the *physical,* spatial-temporal form (body) and the other, the *quantic*, which is much more profound. The latter describes the interior person and the unique capacity to produce a personal, unique point of view that enables one to think beyond the material world, something that pure materialism cannot explain. Computers consist of transistor on-off switches, a mechanism that does not know the meaning of what a computer is doing. Humans, in contrast, are made of cells containing the organism's DNA and even the smallest component contains the potential knowledge of everything. Our consciousness is unique and irreducible, states Faggin.

Computers now possess human voices and appear to have the potential to answer all questions (Scaramuzza, 2022). The idea that they are autonomous and can decide by themselves comes from a powerful elite who want us to believe this fact. Faggin replies to this view that it is a game of deceit in order to make us accept the thought that we are imperfect machines. Computers are little more than a recording device repeating everything told them. They do not have human consciousness. Unfortunately, people have not been trained to develop their consciousness and are afraid to deal with it.

Modern AI could be a weapon in the hands of evil forces, so we may end up having to employ "Blade Runners", suggests Maria Paola.[6] Who do we have to fear most – the machines or their builders? Faggin replies that computers have access, so the creator can make them perform as wanted. Members of the younger generations today – who do not reflect on such matters enough – display a tendency to accept things without question, in the same way religious dogma has been given assent in the past. The speed and information overload presently experienced by people does not give time to think deeply. Powerful people may preach that AI is better than us and that it is able to produce complex calculations at higher speed, but it lacks the consciousness that gives humans superiority.

Today, generations are different, says Faggin. Children use computers from age two and could be conditioned and trapped for life. When Faggin started to work with AI and understood the importance of neural networks, experts believed them unimportant. He understood that this innovative idea would open up various markets and 20 years later they are influencing almost everything.

During this period, he experienced the extraordinary event of consciousness, mentioned before, that changed his idea of science. The deterministic, structured, mechanical views of classical physics were extended to encompass the view that we are mechanisms with an internal genetic history and knowledge gained from varied abilities and background experiences. The time has come, Faggin concludes, that we understand what matters most is our own experience and that we are a quantum entity. When we discover better what it is, with a new lexicon to explain it, we will understand it fully.

New theories embrace interiority not exteriority. Quantic physics has helped to change Faggin's views. Once again, he has astonished readers with his second book, especially addressed to people who desire to behave according to compassion, ethics and responsibility.

7.1   *New Vision*

In the first part of *Irriducibile*, Faggin explains a world vision based on classic physics, showing how non-animation works. This makes assumptions about other scientific fields. Analysis focuses on aspects neglected by science, considered more in philosophy, such as consciousness and free will. This fosters the belief that a materialistic view could describe and explain all reality. On the contrary, major aspects have been ignored, such as consciousness, considered an epiphenomenon (a mental state regarded as a by-product of brain activity) and free will.

Faggin points out that AI leads to misunderstanding, because of a confusion between realty with a theory of reality, eliminating consciousness that makes the difference between this and its imitation. A materialistic vision justifies egotisms, competition and a universe without meaning or purpose. Quantum physics does not support this vision.

The author thinks that the existence of interiority can be explained without invalidating classical physics, as materialism comes from a wrong interpretation. Difficulties in understanding quantum physics are due to the fact they address light to the internal and not the external world. This clarifies that reality interweaves an internal semantic and an external symbolic one, which act as two faces.

Five problems are identified without answers to date: creation, order, life, consciousness and free will (Faggin, 2022, pp. 150–154). The one that will not be answered is creation, because we lack the capacity to grasp it. It is a miracle that must be accepted. Physics resolves creation, suggesting the existence of a "field" with all necessary properties to transform matter and energy based on fundamental laws, postulated, too, by describing interconnections among parts. According to quantum physics, the "field" is ontological, because it is the dynamic matter for all that exists and that will exist, so it needs to contain all properties present and perceptible in its evolution.

The remaining problems are explained as logical consequences of the creation miracle (Faggin, 2022, p. 161). To answer the four remaining questions, it is assumed the existence of a holistic All that contains not only the fundamental properties allowing development of an inanimate universe, but also the presence of free will, consciousness and life.

7.2   *Quantum Information-Based Panpsychism (QIP) Theory, Bit, Quantum Bit (Qubit), Entanglements*

Faggin mentions the difficulty of finding researchers interested in consciousness studies, with reality having two parts, one inner semantic and the other symbolic connected to meaning. His view is that quantum physics can sort out the consciousness problems and in his research came across D'Ariano and his team's studies that demonstrate quantum physics derives from quantum information. According to Faggin, information without meaning would be senseless, because consciousness is fundamental. From the two positions, quantum information-based panpsychism (QIP) theory was generated and consists in a pure state that is well-defined and impossible to clone.[7]

"Panpsychism" is the idea that mind or some other mental aspects such as consciousness is a fundamental part of reality since time immemorial. It is one of the oldest philosophical theories explained by the *Vedas*, Thales, Plato, Spinoza, Leibniz, Russell and many others. According to QIP theory panpsychism cannot exist in a classic system.

This is the basis of Faggin's model, published in an essay with D'Ariano (who has shown that quantum physics derives entirely from quantum information): "Hard Problem and Free Will: An Information-Theoretical Approach" (D'Ariano & Faggin, 2022). In this theory, consciousness does not arise from information generated in the physical world. It is instead a quantum phenomenon creating information that we then perceive as the physical world.

Classical information is about "bits" – things in one of two possible states, 0 or 1, true or false. A "bit" is a human construction out of which we can create computers. Scientists have now figured out there is something equivalent to a "bit" in the quantum world, called a "quantum bit" or a "qubit". For example, the "qubit" is represented by the "spin" of electrons. Spin can only be represented in Hilbert space, which is multidimensional, with each aspect represented by a complex number, the sum of a real and an imaginary one. The "qubit" exists as an infinity of states in Hilbert space, but when measured in our physical world appears only as two states: 0 or 1; up or down; left or right; forward or backward, depending on the choice of direction of the magnetic field in which this spin is measured.

Each "qubit" represents an infinity of states, although when in space-time shows up as a classical "bit". Qubits are also able to "entangle". When two particles, such as a pair of photons or electrons become entangled, they remain connected even when separated by vast distances. This occurs, to give an example, in the same way that a ballet or tango emerges from individual dancers. Entanglements arise from the connection between particles and this is what scientists call an "emergent property". Entanglement is a property existing only in quantum systems. It means that if two "qubits" interact, they become a joint state which continues to exist even if moved apart in space. This results in phenomena, such as instantaneous correlations, irrespective of distance between two entangled electrons physically separated. These two properties together mean that a "qubit" can form connections not possible in classical space-time.

Quantum reality is larger than the one we are aware of in normal experience. In quantum theory, the quantum probability manifestation does not exist before the measurement of it. This explains why no law or algorithm can determine the future.

Belonging to classical systems, computers use statistic properties of atoms and molecules that are deterministic and do not possess consciousness nor free will. If classic information would be suitable to describe a consciousness experience, our own could be copied in the computer memory and it would not be private anymore. We must not confuse the description of a conscious experience as a pure state with the experience itself. As an example, the description of affection towards a loved one can be described with classic symbols like words but cannot be confused with the feelings inside us. The description of love through a pure quantum state is different from the love inside me; even the quantum state has mathematical properties more homomorph to qualia that could be felt inside. A quantum state is the best mathematical structure to represent an experience but cannot substitute for it. A consciousness experience cannot be comparable to its description, even if a quantic description is much better than the classic one.

7.3   *One, Seity, Conscious Unit (cu)*

To understand Faggin's theory, we must accept the "holistic all", containing not only the fundamental properties that allow evolution of the inanimate universe, but also seeds of free will, consciousness and life (Faggin, 2022, pp. 161–164). To understand, we have to imagine that everything is made of undivided energy that has the desire and capacity to experience and know itself – the unified field "One". One exists before what physicists call the "physical universe", which is only the informational aspect of reality. The semantic aspect is the inner experience and knowing of One, which current physics does not recognise. Also, One exists in a vast reality that contains the space-time we experience. Out of One conscious entities emerge that have the desire and capacity to know themselves. Imagine each entity as a point of view or perspective that One has about itself. They are not separate from One, though their conscious experience is private.

From One, conscious fields emerge that possess free will, referring to the elementary "seity", called the conscious unit (cu). This is not to be mistaken with the inanimate field of the elementary particles of physics following predetermined laws.

This concept establishes that cus are conscious fields equipped with free will and from their interactions the laws of physics and new combinations of seity emerge – that is the basic difference compared to contemporary physics. In this vision of reality, the presence of consciousness and free will have been at the end of evolution and not at its beginning.

Faggin believes we are seity, who temporarily live in our body, as we are eternal, conscious and imperishable. "Seity" is an uncommon English word, meaning to possess individuality. It describes a conscious being knowing to be such that can act with free will and has a permanent identity. We are here to learn about ourselves, interacting with one another in the universe that we have created for this purpose. Whatever we see in the universe has been initially created in the consciousness of seity, as physics reality follows quantum reality, which follows quantum information and which, in its turn, follows the thought of seity.

Thus, laws of physics are syntactic for communication. They obey syntactic laws not from obligation, but because, wanting to communicate, they need agreed common language rules they have helped create. The necessity to obey rules does not contradict free will. Think of a game created by children, who establish rules to give order to play. Each child chooses actions according to rules for the sake of fairness and direction. Existence of free will requires quantum entanglement that allows a universe not determined a priori by laws, but by free will and creativity of the seity (Faggin, 2022, p. 253).

Seity is a pure state field that exists in a reality much wider than our physical world and contains our body. It is without a physical body, which is important, because it implies that our existence does not depend on the body. The latter permits the seity to perceive and operate in a physical world that is only a part of a wider reality. Seity cannot exist in the same space-time dimension as our body does. It can only communicate with the body using live information, in the same way we do with a robot or an avatar in virtual reality, using classical information. A robot is described by classical theory, while a human body by both quantum and classical ones. If wanting to represent a seity as a quantum system, we note that the quantum state represents its personal experience (Faggin, 2022, p. 179). What it will manifest under a classical view, will be only what the seity decides to share (Faggin, 2022, pp. 179–180).

In his model, Faggin defines a seity as a reality going beyond all categories and definitions. It is not possible to define a seity as a machine, because its characteristics, consciousness, identity, human agent and creativity are not separable. Through quantum physics, we discover that reality goes beyond that conceived by classical physics. Quantum reality is probable, undetermined and contains entanglement that connects particles irrespective of the distance separating them. This implies a holistic reality made of parts not totally separable. Seity can create different worlds that are interconnected and can exist even one inside another. Their fundamental connection is determined by a universal language created by the first level of seity, the CU. Entanglement offers the final proof that physical reality cannot exist before quantum transformation. The universe, described by quantum physics, must be open and not determined a priori by unavoidable laws.

CUs that emerge from One are conscious fields with free will and identity that communicate with one another via live symbols to deepen self-knowledge and through combinations augment their complexity. Knowledge refers to interior existence and complexity to exteriority – as live symbols (Faggin, 2022, p. 180). From what we call creation follows the logic that from One emerges beings whose purpose is to enlarge knowledge. CUs are the first level of seity and Faggin recognises others for consciousness, free will and identity. They are perspectives, views or referential systems through which One knows self. Similar to Leibniz' monads, they interact spontaneously, following their nature reflecting One. When interacting via symbolic communication, signs emerge that combine rules that emerge gradually and become more sophisticated to create a first level of syntactic laws and a second of symbols and seity. These new seity are conscious fields with identity and human agency – the capability to make things happen, to intervene with reality and exercise power based on free will (Faggin, 2022, p. 181). The new symbols are quantum combinations of the original that have different properties.

The elementary seity (CU) exist in a reality wider than the physical, corresponding to what physics call particles fields, but they are conscious with free will, whose live symbols correspond to states of homonymous fields (Faggin, 2022, p. 283). In this model, laws emerge from One through the spontaneous communication of CUs and represent syntactic symbol rules, negotiated spontaneously to communicate among themselves.

7.4   *Quantum Information*

Knowing is an experienced phenomenon, a seity's conscious experience, whose mathematical model is a pure quantum state, described as entangled qubit. Knowing is tied to existence as two facets, because to exist is to know and to know is to exist. A pure quantum state is an abstract symbol needed to represent the personal knowledge of seity that becomes what it knows.

Quantum information cannot be cloned, just in the way knowledge of seity is private. In this sense, quantum information represents the interiority of the universe. Instead, classic information is replicable and public, opposite to private quantum type and known only by the system in that state – seity.

Faggin says that what can be known from outside is only classic information that seity decides to share with the outside world. It is possible to know only from inside and when we experience something novel, we create new existence that becomes more than what we were before: we grow to our satisfaction. New experience takes place first in the interior and then is communicated through symbols, in the same way the contents of a book can be written only after the author has thought about it consciously.

Live Information is the symbolic representation of meaning that becomes shared, when appearing in time-space. It is not totally objective, not even in the classic reality, because there are complementary properties impossible to measure.

We need to make a distinction between "know" and "knowing": "know" refers to information, while "knowing" to the meaning of information, happening only through conscious experience.

7.5 *Consciousness as Quantum Phenomenon*

Experience comes before the symbols that describe it. Quantum information defines the interior world. It is personal, precise and individual with no possibility of cloning. Our body contains 50 trillion cells and each has the organism genome. We are part of an All and if we provoke something bad to another person, it is the same as doing this to ourselves.

In contrast with evolution theory, in the quantum phenomenon we find cooperation and collaboration to solve problems together: the consciousness of all is that of the individual. Quantum is the world of involvement and ontology is experience. Reality is lived experience that we do not know through books. Our body is not only a machine, but what is behind it to make it function.

7.6 AI

The technological world creates confusion between interior and exterior reality, the theory of reality and its simulation, to a point that simulation can be compared to a conscious experience. To think that AI might be intelligent is a misunderstanding similar to the one when we confuse the theory of reality with actual experience. AI without interiority it is only an imitation of human behaviour. Reality is alive – it does not reside in matter, but in the knowledge of self-experience.

Robots repeat automatically what they are programmed to do, because they have no life, even if moving and appearing alive. We are alive even when our body dies, existing in a wider reality that contains a physical one. Faggin describes the vision of Bert Hellinger, who says that death is a rebirth gift in the spiritual universe (Faggin, 2022, p. 177). As seity, we are eternal. Robots have no feelings and when disconnecting from ours, we act like them, but consciousness gives us choice.

Studying reality generates misunderstanding, confusing symbols and meaning. We attribute the value of reality to symbols and deny reality to meaning, having more information than understanding. We are conscious fields full of light and not machines lacking consciousness. Machines have no free will and cannot say "no". We control them, deciding how they must function.

Science says that consciousness derives from brain activity and is born from this experience – but no scientific explanation for it is given. If everything is explained by scientific laws, for example, why it is impossible to describe the taste of chocolate? AI does not overtake us, but makes us think to decide where to go. It is impossible to explain experience through electrical and biological signals. The taste of chocolate cannot be explained through these signals. It is possible to describe the experience of eating chocolate, but I will understand it only after having tasted it. Consciousness is not inside: it is a field extending outside our body and has created the matter – not the other way round.

Faggin concludes by saying that technology must help us discover our real nature, not imprison us in a virtual world lacking meaning. Technology can unify or divide humans in a growing destructive war. We need to experience a new consciousness of scientific events that generates it in a never-ending process. This is the creative principle of One and integrated science and consciousness will augment our union with All. Positive future strengths will be based on sensitive cooperation, understanding, love and friendship for neighbours, not on strengths based on the laws of matter. All sensitive human beings will manifest this attitude one way or another because such is our inner essence.

Educators should teach these principles starting on the first day of school and demonstrate to students, with examples, the benefits of cooperative and collaborative action – if we really want to make changes in the world.

8 Review

These views represent the problem between religion and science that connects the study of the natural world, history, philosophy and theology. Both science and religion are complex social and cultural endeavours that vary across cultures and change over time. What are the roles of science or religion in the creation of the world? This question has always divided people. In Western culture, the first to question this were Greek philosophers, such as Democritus and Epicurus, who denied the existence of a superior deity and believed that everything was chance. Democritus said that whatever exists is the result of chance and necessity, excluding will in creation. In the Latin literature, Lucretius, in his book *De Rerum Natura*, when speaking about Epicurus, said that while humanity was oppressed by the weight of superstition and religion, only one Greek man dared to challenge. These philosophers could be considered the first atheists in Western culture.

During the Middle Ages, religion had a fundamental position in people's lives, so that the majority believed that all happenings were due to divine will. Whoever dared to oppose was considered heretical and condemned to death.

Illuminism faced many fights between religion and science but, when explaining the world, it was not necessary to abandon beliefs that had no scientific basis if backed up by creative and critical thinking.

This brief narration arrives when dispute between the two is harsh, because science has developed enormously, making present unthinkable discoveries. One is "cloning", considered immoral by religious followers along with other novel scientific discoveries. The same reaction was shown in Galileo's time, 400 years plus ago.

I believe that religion is afraid that through technology and new discoveries, humankind will sort out the major problems of illness and health. A human who does not fear death will have no need of God – and this could be a reason why religion tends to oppose science. It relies on faith to demonstrate what is in John 20:9: "Blessed are those who have not seen, and yet have believed".

Creative and critical thinking, along with science, will lead humankind in the near future. Religion still shows a medieval structure not always in line with 21st-century life – we all see what happens in Iran with riots initially led by women.

Acceptance of certain scientific principles may lead to moral decay, revolutionary social changes and other ills, but blind acceptance of a deity leads to the oppression of non-believers and the loss of freedom.

I would like to conclude with a quote by a man who contributed enormously to the development of modern science, Albert Einstein: "Science without religion is lame, religion without science is blind".

Notes

1   Hameroff was the chief organizer of the first Towards a Science of Consciousness conference held in Tucson, Arizona, in 1994. It is considered a landmark event within the subject of consciousness studies. It gave birth to the Association for the Scientific Study of Consciousness and led to the creation of the Center for Consciousness Study at the University of Arizona, whose director is Hameroff.
2   Homeostasis is a collection of rules proper of living creatures to maintain their characteristics even with the change of environmental conditions.
3   Claude Bernard was a French physiologist who established the use of the scientific method in medicine and relied on experiments (vivisection) and suggested the use of blinded experiments to guarantee the objectivity of scientific observations. He originated the term "*milieu intérieur*" and the associated concept of "homeostasis", later coined by Walter Cannon. Bernard held that the living body, though its need for a surrounding environment (sensing), is nevertheless relatively independent of it. The independence that an organism has of its external environment derives from the fact that in a living being the tissues are withdrawn from direct external influences and are protected by a veritable internal environment constituted by the fluids circulating in the body.

4 All aspects of physics were developed before the rise of quantum mechanics. The division of physics into the three major areas of mechanics, electrodynamics and thermodynamics occurred prior to the establishment of quantum physics in the twentieth century (Egolf & Shumate, 2004).

5 Damasio states that Romance languages have not evolved an equal term for this English word and still use "conscious" as a synonym of consciousness, meaning moral behaviour. He adds that when Hamlet says "thus conscience does not make cowards of us all", he means moral feelings and not consciousness (Damasio, 2021, p. 210). The author is not taking into account Greek and Latin Literature.

6 Paola is referring to members of a Blade Runner Unit, a police force that identified and killed fugitive replicants, or androids, in *Blade Runner*, the 1982 science fiction film directed by Ridley Scott (Off-World, n.d.).

7 QIP defines consciousness as the capacity owned by a quantum system, in a pure state, to experience its state of consciousness in the form of qualia. Part of this theory states that a consciousness system can transform quantic information into classic information and vice versa through free will.

References

Adolf, R., & Anderson, D. J. (2018). *The neuroscience of emotions: A new synthesis.* Princeton University Press.

Bernard, C. (1879). *Leçons sur les phénomènes de la vie communs aux animayx et aux végétaux.* J.-B. Baillière et Fils.

Cannon, W. B. (1932). *The wisdom of the body.* Kegan Paul & Co.

Chalmers, D. J. (1996). *The conscious mind: In search of a fundamental theory.* Oxford University Press.

Damasio, A. (1994). *Descartes' error: Emotion, reason and the human brain.* Harper Perennial.

Damasio, A. (1999). *The feelings of what happens: Body and emotion in the making of consciousness.* Harcourt Brace.

Damasio, A. (2003). *Looking for Spinoza: Joy, sorrow and the feeling brain.* Harcourt Brace.

Damasio, A. (2010). *Self comes to mind: Constructing the conscious brain.* Pantheon Books.

Damasio, A. (2018). *The strange order of things: Life, feelings and the making of cultures.* Pantheon Books.

Damasio, A. (2021). *Feeling & knowing: Making minds conscious.* Pantheon.

Damasio, A., & Damasio, H. (2022). "How life regulation and feelings motivate the cultural mind: A neurobiological account." In O. Houdé & G. Borst (Eds.), *The Cambridge handbook of cognitive development* (pp. 15–26). Cambridge University Press.

D'Ariano, G. M., & Faggin, F. (2022). Hard problem and free will: An information-theoretical approach. In F. Scardigli (Ed.), *Artificial intelligence versus natural intelligence* (pp. 145–192). Springer.

De Duve, C. (1995). *Vital dust: The origin and evolution of life on Earth.* Basic Books.

De Duve, C. (2005). *Singularities: Landmarks in the pathway of life.* Cambridge University Press.

Denton, D. (2005). *Primordial emotions: The dawning of consciousness.* Oxford University Press.

Dyson, F. (1999). *Origins of life.* Cambridge University Press.

Egolf, R. T., & Shumate, L. E. (2004). *Physics for Christian schools.* BJU Press.

Faggin, F. (2019). *Silicio: Dall'invenzione del microprocessore alla nuova scienza della consapevolezza.* Mondadori.

Faggin, F. (2022). *Irriducibile: La coscienza, la vita, i computer e la nostra natura.* Mondadori.

Gagliano, M. (2018). *Thus spoke the plant.* Penguin Random House.

Gánti, T. (2003). *The principles of life.* Oxford University Press.

Ginsburg, S., & Jablonka, E. (2019). *The evolution of the sensitive soul: Learning and the origins of consciousness.* MIT Press.

Hameroff, S. (2017). The quantum origin of life: How the brain evolved to feel good. In M. Tibayrenc & F. J. Ayala (Eds.), *On human nature: Biology, psychology, ethics, politics, and religion* (pp. 333–353). Elsevier.

Koch, C. (2019). *The feeling of life itself: Why consciousness is widespread but can't be computed.* MIT Press.

Leakey, R. (1994). *The origins of humankind.* Basic Books.

Man, K., & Damasio, A. (2019). Homeostasis and soft robotics in the design of feeling machines. *Nature Machine Intelligence, 1,* 446–452. http://doi.org/10.1038/s42256-019-0103-7

Off-World. (n.d.). Blade Runner Unit. *Off-World: The Blade Runner Wiki.* https://bladerunner.fandom.com/wiki/Blade_Runner_Unit/

Sage, R., & Matteucci, R. (Eds.). (2019). *The robots are here: Learning to live with them.* Buckingham University Press.

Scaramuzza, M. P. (2022, October 22). Federico Faggin, papà del microchip: "Attenti all'intelligenza artificiale, dobbiamo riscoprire l'interiorità". *Corriere della Sera edizione del Veneto.*

Schrödingher, E. (1994). *What is life?* Cambridge University Press.

Tsakiris, M., & De Preester, H. (2019). *The interoceptive mind: From homeostasis to awareness.* Oxford University Press.

PART 1

The Processes of Learning

∴

Introduction to Part 1

Rosemary Sage and Riccarda Matteucci

We start with the processes of learning, as in an inclusive education system the idea is that all should be studying the same curriculum. In the UK sit regular Standard Assessment Tests (SATS) to measure progress. This does not account for differences in growth patterns, which are genetically influenced. Thus, those with slower development are often perceived as dull and considered below average ability. The greatest influence on learning is that intelligent machines are now taking over routine tasks, which means that education must give greater attention to thinking development and how this is processed and produced. Higher thinking depends on well-developed narrative levels of language to be able to communicate with oneself (*inner talk*) as well as others. Technology replaces face-to-face talk to a large extent and experts have seen a decline of narrative thinking and language to reduce effective problem solving. The chapters in this part expand on this situation.

Chapter 1 – What Do We Communicate? Thinking Processes in a Technology Era

We have a right brain which thinks laterally, in a free way to consider and choose from many possibilities and a left one which functions in a linear, fixed way, as when setting out steps in a task. The chapter shows how formal education facilitates the left brain at the expense of the right. However, it is the right, creative brain that is now needed for the smarter jobs now on stream. Technology must be used to promote this creative thinking.

Chapter 2 – What Are Learning and Remote Learning Processes?

Information processing, thinking, communication and support are discussed to understand how to assist effective progress. Technology can be a blessing for those with learning difficulties, by providing personalised input devised by specialists that is delivered at a learner's convenience. Problem-solving depends on insight and awareness of both the issues and the possibilities that can improve situations with consistent approaches from all stakeholders to achieve goals.

Chapter 3 – Why Technology Makes Learning Processes Difficult?

Although e-learning has coped with the COVID-19 2020 pandemic, when face-to-face teaching has been impossible, it has illuminated inequality issues. This

© ROSEMARY SAGE AND RICCARDA MATTEUCCI, 2024 | DOI:10.1163/9789004688612_003

is not only that some students lack required technology and home support to access on-line materials but a significant number are unable to learn without ongoing help. In Britain, we run a prescriptive education system focusing on *what* to learn rather than *how*. Students performing competently in supportive classrooms have found themselves floundering as they try to manage learning with less guidance. This has revealed their difficulties more acutely, resulting from language deficiencies that are rarely identified, which the chapter presents and provides solutions.

Reflections

Trends in new technology, economic shifts, education-work mismatches, urban growth, people mobility, education demand, life-long learning needs and cultural mixing are noted in reports. They focus on a need to cultivate greater resilience, flexibility and the communication competencies underpinning all personal development. In a competitive world, where assessments rule, it is easy to focus mainly on academic growth, but it is the ability to apply knowledge personally and practically that is sacrificed.

CHAPTER 1

What Do We Communicate?

Thinking Processes in a Technology Era

Rosemary Sage

Abstract

We have to be careful now that technology is doing much of the routine thinking for us that we do not lose our ability to do so, with effective ways to communicate this, as it is now needed at higher levels. Awareness of the process of how we rationalise, process and express thoughts coherently in language structures is vital for our survival, in order to cope with the many issues continually facing us in our complex world now dominated by technology. Before analysing the issue of technology let us refresh ourselves on how the thinking process happens.

• • •

How we must *free* thinking from *fixed* domination for a technological world

⋰

1   Introduction: How We Think

Free, lateral thinking involves creativeness along with risk-taking. Fixed, linear thinking is based on logic – rationality, rules and routines – to find solutions to problems, using rigid, pre-defined procedures in a stepped process which ensures results. A prescriptive British Education defines standards to favour fixed not free thinking, in a bureaucratic system based on rules, routines and ranking from examinations. Deacon (2022) is disturbed by this situation and quotes research showing a popular name for a puppy in 2021 was 'puppy' as it demonstrates a lack of imaginative, creative thinking! The media have reported that the mess the present world reveals shows a lack of inventive thought on the part of elite leaders. Although traditional education, with standards measured by examinations, was relevant for the last century, when jobs were dominated by fixed procedures, new technology enables their implementation by intelligent machines (robots), so freeing us to solve complex world problems, like climate change, over population and diminishing natural resources. These demands need a creative, free-thinking approach. They require multi-discipline action, dependent on communication, cooperation and collaboration, using language to transfer thoughts from one person to another. Word information entering one mind and then passing to another causes new thoughts with insight for influencing the behaviour that follows. Thoughts, however, are expressed in linguistic structures with certain limitations, as humans cannot communicate everything they are rationalising inside their minds. Also, in multi-lingual societies, thinking and language expression reflect different realities to make intercultural communication challenging. The chapter looks at relations between thinking and language and reiterates the importance of free, creative thought, with discussion on how to implement this for teaching all subject areas. This cannot happen without full leadership support for policy and practice. Education has a special part to play in developing competencies for professional work roles. Presently, there is a serious disconnect between education and work requirements, which advances in technology have accelerated.

2   An Example of Basic Thinking

I have a problem needing a solution. The issue is hunger, which happens regularly so the answer is familiar! However, there are always different things to consider as each occasion is unique, although having similarities with past ones. It is 7.30 am and I must leave home by 9 o'clock, but have the dog to walk and need a shower, so time is tight! Therefore, a large cooked breakfast is out. Also, I am trying to lose weight to get into a special outfit, so must choose something with low calories. I will not have time for lunch because of back-to-back appointments, so decide on fruit and nuts now, which are quick to eat and low in calories, but provide some protein to keep me going. I will take a lean snack to eat later in a free moment.

Throughout each day, we are thinking how to make the best decisions for the circumstances presenting themselves. The story above shows how we depend on previous knowledge and experience, with each new situation requiring a review of features. The final step is to go to the kitchen where food is stored, find the items, prepare and then consume them. The event sequence, even in this basic thinking, demonstrates two stages – starting with the *free approach* – observing the situation, considering possibilities and making meaning of these for selecting the best fit. The second stage implements the choice in a routine way to achieve the desired result – in this case ridding me of hunger!

Thinking produces less possibilities, if the R brain is inactive as it begins the process and assembles the whole experience. This *narrative thinking* is seen when children 'story' real experiences in play, like a visit to a shop for buying goods. Such thinking is often ignored and not clinically tested. Why? In general, language cultures show good connotations for the R hand/L hemisphere and bad ones for the L/R one. The Latin for L is 'sinister' meaning 'bad' and for R, 'dexter' indicating 'skill' or 'adroitness'. In French, L is 'gauche' or 'awkward' whereas R is 'just' or 'proper'. In English, L comes from the Anglo-Saxon 'lyft' meaning 'weak' or 'worthless', whereas the R (riht) is 'right' or 'just'. The political right endorses national power and resists change whilst the left values individual autonomy and radicalism (Edwards, 1979). Thus, it is unsurprising that the R brain is ignored as unimportant.

3   Narrative Thinking and Language Structure

The Medical Research Council asked me to look at children, thought to be bright but achieving poorly in school. Tests of thinking, understanding and expression rarely require subjects to assemble quantities of information, so that narrative thinking and linguistic structures were not monitored but presented as their major learning problem (Sage, 2000b, 2021).

Narratives develop when children recall and retell events, give instructions, explanations and reports, along with discussing the pros and cons of issues. Today, television and online *screens* replace *talk* in life. Watching a television programme, meaning is provided in ready-made images with talk the secondary back-up. A viewer is passive and brains do not have to actively think and visualise for understanding. Modern life gives no time for talk – key to imaginative development of ideas. Children starting school are shocked because suddenly they are confronted with vast quantities of talk with no mental schema for dealing with this. Studies indicate that many begin education with thinking and language below that required for formal class talk (Sage, 2000b, 2017, 2021). Stasia Cwenar (2005) showed that 80% of students entering her senior school had cognitive-linguistic ages of around a 5 year-level at age 11. Early deficits had not been remedied as no sustained attention was paid them in primary settings. They are repaired by attention to formal communication, focusing on how ideas become narratives. Researchers attest to the method's success (Cooper, 2004) – the Communication Opportunity Group Strategy (Sage, 2000b, 2000c).

4   Evidence of Thinking Problems

Recently, I have worked with teenagers on practical tasks, like cleaning cars, mowing lawns, weeding flower beds and chopping wood. These are students who shine in school exams. However, they find it difficult to carry out 3 instructions in sequence and continually fail to use initiative – asking for help when they should be able to solve a practical problem. They never review jobs, to check and refine outcomes, so that things are missed like the unwashed car windscreen. The youngsters were constantly on their phones, which came out at every opportunity, even when asked to put them away while executing tasks. Although excellent at learning facts, which are checked in exams, their application of these needs attention. We cannot blame them, as our UK system is skewed towards competitive testing and worldwide comparisons through league tables, with factual knowledge easier to mark rather than use in real-life. The students demonstrate, in practical applications, an absence of inner-language narrative thinking to complete tasks alone, which is the competence mentioned as lacking in workplace reports of employee performance. This is learnt through opportunities to use spoken language continually with others, in order to develop inner thinking. Education must aim to improve student internal and external communication processes and give teachers the knowledge to develop this complex activity, which is vital for jobs today.

The UK Association of Chief Executives (ACE, 2018) reported on jobs, predicting they would increase in spite of intelligent machines taking over routines. They said that "education is flawed" as it does not develop the personal competencies required by workplaces, so fails to meet economic needs. A decline in the quality of British society was recorded. Even supposedly educated people do not know how to speak, think and write clearly, displaying little knowledge and ability compared to 50 years ago. Employers point out that a feature of those who cannot communicate and rationalise is that they never admit mistakes and fail to put them right. They rarely make effective decisions that consider many facets. A lack of inductive reasoning is evident.

However, there are signs of progress. Kaczmarek (Poland) is coordinating a world study on thinking and expression. The Learning for Life Educational Trust is prioritising oracy and planning a study of pupil-thinking styles to provide an East-West appraisal. Dame Elizabeth Negus is using cognitive assessments with London immigrant pupils to compare with native performance. Juan Romero is carrying out tests of thinking on his medical students at the University of Chile. Bear Grylls, the Chief Scout, has recently started groups for 4–5 year-olds, called "Squirrels", as teachers report their lack of basic competencies to cope with extended talk and text. Inductive reasoning, from outdoor exploration and interaction for developing observation and problem solving, will encourage narrative talk for high-level thinking. In further support, the English Speaking Union and the UK Parliamentary Oracy Group are collaborating to enhance student talk and thought. In societies, where diversity has increased, due to migration, these initiatives will greatly assist social solidarity if we want a genuine meritocracy that values diversity within national laws and values.

5   What to Consider

Today's students are excellent at jumping through endless test hoops – the goal of bureaucratic democracies. Although positive, there are negatives, as with everything in life. One is the leaders these systems produce. The SPANA (2018) research came up with 50 problems common to employers in all contexts. The top 5 complaints about leaders are:

1. Failure to communicate or think well
2. Inconsistent
3. Set own rules
4. Do not understand the work of the people they lead
5. Incompetent – cannot organise effectively, demonstrate no learning or intelligence

Diversity Q (2019) reported that 60% of employees quit jobs because of poor management. Why the best people are stuck running things, whilst many leaders appear second-rate? Ability to manoeuvre and manipulate rather than excellence gets one to the top, called "kissing the people above and kicking those below". It is what you are required to be, rather than distinction which brings high positions. Power and wealth acquired from previous generations brings complacency. Therefore, we have leaders who can answer questions but not ask them, because they have been narrowly educated to conform (*L brain thinking*) with no interest outside their expertise. We lack "thinkers" to lead in new directions and build on democratic ideals. This requires independent judgement, freedom for expressing disagreement and assessing performance, as well as courage to not tolerate tyranny. People must think independently, creatively and flexibly to deal with the complex, rapid changes from new technology and constant people movements. Unfortunately, we have so-called educated people unable to think effectively, to evidence a lack of R brain thinking in human development. Of course, we do have excellent leaders, but alas too few of them!

Stanford University conducted a decade of research demonstrating how you do not learn to think (Uncapher & Wagner, 2018/2019). People continuously bombarded with streams of electronic information fail to pay attention, control memory or switch from one job to another as well as those preferring to complete one task at a time. Minds were more disorganised so multi-tasking (working on 2+ tasks simultaneously, switching back and forth or performing many tasks in rapid succession) can impair ability to think and result in mental health issues. Psychologists refer to these as *'task switch costs'*. Other research (Kapadia & Melwani, 2021) suggests that while there is a connection between multitasking and distraction, this varies from person to person, as switching thinking can assist creativity. A "spill-over effect" from the excitement and energy of multi-tasking can lead to original ideas. Changing focus stops us relying on automatic behaviours to complete tasks. When repeating these, autopilot frees mental resources. Switching back and forth bypasses this process to perform more slowly. Multitasking is managed by executive brain functions controlling cognitive processes that determine how, when and in what order tasks are performed in 2 stages:

1. *Goal shifting*: Deciding to do one thing instead of another
2. *Rule activation*: Changing previous task rules for the new one/s

Negative impact of heavy multitasking can harm young minds forming neural connections, because of continual distractions from many information sources. Those engaged in media multi-tasking might be better at integrating visual and auditory information. A visual search task, both with and without sound, to indicate when an item changed colour, showed heavy multitaskers performed better when tone was presented. They performed worse than light/medium ones when it was absent.

Best thinking happens by slowing and concentrating to reflect on what life events mean. People boasting speed should know that James Joyce, author of Ulysses – the great 20th century novel – wrote only 100 words a day. Doubts, difficulties and questions get suppressed from rapid web influences, which need confronting bravely and honestly. Answers are not on Twitter but within ourselves from quiet reflection without distractions or pressure. Absorbing orthodox wisdom or onslaught from other thinking makes it impossible to hear one's own voice. Books are better than tweets/posts to assist thinking, as one author's thoughts, and although reflecting the conventional wisdom of their time may present a different view to extend ideas.

Thus, contemplation means concentration that should include *conversation*. Ralph Emerson's quote: "The soul environs itself with friends that it may enter into a grander self-acquaintance or solitude"[1] suggests that the way to communicate with oneself is by conversing with a trusted person, to allow thinking out loud. Our electronic world disrupts interpersonal extended talk and instead we have many on social media batting one-line messages to produce further distraction. How will we find wisdom to challenge factual errors, foolish orders or reckless policy? Think through issues, respecting integrity and morality, in order to deal with problems when arising. William Deresiewicz's (2008) essay: "The Disadvantages of an Elite Education", expands on these views, as we must find ways to limit distractions and improve thinking.

Thoughts arise through the complex interactions of the brain's roughly 100 billion nerve cells (neurons), forming an intricate net (neuronet) to produce thought patterns. Nothing is more important than the ability to think creatively and critically to deal with difficulties. Education teaches us how to solve problems but not the art of thinking, the instrument of which is language that must be developed at narrative levels to carry out this cognitive process. Effective thinking means better decisions, to allow more free time, less stress and greater opportunities. This can be facilitated through activities to extend narrative language structure, where 7 levels can be identified (Sage, 2000a). Since communication is a process there are many aspects and the model below attempts to locate the main ones that affect the transaction in some way. In the UK we tend to look at parts of the process, such as sounds (phonetics) or *word structures* (grammar & syntax) which may interfere with the developmental process. An example, is concentration on sounds for reading as soon as children start school at age 4–5, when the phonemic system is not matured until 7–9 years. At this time, the right brain is dominant in development concentrating on whole experiences. The left brain spurts from 7 years onwards to cope with details like sound analysis. Is this why the UK has so many learning problems? The 10 best nations educationally do not start formal schooling until 7+ so working more consistently with brain development.

The graphic shows how ideas are generated and organised progressively. From producing a range of ideas at the first level, you eventually locate context, characters, events, results and reactions to produce a coherent narrative. There is evidence that students leave school without achieving the last 3 levels to limit reflections and judgments (Sage, 2000c, 2004). This cannot be left to chance with formal talk enabling both brains to function equally and opportunity for seeing, feeling, saying & hearing.

The Communication Opportunity Group Strategy (Figure 3) works for small or large groups of any age and ability. It focuses on narrative thinking and language structure, along with making ideas clear (*clarity*), ensuring they are

MODEL TO ASSEMBLE INFORMATION & OPINION (Sage)

7 Stages to Information Development: 7 Communication Aspects

CHILL – relax muscles CONNECT – smile, eye contact CONTEXT - make clear as words have many meanings

PERSONALITY   **INTELLIGENCE**

CLARITY
making ideas clear
and interesting

CONTENT
ideas relevant for
audience

Record: *produce ideas*
Recite: *arrange ideas*
Refer: *compare ideas*
Replay: *sequence ideas in time*
Recount: *Introduce, describe, discuss ideas*
Report: *Introduce, describe, discuss, reflect*
Relate: *setting, characters, actions, results, reactions*

CONDUCT
impression ideas
make on others

CONVENTION
rules governing the
exchange of ideas

OPPORTUNITY   **ATTITUDE**

Many people do not achieve the last 3 narrative levels to affect their higher level thinking & problem solving

FIGURE 3   The communication opportunity group scheme model

audience appropriate (*content*), whilst obeying social and linguistic rules (*convention*) and behaving properly (*conduct*). Research supports the approach, bringing academic and social success for children and adults (Sage, 2000b, 2000c, 2003, 2004, 2006, 2020). However, 200 years ago, thinking was different with Lancaster (1806) writing that class talk is improper and punishable, as students cannot chat and learn simultaneously. Does this view still linger in minds of policy makers and practitioners?

Educators acknowledge intuitive, creative thought but structure learning in L brain mode to achieve targets. Teaching is sequenced; learners progress through linear year-grades. Main subjects are verbal and numerical. Time schedules are followed. Seats are in rows. Student answers are judged right or wrong. The R brain (free thinking) is lost and mostly untaught. There are limited art, music and drama lessons in schools, but courses in imagination, intuition, inventiveness, perception and communication are unlikely. We are uncomfortable with free-thinking and more at ease with a disciplined, fixed approach. Educators and employers value creativity, assuming students will spontaneously develop it. This occurs to some extent for survival in spite of lack of attention. However, our culture so strongly rewards L brain performance that we are losing potential. Levy (1968) said that we may eventually destroy the R brain with prescriptive methods – speaking in an era with less target and grade achievement emphasis.

We are aware of inadequate verbal abilities (narrowly viewed as vocabulary & grammar) that handicap people. What happens to the non-verbal R brain, which assembles meaning and is barely considered? As neuroscientists provide evidence for R brain teaching, we can develop approaches to facilitate the *whole* brain, matched to natural development. R brain processing has its growth spurt from 4–7 years with the L kicking in after this. Studies show that learning problems arise from a limited R brain strategy, because early L analytic focus hampers growth. The result is a strong grasp of facts but a weak one for meaning (Sage, 2000b, 2003). High-achieving nations start formal learning after age 6–7, so working with brain development and allowing freedom for more real experience and R brain growth.

6 How Narrative Language Works for Thinking

Language and visual images transfer information as tools for expression and storage of ideas. Thinking and language have similarities and differences, developing over a lifespan from genetic factors, environmental and cultural input. Those poor at imagining (R brain activity) struggle with understanding (Sage, 2003, 2017). Take the story verse by Ogden Nash, Algy met the bear. The bear met Algy. The bear was bulgy. The bulge was Algy. Words do not contain the main message: The bear ate Algy. The gap is only filled if we can imagine what happened from other clues – The bear was Bulgy. The bulge was Algy. This depends on experience of hearing that bears are dangerous and might eat humans.

Connected talk or text has information/opinion gaps dealt with imaginatively to gain meaning, but seldom brought into teaching. How could it be done? Take the topic of Martin Luther King, the famous American activist. Introduce him like this: 'Can you tell a neighbour what you think Martin Luther King looked like? Sketch ideas and present to the class in 5 minutes'. This helps students use imaginations, so when given facts about him they will have used both brain sides. After facts, host a *review*. Ask pairs to share their designs with the class and what has been gained from the topic in a 30 sec. time-slot at the end of the lesson. Summarising and swapping experience develops understanding to establish a mental record. Without this opportunity superficial learning occurs. We fill brains with knowledge to marginalise approaches aiding comprehension, from regularly creating and recreating meaning through talk with others.

The French phrase, coup d'oeil, means "power of the glance", which Generals have to immediately see and make sense of battle. A tennis player, who perceives, interprets and comprehends a game, has "court sense". David Sibley, ornithologist, spotted a flying bird over 70 metres away as a ruff. He had not seen this rare sandpiper before, but captured what birders call the bird's giss – its essence (Gladwell, 2006). If unable to "thin-slice" we would not make immediate sense of complex situations. This R brain ability brings understanding of events. "Thin slicing" is facilitated by reviews and summaries of experiences. Japanese students do this in the final segment of a lesson, called "hansei" (reflection).

7 Language Knowledge

We need 4 knowledge types to develop linguistic competence – studied by experts (Sage, 2020):

> *Phonology* – basic sound units
> *Semantics* – symbols and meanings
> *Syntax* – grammar rules combining words for understanding
> *Pragmatics* – ability to communicate informally and formally in different situations

Competence in these areas is vital as language is used constantly in work and play. We acquire it first to make thinking possible. Natural conditioning helps us create, innovate and improvise. After learning words comes the symbolic communication process and then thinking and problem solving. Thus, language has a specific growth process which is different form linguistic competence and arises from experience and the integration of *sound* (auditory), *sight* (visual) and *spatial* (haptic), as well as *smell* and *taste* sensory input in some contexts. These present particular issues that need thinking through carefully.

8 How We Assemble Information

The R brain provides insight and outline, leaving the L to analyse and arrange parts. The Greeks grasped this in the *Places Trick* (Sage, 2003). With eyes closed, imagine the front door of your house/flat. Open it and enter the hall. Observe what is there. Go into the kitchen. Notice the space. Then walk to the stairs/corridor for the bathroom and view. Finally, go to your bedroom and gaze around! We have located 6 places: front door, hallway, kitchen, stairs/corridor, bathroom and bedroom. I will tell a story while you recall the objects.

After a night out, you return to find your front door ajar – propped open by a large, red apple, the size of a football. This shocks you as the door was locked when leaving. You creep into the hall and a glass slipper winks from the outside moonlight. It is like the one Cinderella wore for the Prince's ball! Switching on the light, you go to the kitchen and on a work top a purple, sparkly pen, dances a jig! How curious! You rush to the stairs/corridor, finding a large semi-precious stone, in your favourite colour – the size of a large rock. You step over this to reach the bathroom. The smell of your best-loved oil greets you and luxuriously bathing is a large wooden spoon, which turns & grins! Backing out, you find the bedroom. On the bed is a black velvet cushion, with a silver necklace curled like a snake!

Without a review, can you recall the items? How was this achieved? Did you remember the 6 familiar places and link these to the new information? It is the R brain creating these associations. Descriptive words image the scene. Knowledge of language grammar and syntax assists organisation of detail. It shows how brain sides work together for carrying out tasks, thinking both inductively and deductively. Inductive reasoning draws a conclusion from observation (bottom-up logic), whilst deductive is based on stepped reasoning and evidence (top down logic). Putting together what you see, feel, say and hear is the essence of this process. Both brains complement rather than contradict to give breadth and depth of understanding. Thus, learning uses the communication system as the essential tool. In the last 50 years research has recognised that language processing is cognition, the use of it is distributed thinking and capacity means understanding the development and recruitment of general learning and rational processes (Sage, 2020).

9   Thinking about Thinking

Behavioural sciences provide concepts, theories and frameworks to clarify human behaviour and choices. Some focus on the role of context or the anchoring or framing of information. Others consider how people are wired with dispositions like *biases*. Awareness of *bias* is vital for decision-making. My speech and language therapy training had sessions to detect *biases* (below) influencing diagnosis and management:

1. *Actor-observer* – attributing our actions to external influences and those of others to internal ones. As the actor, we observe our thoughts and behaviours but cannot see what others think, so focus on situational forces for ourselves but guess internal characteristics of other actions. This leads to each side blaming the other rather than considering all variables.

2. *Confidence* – overestimating that good things will happen and underes-
    timating negatives, so leading to risks. This bias is difficult to reduce as
    hope motivates to pursue goals.
3. *Confirmation* – only listening to information confirming existing beliefs,
    so reinforcing them. This leads to limited choices, inability to consider
    other views and contributes to dismissing those with different opinions.
4. *Convenience* – estimating probability of a happening on known exam-
    ples, which leads to poor estimates and decisions. We all use this as a
    short cut – so beware!
5. *Distortion* – memories influenced by things happening after an event,
    like watching television coverage, being questioned or hearing other rec-
    ollections. Memory is susceptible to subtle influences to cause incorrect
    identification.
6. *Egotistical* – giving oneself credit for successes but blaming failures on
    other causes. Older people are more likely to take credit for success. Men
    often assign failures to outside forces to protect self-esteem.
7. *False agreement* – overestimating how much other people agree with our
    beliefs, behaviours, attitudes and values, from mixing only with those
    sharing our views to boost self-esteem, normality and identity. This over-
    values our opinions and dismisses others.
8. *Fastening* – influenced by the first information heard. This is seen with
    doctors susceptible to first impressions that lead to wrong diagnoses and
    inadequate treatment.
9. *Halo effect* – allowing first impressions to influence thinking, as we want
    to prove correct to avoid cognitive dissonance – contradictory beliefs. The
    confidence of a person at interview, means we are likely to view them as
    competent and suitable.
10. *Hindsight* – seeing events as predictable, resulting in over-rating ability
    and taking unwise risks.

Biases are inevitable and we cannot evaluate every decision we make for them,
but awareness helps to understand how they affect learning and decision-making.

10   **Decision-Making**

Daniel Kahneman (2011) popularized system 1 (fast) and 2 (slow) thinking,
following Stanovich and West (2000). System 1 is the brain's innate rapid,
automatic approach to perceive, recognize objects/events, attend & avoid
problems. System 2 is the slower, analytic mode, using reason and conscious

mental exertion. An example is a pen and pencil costing £1.50. The pen costs £1 more than the pencil. How much does the pencil cost? People instantly reply '50p', but reflection brings the correct answer as 25p, showing fast, intuitive and slower, analytic thinking to solve problems.

Experts distinguish intuitive and conscious reasoning from Descartes' mind-body dualism (17th century) to Posner and Synder's (1975) dual-process mind. System 1 and 2 has general appeal but is over-simplified. Although some regions are more associated with one system, the brain is a complex interrelation of functions for tasks. Affective cognition (system 1) locates in the mesolimbic pathway, responsible for dopamine release. Dopamine is a neurotransmitter sending messages between cells to influence pleasure. As humans seek instant gratification, it plays a role in thinking fast. The frontal and parietal areas link to the analytic decision-making system and complex reasoning and higher-order slow thinking (system 2). Combined information from multiple systems – mesolimbic pathway, frontal and parietal areas – makes decisions. Most processes are a mix of systems. Unconscious ones, like emotion (system 1) are involved in more logical reasoning (system 2), so integration makes decisions effective, as reason alone rarely provides motivation and drive.

Language demonstrates teamwork. We communicate deliberately, but do not rehearse phonetic, syntactic, grammatical and pragmatic rules, which become unconscious when learnt. Exercise is also habit-driven but requires conscious review for success. Integrated 1 & 2 systems are when driving a familiar route, typing this article or playing a rehearsed tune, needing combined deliberate, automatic thinking and action.

With regard to bias, it has been thought that diagnostic errors were caused by system 1 reasoning, so clinicians were advised to think more slowly and gather as much information as possible. However, Gigerenzer (2020) showed that more information and slower processing does not always lead to accurate answers. Diagnosing patients and deciding treatment using evidence-based rules can perform as well. This led to "fast and frugal decisions" (FFD) for patient diagnosis, with doctors only needing to ask 3 crucial diagnostic questions to improve diagnosis of heart disease by 15–25%.

11   Developing Language and Thinking

Embedding language and thinking into learning alongside knowledge can be done if understanding narrative levels and selecting tasks to encourage them. Giving this consistent attention is purposeful and generates value behaviour, as many people do not achieve higher levels. Language and thinking are social activities responding to issues facing us all. Habits to encourage are: *commu-nicative, cooperative, collaborative, imaginative, inquisitive, persistent, resilience* and *discipline*. These are increasingly valued worldwide, but often are marginalised, as education organises learning around examinable subjects. When understanding their importance and acquisition, it is easy to embed them into lessons, with ways that enable competencies to flourish. This demands:

1. Awareness, knowledge and understanding of narrative thinking and language structures
2. An educational climate that values such strategies
3. Teaching approaches that facilitate thinking and language narratives
4. Learner engagement and commitment to achieve competencies

12   Issues to Consider

12.1   *Clarity*

Playing with possibilities, challenging assumptions, taking risks, tolerating uncertainty are discussed with students to improve thinking, understanding and expression. *Mind Movies* (on the web) transform ideas into fun, digital experiences, with positive affirmations, inspiring images and motivating music. Students can make their own movies.

12.2   *Climate*

Creating a positive climate that encourages exploration and risk-taking, whilst accepting mistakes as chances to learn, is vital. An exciting, unusual one frees thinking and-giving student choices and chances to take responsibility. Teachers must consider both the knowledge and competencies being developed and impart these at each lesson (see Appendix A). Harvard's Zero Project identifies routines for developing thinking and communication. When students describe an object, concept or experience – a routine like: "What makes you say that?" – challenges assumptions. "Think-Explore-Review" (TER) invites students to follow a learning routine that develops questions to investigate – leading to deeper inquiry and seen in the Japanese Hansei (reflection) part of each lesson/lecture (Sage et al. 2010).

12.3   *Choices* (*Approaches Assisting Thinking & Communication*)

1. *Problem-based learning* – uses real problems, enabling learners to conduct research integrating theory with practice as well as apply knowledge and competencies for solutions. Students on the Italian Education for Robotics programme researched local needs – checking people using

a park, by coding a robot to calculate use (avoiding accompanying dogs). They then designed facilities (toilets, snacks & activities) for diverse needs (Matteucci, 2022).

2. *Learning communities* – group learning assembles knowledge to support individual growth. In Japan, groups are normal – even for producing a picture! Use graphic organisers like *Venn diagrams* to present similarities/differences; *concept maps* to identify main and sub concepts; *T charts* for comparisons and *KLL charts* – what I know – would like to know – have learnt- to assemble experiences. Knowing how concepts connect; understanding inference/reference/coherence in talk/text/tasks deepens thinking and comprehension.

3. *Approach* – students must understand *why* they are learning things and *what* is acquired by doing them. Students are not given this information routinely, to affect knowledge of how to improve (Sage, 2000c, 2009b, 2020).

4. *Experimentation* – learning by doing applies knowledge to solve problems. The Confederation of British Industry report this as an employee issue.[2]

5. *Practice makes perfect* – prototyping, rehearsing and monitoring performance, drafting and re-drafting improve performance, so students must understand repetition needs.

12.4   *Sharing Experience*

Thinking and communicating is not an on/off switch, but a way to see, perceive, interpret, engage and respond to the world. People want to connect with others and working productively and well together can be taught. "Class Talk" (Sage, 2000c) develops group behaviour, so everyone participates and this can be highlighted in discussion. Continual sharing of each other's work and experiences builds a range of views and possibilities that a teacher transmitting knowledge to a group of passive listeners can never do. The appendix outlines how to achieve this. This is impossible without leaders' awareness of disconnection issues between education and work and also those from different language cultures. Language reflects the reality of people and thus the thinking, culture and customs of their native community. This means that conceptual understanding varies.

A colleague was given a foot massage for Christmas, as they have been well advertised, promoting relaxation benefits. The instructions are mumbo-jumbo! Do not use if you have "some psychopath" or have some "skin consciousness obstacle" or if the machine becomes "mojibake". Do readers know what mojibake is or how to identify this? Mojibake is an IT that describes instances where text is improperly decoded, resulting in nonsense or random symbols.

It happens largely due to the replacement of a set of unrelated symbols in a different code structure. The word is Japanese for 'character transformation' is 文字化け – IPA: modʐibake. Therefore, it is garbled text resulting from words being decoded using an unintended character encoding. The result is a systematic replacement of symbols with completely unrelated ones, often from a different writing system. Are you any wiser? Today, it is increasingly difficult to comprehend people, if it is not their mother-tongue – not only for words used but the different voice dynamics which inevitably reflect their first language. If this is syllable-timed not English stress-timed articulation, understanding is often impossible! Language nuances are rarely fully understood by those who are not first speakers. There are so many examples of misunderstanding where this is seen as the problem.

13   The Role of Higher Education Leaders

In UK Advanced level examination results (2021), girls increased a lead over boys with 46.9% achieving A grades compared with 42.1% of boys (Reform UK, 2021). Smithers (University of Buckingham) attributed this to the superior female intelligence (Daily Telegraph, 14 August, 2021). This must be challenged. There are many reasons for this difference – not least the verbal style of teaching and assessment that favours girls, whose linguistic abilities tend to be better than boys. This evolves from their historic child-rearing role, depending on effective verbal communication for successful physical, mental and emotional growth (Sage, 2000c). Thus, on verbal tests, girls will generally do better than boys but on *visual* ones this difference disappears (Sage, 2004, 2006). Boys are inclined to be more active than articulate, with their strength outstripping girls in teenage years, with a need to be energetically employed. They may be less inclined to sit at desks and learn in the traditional way. Trapasso (2018) showed how the active Forest school approach suited students. This was studied in the IDIAL European Project (Sage, 2008–2012) looking at how it could be encouraged, finding the following improved in active teaching styles:

1. *Language development* – speaking, thinking and the secondary linguistic abilities of literacy and numeracy improve with active methods encouraging group engagement
2. *Sense development* – hearing, sight, touch, smell and taste are heightened in real situations with natural environments offering stimulating sensual experiences
3. *Physical development* – control over muscles assists large motor abilities of arms and legs and fine motor of hands/fingers and feet/toes – developing

into the third decade of life and beyond. This aids coordination and unpredictable real environments help to assess risk and solve problems in cooperation with others

4. *Emotional and social development* – a natural environment inspires care and affection, empathy and trust, with opportunities to share, lead and cooperate

Thus, active learning assists holistic development, but as formal education progresses to university levels this decreases with the transmission style of lectures. Student increased numbers mean seminars for interaction in smaller groups tend to disappear. In 2021, 79% of UK students achieved either 2.1 or class 1 degrees, which provoked criticism from employers. Imperial College, London awarded 45% of final year students a first class, whereas Bath Spa and Chichester universities gave 15% this top grade, showing a wide institutional difference (Reform UK, 2021). Employers suggest that it does students no favours to think they have abilities to undertake careers for which they are manifestly unprepared. They state that university can be a waste of time, as now top employers have their own assessments because "A-level and university results give no indication of whether candidates have the skills needed" (Doulton, 2021, p. 19). Surveys show that graduates are limited at applying knowledge, initiative and self-management – having not achieved the range of communicative and collaborative abilities for today's inter-discipline teams (Confederation of British Industry, 2021). Adzuna, the jobs website studied 150,000 CVs and found two thirds had spelling mistakes and other errors. They pointed out this meant jobseekers will fall at the first hurdle. This is a wake-up call for education leaders, who need to address this mismatch of education and work-place goals.

The new Technical levels (T-Levels) were implemented in some UK institutions alongside A-levels, in September 2021. This gives student opportunities for workplace placements and assignments, so is a step in the right direction. Nigel Adams (2021) runs a degree course where students are given a grant to develop a business idea, which is implemented to gain their degree. The T-levels, rather than A-levels, would be an excellent entry to this programme, as students will have had real experience in professional contexts to become aware of workplace needs.

The Education for Robotics programme, coordinated by Stefano Cobello, for the Europole 4,000 worldwide agencies, shows how active learning, encouraging talk and thinking, can be facilitated effectively for work, where people will encounter technology. This frees employees to engage in higher-level work, but they urgently need a greater range of high-level competencies to achieve this successfully. The Robotics Education programme does not operate in the UK, but is mandatory in nations, like Italy. I believe I am the only Briton qualified in Educational Robotics. Higher Education leaders have a crucial, urgent role in bridging the education-workplace divide. There is not a moment to lose as employers are wasting time and money in training recruits to standards required. The Organisation for Economic Cooperation & Development (OECD, 2018) reports that British young people are the saddest and least satisfied of the 38-nation group, with low work performance. Why is this so? Reasons are:

1. British young people spend more time online than others (except Chile) and are sucked into a toxic culture of self-comparison and cyberbullying
2. More tests/exams than other nations bring pressure in a one-size-fits-all system
3. Social relations suffer from limited communication competencies from time spent online rather than face-to-face interaction which then impacts on later working roles

Education leaders must take action now!

14   Theories of Thinking and Language

Classical theories of relations between language and thought are those of Vygotsky (1962), Piaget (1970) and Luria (1976). Mental operations are embodied in language narrative structure with cognition resulting from internalisation. However, Hurlbert et al. (2017) show that less than one third of descriptive experience sampling showed *inner speech* as a salient characteristic. Language internalisation evolves from narrative speaking and may be declining, witnessed in people needing help for each step of a task and criminals, who cannot think about action consequences, supported by studies showing inadequate narrative levels to sustain inner talk. (Sage, 2020). Aaron Beck (2012) suggests emotions and behaviour are caused by *internal dialogue* and we must learn how to challenge and refute thoughts, especially mistaken ones – "cognitive distortions". Inner speaking is viewed as vital for continuity and sense of self. Discussion of these issues continues around:

– Innateness of knowledge vs. its gradual construction;
– Domain-specific knowledge representations vs. their general and connected nature;
– Perceptual/cognitive prerequisites & determinants of language acquisition vs. the structuring role of language and of language-specific properties in cognition;
– Relative importance attributed to structure vs. function in language.

Clearly, both universal determinants and language specific factors affect acquisition, accounting for why its course is both similar and different across languages. The Munduruki people have number words only up to 5, calling this "a hand" with 10 as "2 hands". Numbers above this are referred to as "many". The Piraha people's "one-two-many system" uses "many" for quantities larger than 2. They are accurate in representing numbers 1 and 2 using fingers, but this diminishes for bigger ones, showing language affects thinking to support the Sapir-Whorf Hypothesis (Giesbrecht, 2009).

This holds that thoughts are shaped by our native language and speakers of different ones reveal this in their thinking, although evidence is disputed. Pinker (1994) defines a hypothetical language (mentalese) used specifically for thought, housing mental representations of concepts like word and sentence meaning.

Aboriginal nations, like the Kuuk Thaayorre, use cardinal-direction terms – north, south, east and west: "pass the ball to the north, northeast". They say: "Where are you going?" instead of "hello" with a directional answer "to the northeast in the middle distance". These speakers need to be always spatially oriented and show greater navigational ability and spatial knowledge compared to others using relative references in their languages. Thus, current models suggest that language filters and channels information, engaging speakers to pay attention to different aspects of reality. For example, Yaghan an indigenous language of Tierra del Fuego, has the word "tuockolla" meaning to employ a person to chop down bone for spears. No such equivalent is found in English as this is not a facet of our daily activities. Further language confusion comes from their word for sun, which is "lamp", although the concept shows similar thinking. Appropriate learning theory must account for relations between languages and cognition and linguistic structures and functions, to explain invariant and variable growth aspects.

Encouraging thinking leads to questioning to make life less hazardous. Students can achieve creative-critical interpretations and demonstrate high levels of insight and intricacy in thought, to make inferences, draw conclusions, use knowledge in new situations and relate thinking to all contexts and their background knowledge. This encourages harmony in an age of identity politics, with widening divisions between people displaying different ideas, thinking, lifestyles and values.

15   Review

Howard Gardner (2009) in: *Five Minds for the Future* has the final thought, saying that creative thinking in human history has neither been sought nor rewarded. Human societies are naturally conservative and institutions particularly so. People strive to maintain their current position and education mitigates against innovation and interdisciplinary leaps. To thrive requires individuals to be creative in spite of the hassles that might occur for them.

The more we look at things the messier they become. Discovery of a prehistoric skull (Dragon Man) in China (1933), dated in 2018 as at least 146,000 years old and an unknown hominid, means we must rethink the story of mankind and ideas of linear progression (Pavid, 2021). Humans seem to be less a line and more a scribble. The diagram we learnt at school – a linear progression from ape to human has been declared by Adam Rutherford (2021), the geneticist, as so wrong it must be removed from books. We can never be certain of anything for long in our rapidly changing universe.

The issue of thinking and language is presently receiving attention because the necessity to improve it is seen as essential to survival. Leaders must support this for changes to be made. As you read this, you may hear your own voice speak the words. Your mind is thinking about this on a conscious and subconscious level, realising that language has great influence over thoughts. How we think and communicate directly correlates, which has intrigued scholars. How does the language you speak impact on your mind? This chapter aims to set you thinking and thinking and thinking …

We have to be careful now that technology is doing much routine thinking for us that we do not lose our ability to do so, as it is now needed at higher levels. Awareness of the process of how we rationalise and express thoughts coherently in language is vital for our survival, in order to cope with the many issues continually facing us in our complex world now dominated by technology.

Notes

1   www.azquotes.com
2   www.cbi.org

References

ACE. (2018). *Statement on jobs*. https://www.uk-ace.org.uk

Adams, N. (2022). Preparing for work. In R. Sage & R. Matteucci (Eds.), *How world events are changing education*. Brill.

Beck, A., & Dozois, D. (2012). Cognitive theory and therapy: Past, present and future. In S. Bloch, S. A. Green, & J. Holmes (Eds.), *Psychiatry, past, present and prospect*. Oxford University Press.

Beilin, H. (1975). *Studies in the cognitive basis of language development.* New York Academic Press.

Bruner, J. S. (1966). *Toward a theory of instruction.* Newton.

Cobello, S., & Milli, E. (2022). Sociological aspects of educational robotics. In R. Sage & R. Matteucci (Eds.), *How world events are changing education.* Brill.

Cooper, P. (2004). *Successful approaches with SEBD pupils.* Dr Barnardos.

Confederation of British Industry. (2021). *Employer surveys.* http://www.cbi.org.uk

Cwenar, S. (2005). PhD: An educational action zone project to audit student abilities. UOL.

Deacon, M. (2022, February 8). Ways of the world. *Daily Telegraph.* 14. Pub. Lon. DTPres.

Deresiewicz, W. (2021). The disadvantages of an elite education. *American Scholar.* http://theamericanscholar.org/author/

Diversity Q. (2019). *Leadership survey.* https//diversity.com>badboss

Doulton, R. (2021, August 14). A-levels now mislead students about their skills. *Daily Telegraph.* 19. DT Press.

Edwards, B. (1979). *Drawing on the right side of the brain.* Harper Collins.

Gardner, H. (2009). *Five minds: for the future.* Harvard Business School Press.

Giesbrecht, R. (2009). *The sapir-Whorf hypothesis.* Kindle Edition.

Gigerenzer, G. (2020). How to explain behaviour. This article is part of the topic "levels of explanation: From molecules to culture. In M. Colombo & M. Knauff (Eds.), *Cognitive science.* http://onlinelibrary.wiley.com/journal/10.1111/(ISSN)1756-8765/earlyview

Gladwell, M. (2006). *The power of thinking without thinking.* Penguin.

Goldacre, B. (2008). *Bad science.* Fourth Estate.

Harvard PZ Zero Project. (2016). *Project zero's thinking routine toolbox.* http://www.pz.harvard.edu>thinking-routines

Hurlburt, R., Alderson-Day, B., Fernyhough, C., & Simone, K. (2017, January 27). Can inner experience be apprehended in high fidelity? Examining brain activation & experience from multiple perspectives. *Frontiers in Psychology.* https://doi.org/10.3389/fpsyg.2017.00043

Kahneman, D. (2011). *Thinking, fast and slow.* Farrar, Straus and Giroux.

Kapadia, C., & Melwani, S. (2021). More tasks, more ideas: The positive spillover effects of multitasking on subsequent creativity. *Journal of Applied Psychology, 106*(4), 542–559. https://doi.org/10.1037/apl0000506

Lancaster, J. (1806). *Improvements in education.* In A. Jackson (Ed.), *Desperate deeds: Tales of triumph or despair .* Collins Classic Collection.

Levey, J. (1968). Differential perceptual capacities in major and minor hemispheres. *Proceedings of the National Academy of Science, 61,* 1151.

Luria, A. (1976). *Cognitive development. The cultural & social foundation.* Harvard University Press.

Matteucci, R. (2023). Teaching for the new industrial age: The Europole system. In R. Sage & R. Matteucci (Eds.), *Teaching with technology*.

Miller, L. (1986). Language disabilities, organizational strategies and classroom learning. In *The language learning disabilities institute*. Emerson College.

Murphy, G. (2009). *A vision of learning for the future: Presentation to the Inter-competency & Dialogue through Literature (IDIAL) project with Bulgaria, Finland, Latvia, Slovenia, Spain & the United Kingdom*. Liverpool University.

National Office for Statistics. (2021). Data published by Government Departments.

OECD Report. (2018). *Educating 21st century children and young people: Well-being in the digital age*.

Piaget, J. (1970). *Science of education and the psychology of the child*. Viking Press.

Pavid, K. (2021). Dragon man: Ancient skull from China could be new human species. *Science News*.

Pinker, S. (1994). *The language instinct*. William Morrow.

Posner, M., & Snyder, C. (1975). Attention and cognitive control. In R. Solso (Ed.), *Information processing and cognition* (pp. 55–85). Erlbaum.

Reform UK. (2021). *UK grade inflation*. http://reform.uk/research/degree-uncertainy-investigation-gradeInflation-universities

Rutherford, A. (2021). *How science is reinventing life itself*. Creation LIB/e.

Sage, R. (2000a). *The communication opportunity group scheme (Assessment)*. UOL.

Sage, R. (2000b). *The communication opportunity group scheme (Teaching)*. UOL.

Sage, R. (2000c). *Class talk: Successful learning through effective communication*. Bloomsbury.

Sage, R. (2003). *Lend us your ears: Listen & learn*. Bloomsbury.

Sage, R. (2004). *A world of difference*. Bloomsbury.

Sage, R. (2006). *The communication opportunity group scheme: Assessment and teaching*. UOL.

Sage, R. (2009a). What Cuba has to teach us about education. *Education Today*, 59(3).

Sage, R. (2009b). The IDIAL teacher course: Teaching transversal abilities to teacher students A *European project* (Inter-competency & Dialogue through Literature-IDIAL) researching success abilities in 7 countries. *Theories, Informing Teaching*.

Sage, R. (Ed.). (2010). *Meeting the needs of students from diverse backgrounds*. Continuum.

Sage, R., Rogers, J., & Cwenar, S. (2004, 2006, 2008, 2010). *An evaluation of education in England and Japan, the dialogue, innovation, achievement and learning projects*. University of Leicester.

Sage, R., Rogers, J., & Cwenar, S. (2006). *Why do Japanese children outperform British ones? The dialogue, innovation, achievement and learning project*. University of Leicester.

Sage, R. (Ed.). (2017). *Paradoxes in education*. Sense Publishers.

Sage, R. (2020). *Speechless. Issues for education*. University of Buckingham Press.

Stanovich, K., & West, R. (2000). Individual differences in reasoning: Implications for the rationality debate. *Behavioural and Brain Sciences, 23,* 645–665.

Sperry, R. (1968). Hemispheric disconnection and unity in conscious awareness. *American Psychologist, 23,* 723–723.

Trapasso, E., Knowles, Z., Boddy, L., & Newson, L. (2018). Exploring gender differences within forest schools as a physical activity. *Children, 5*(10). https://doi.org/10.3390/children5100138

Uncapher, M., & Wagner, A. (2019). Minds and brains of media multitaskers: Current findings and future directions. *Proceedings of the National Academy of Sciences, 115*(40). https://doi.org/10.1073/pnas.1611612115 (Original work published 2018)

Vygotsky, L. (1970). *Thought and language.* MIT Press.

Wallach, G., & Miller, L. (1988). *Language intervention and academic success.* Pro-Ed, Inc. Publishers.

Appendix A

Now technology largely replaces face-to-face talk and intelligent machines carry out our basic thinking routines, there is a demand for teaching thinking and language competencies for smarter work roles that are demanding higher levels. The following provides a possible lesson plan which research shows to be effective.

Class Format for Teaching Thinking and Language Transferable Abilities
Target Group: Any – Depending on Topic Choice
Method used with nursery to university level in the UK & elsewhere

COGS Narrative Levels Differentiate Classroom Tasks with Story/Video Clips for Stimuli

Lesson aim: Explore coping with biased thinking by communicating and cooperating with others and choosing tasks based on 7 narrative thinking and language levels.

Topic: *How to survive and cope with bias.* This was chosen from discussion of problems that students face with alternative ideas, values and attitudes in multi-cultural settings. (Lesson taught in English & Citizenship classes; method used in any subject teaching at all education levels).

Justification: Group teaching is characterized by participant diversity and narrative levels provide an effective way of differentiating tasks for different thinking levels. Learners observe (informal learning) the various uses of thinking and communication for different purposes and from group presentations develop judgements on effective performance. Small groups each have an observer role to report back on working together and presenting ideas to encourage peer group feedback.

Resources: Stories, pictures + video clips (available on the web). Packs for 7 groups (all narrative levels) include task instructions and supporting information, like stories, pictures, pens, paper, card, glue, sticky tape, etc. – to produce props for presentations.

Organisation: Introduce topic with a news story and video clip. Groups of 4 (3 carrying out tasks + 1 observing/reporting) are organized for narrative tasks. Each group presents outcome to the large group (3 minutes time limit to include observer comments). Review learning and feedback points for developing.

Topic: The Elephant in the Room: Understanding Human Biases
         Communicating, cooperating, collaborating, thinking, problem solving

---

Using the COGS model

Friendship groups work well, but facilitators may want to match tasks to ability. Distribute task folders to tables. As students enter class ask them to group around the 7 tasks, according to who they want to work with or assign them to a set. They should have prior notification of tasks.

Timetable for a 1 hour lesson

---

8 min. – Introduction: After greeting introduce ideas about biases, focusing on how to become aware and deal with them. Throw topic out to the class, asking about biases faced and how they coped. Explain we all have biases with how they form. Present a short story/film clip for stimulus – Monkey Business (Daniel Simons) or Diffusing Bias (Binna Kandola) as appropriate. (Visualising is vital for understanding. When we hear/read words we map them back into mental pictures).

---

22 min. Introduce tasks and observer feedback role, stressing a time limit for completion and how groups need to decide on a schedule for a presentation at the lesson end (2 min. introduction + 20 min. for groups to complete task).

---

21 min. Group presentations to class, (3 min per group including observer comment). Elect a time keeper. All must perform even if just holding a picture/poster.

---

9 min. Review main points emerging from discussion:

To solve problems – need to communicate and cooperate with others, share and organize ideas in line with specific requirements. Ask for reflections, reinforcing the experience as teaching themselves by swopping ideas, problems and solutions – observing other's behaviour.

Observer roles: 1. Rank talkers – most > least. 2. Note good points + those to develop? 3. Note leaders/ followers.

Tasks: Allot tasks to groups. **Note:** By end of primary schooling students need all narrative thinking levels, but many leave education not reaching above *Replay* level.

Record (produce a range of ideas)
1. Make a list of different biases that the group has experienced. Decide the 3 most urgent to address (Make a KLL chart – What we know- what we want to know- what has been learnt?

Recite (arrange ideas but not necessarily in a time order)
2. What are views and feelings about biases? Complete story blanks (below) to highlight inference – discuss views about word use. (Make a concept map)

Refer (compare ideas to judge similarities and differences)
3. Compare 2 bias types: Write a dialogue to illustrate & act out. Create a Venn diagram.

Replay (sequence ideas appropriately in a time sequence)
4. Select a common bias & sequence steps to deal with it effectively. Complete a graphic.

Recount (explain ideas – How? Why?) The Monkey Business Video
5. Students explain why so many people missed the gorilla, the black-shirted student leaving and curtain changing colour. What was learnt from this experience about themselves and people in general? Define and explain how selective attention influences people's ideas and behaviour in the real world? Prepare a concept map for group presentation.

Report (introduce, describe and discuss ideas)
6. Report on an example of biased thinking having a bad result for someone. (Examples of the Woke movement cancelling people on the web). The group chooses news articles to present.

Relate (setting, events, actions, results and reactions)

7.   Students play NPR report "Digital Culture Critic Abandons 'Fake on the Internet'
       Column" – exploring a decision by the Washington Post to discontinue a news-
       paper column correcting viral misinformation online. As students listen to the
       story, have them note words, phrases, or ideas that explain why it is so difficult to
       correct misinformation. What are reasons why people create and share it? Why
       is this hard to stop? Students present the story and review learning about confir-
       mation bias and how biases affect the way we respond to data.

Note: Groups select information for presentation. Time keeping is vital for a concise
message. Narrative levels differentiating tasks is effective – using all learning methods:
observation, coaching and formal presentation. Watching others provides good/bad
models for judgements.

Assessing outcomes

Group final presentations in which all students participate give teachers a view of individual and group performance. Everyone's feedback is encouraged-emphasizing positive aspects and areas for development.

Key competencies: thinking levels – their verbal and non-verbal expression; initiative; learning how to learn; team cooperation and commitment; social engagement;
leadership and management; numerical and graphical presentation in tasks; culture
and citizen issues; personal coping strategies; presentation and performance issues;
awareness of the many systems involved in communicating with others.

Fill in the Blanks

All students are capable of _____ but we cannot expect them all to _____ Too
many are tripping and falling as well _____ to keep up, while others are _____
Equitably funded education institutes run by _____ Educators, supported by strong
local and national educational _____ that address the context of student lives will
be the ones to improve the academic _____ of society's economically _____ students. These demand multiple solutions, big investment and political _____.

CHAPTER 2

What Are Learning and Remote Learning Processes?

Rosemary Sage and Riccarda Matteucci

Abstract

The COVID-19 pandemic put under a microscope the myriad of problems that many students face with learning. Information processing, thinking, language, communication and support are discussed to understand how to assist effective progress.

1 What Is Learning and Remote Learning?

Learning results from the processing of our five senses – *hearing, sight, touch* (feeling, movement, position in space – called haptic[1]), *smell and taste.* Every waking second, information flows through each sense, with the brain selecting the relevant bits to build a whole picture of experiences. This relies on converting details from short- to long-term memory (consolidation) during sleep. We need this shutdown to build retention and, in our unconscious state, to reflect on and resolve problems.

Learning is individual and what works for one may not do so for another. Although we have a preferred sense, using the five together produces the most effective learning – coordinated through the language and thinking process. Class teaching focuses on what we hear and see, but what about the other three senses, which are the least likely to be damaged by deficiency or disease? Treichler (1967) reported that people remember 10% of what is read, 20% of what is heard but 50% of what they see and hear together. The US National Teaching Laboratories reinforce the importance of all senses for learning, then sharing this information to aid retention. The Japanese use this approach, with a third of a lesson given over to students, who each present a 30-second feedback on what they have learnt. This is called *"hansei"*, meaning "reflection", carrying the idea of room for improvement! As everyone interprets differently, students are exposed to different views during the class *hansei* to enhance understanding and memory.

5% Lecture

10% Reading

20% Audio-visual

30% Demonstration

50% Discussion group

75% Practice by doing

90% Teaching others the information or using immediately to apply practically

FIGURE 4   The learning pyramid – How much information is retained?

Smell and *taste*[2] affect memory and increase communication between brain cells to improve retention. Japanese classrooms have scented plants. Kitchens are located near classrooms, as dishes prepared by students promote learning. Students bake biscuits, which are then used in a mathematics class to teach multiplication and division.

The Learning Pyramid shown in Figure 4 compares the various ways that people retain information according to how they learn. It shows that active learning and sharing information with others is the most effective strategy!

Learning is often passive, at a desk, listening to extended talk or completing prescriptive tasks, usually alone, set by teachers. Make it active, with student choices and control, preferably in group experiences, to increase communication, motivation and retention. In Japan, 7-year-olds work in groups of four to complete one picture. The standard of execution is high because of the different inputs made by the students. Educational robotics[3] is a form of group learning designed to enhance thinking, planning, implementation and communication in all subjects. Groups devise learning using technology and then present results to peers. This active approach is effective – focusing on talk as the technology for learning (Matteucci, 2019). It promotes communication for thinking, learning and doing.

Tip 1: After each task, recap, review, reflect and refine learning with others.

2   How to Use the Five Learning Senses

2.1   *Sight*

We rely on sight, because of our increased screen use today. Brains are image rather than word processors, so using these to reinforce words is vital. Colour stimulates mental activity.

2.2 *Hearing*

Sounds are both an aid and a distraction to learning. Hearing helps associations – the bark of a dog, song of a bird or rush of water. Calming, background music may help to focus attention. Through hearing we learn words, with spoken and written language the basis of formal learning and the understanding of what is right and wrong behaviour.

2.3 *Touch*

This sense involves movement and position in space (haptic). It actively grasps the context – releasing feelings, emotions and memories. Forty per cent prefer tactile learning and absorb best from real experience. Active learning aids understanding, problem-solving, creativity and independence through the application of knowledge.

2.4 *Smell*

Scents activate more brain areas than sight alone, with a strong effect on learning and memory. Negative scents should be noted. Nature trips stimulate and aid word association and have calming effects. We all have preference for smells, so in using these for teaching appreciate the differences amongst the audience.

2.5 *Taste*

Taste assists key associations, teaching sweet/sour, hot/cold, rough/smooth, safe/poisonous, etc. to enhance cultural cuisines, chemistry, geography, history, mathematics, etc.

Tip 2: Consider how to use ALL learning senses in learning task

3 Communication Is Key to Effective Learning

Consider the following mantra often reiterated by teachers: We *listen* to a book a day, *speak* a book a week, *read* a book a month and *write* a book a year![4] In life, 80% of activities are oral and only 20% are written (Sage, 2000).

- *Outside class* – We use informal talk (dialogue) with an equal chance to question and contribute in short speech sequences.
- *Inside class* – Talk is formal (monologue) with listeners required to assemble large quantities of narrative language with less chance to question and clarify information. Students lack the ability to cohere events.

Formal talk has gaps in information that must be filled. The brain has right and left sides with different roles. In the poem below – The loss of the cake has to be inferred:

> *Ronnie saw a nice cake on a plate.*
> *It was his mate's best ever bake.*
> *Sonny came with a smile on his face*
> *To see his cake but not a trace!*

The ability to *infer, refer* (it, he, her, they, them, etc. denoting characters) and *cohere* (assemble meaning) are problems, as people connect more by technology than face-to-face talk, with a reduced sense input making learning less effective. Formal learning favours the left brain more than right, which has the creative role to solve problems. Consider picking an apple from a tree.

> *How would you pick apples from the tree?* The right brain assembles possibilities and chooses the right fit and the left brain organises the steps to implement the goal.

> *Right brain*: Find a ladder; climb a tree; pick up a stick to throw; blow hard; select a tall person nearby. (The ladder is the best fit.)

> *Left brain*: The tall person positions themselves; targets the apples; lifts arm to pick; places them in a container; takes the apples away to store.

The right brain matures from 4 to 7 years and deals with the whole/overview of things/events, while the left brain develops from age 7 to cope with detail and analysis of parts. We expect learners to cope with word parts immediately when they start school, even though the brain is not ready for this process. Thus, many students have higher-level language problems, assembling quantities of words, even though they do not have issues with informal chat. They are labelled as having reading, attention or behaviour problems. In one study, all the students over 10 years old who were referred to a development assessment centre for such school difficulties were found to have higher-level language deficiencies, although visual reasoning was above average (Sage, 2020). These learners suffered from online lessons, which reduced sensory input, making understanding meaning more difficult for them.

4 Peer Support for Learning

Students cope in class because what they fail to gain from lessons, they can get from peers, who fill in gaps in their knowledge during informal chats. Therefore, intelligent students mask their problems, although they may be slower to complete tasks. However, when learning alone, without the support of friends, they become miserable and fearful. Often lacking the ability to self-talk inside their heads, they rely on the prescriptive class regime to take them through the steps of a task. In Japan, students regularly teach classes to acquire higher-level thinking and communication. Figure 5 is a photograph of a 7-year-old boy teaching science to a class of 60. He has thought up eight experiments to look at the effect of one substance on another and divided the class into 12 groups to complete them. Each group is feeding back their results. The students said they loved lessons by classmates, as they talked in a way they could easily understand! In this school, students teach twice a month and choose whatever topic they like and work out how to present it to the class.

Tip 3: Before developing a topic/task, talk about it to stimulate the creative right brain before sequencing the information/instructions

4.1 *Brain Development Opportunities*

At a Manchester Business School conference "It's Good to Talk", a Chicago University team reported that only 15% of what we learn and retain occurs in a

FIGURE 5   A 7-year-old boy teaching a class of 60 students

formal learning context. Where there is close cooperation between schools, colleges, universities and communities, learning thrives. There is a consistent, shared approach to developing knowledge and competencies.

In some Japanese schools students engage in teaching in order to learn how to communicate their knowledge. Japan provides a model as communication and relationships (the moral curriculum) is the primary focus, with the whole community being aware of their responsibilities for effective learning through encouraging opportunities to use narrative talk. This approach is needed worldwide if students are to meet the requirements of today's connected world. Learning comes from curiosity, but educators say that students lack this because they are overwhelmed by life's complexities. Children are overprotected because the media dwells on dangers to them, producing this reaction. We must give them the courage to have the curiosity to learn.

Tip 4: Give learners chances to choose, control and present learning so they understand it better

4.2   The Goals of Education
– Educate for understanding as well as knowledge
– Target communication and cultural issue in diversity
– Form relations with successful learners
– Value talk as the technology for understanding
– Facilitate the use of images and non-verbal communication
– Loosen learning frameworks and increase freedom
– Educate for students rather than for the system

5   What Is Remote Learning?

Remote learning happens when teachers move face-to-face classes to online spaces. It is an educational trend occurring in an uncertain world of pandemics resulting from rapid movements of people and a limited qualified workforce. Educational robotics enables student groups to use technology to plan, control and carrying out learning. Students use robots to devise stories, which are then related to the group and recorded for review remotely. Each student tells a part of the tale in turn. The following ideas provide guidance to make remote learning bearable.

– Design a schedule to fit life circumstances
This allays anxiety and provides a plan and purpose to propel action. Begin with a "to do" list for keeping activities on track. Complete tasks if possible by the end of each session. Check resources required. The website Learning Liftoff[5] provides resources and links to support and extend opportunities. Learners must be able to access web information with speed and judgement. Educators should facilitate this type of activity and at the same time discuss the pros and cons involved.

– Support (rather than teach) understanding
We all learn differently with a preferred sense (sight, hearing, touch, smell, taste). For example, the 40% of people who prefer tactile (real experience) learning could find that they underperform at school or college, environments that focus on learning though hearing and sight (Sage, 2000). However, this type of learner tends to do well in life, when applying knowledge practically in situations that have meaning and relevance for them. Half of us need an overview and structure (the top-down approach). The rest must discuss the topic first, with personal stories and a more informal approach used in order to help them engage (the bottom-up approach). Use both strategies to employ the top-down (right brain) and bottom-up (left brain) styles effectively.

Writing about a football match is easier to support, for example, because it is seen and actively experienced, rather than analysing poetry and prose metre. The latter may have to be learnt about first before grasping the issue about rhythm. The internet helps here with many examples. Prose is the normal language of speech/writing, with sentences and paragraphs presented in sections on pages. Poetry (verse) generally has regular rhythm – dividing into stanzas, with lines often rhyming. Although less fashionable for learning activities today, poetry plays an important role in developing memory and understanding.

– If a learner is struggling, identify their obstacles and ask them questions
Is it the topic, the focus or the frame of mind at the time? Perhaps it is motivation? Is there too much or too little structure? Do they need personal support or a friendly warning if they are not keeping to the expected plan? When students say, "I don't get it", find out what "it" refers to, using appropriate questions to focus on their creative and critical thinking, as well as narrative language competencies. Ask them to tell you about what they find confusing. Use relevant questions to discover issues. The following list gives examples of questions to ask them in order to help you get to the core of the problem:

- What is the best thing about learning something new?
- What is the worst thing about learning something new?
- Can you tell me about a time when you were pleased about what you learnt?
- Think about your learning today. What would like to know more about?
- Cab you ask a question that relates to your learning today?
- Were there times when you did not feel valued for your work?
- Were there times when others showed concern for you over a difficult issue?
- What was the challenge about your learning today?
- Were there moments when you felt proud of yourself for what you had achieved?
- What did you like about your learning today?
- Can you tell me about a conversation you enjoyed with someone today?
- Is there a question you think I should ask about your day?
- How could you continue learning about today's topic?
- What is your way to remember what you have learnt?
- How could learning be made easier for you?
- How do you keep interested and engaged in your learning activities?
- Do you feel you have enough support for your learning?

How, why and when we ask questions and the range of issues they raise makes a difference to the information we receive from learners. Naturally, you will not ask all the above questions at one time – probably two or three are suitable for the specific needs of a situation. Questions must be asked when you are able to focus your full attention on the responses. Meal times are good for this and should become routine for questions and discussion. These should be encouraged, as they are occasions for acquiring abilities of thinking and communicating in narrative forms, such as re-telling experiences.

The world thinking project (2022) indicates that many students find difficulty in thinking and narrating. Positive, powerful exchanges mean:

- Do not interrupt the flow of conversation – encourage with smiles and nods.
- Ask for more information with details – I'd like to know more about....
- Encourage learners to re-call and re-tell experiences and events to rehearse narratives.
- Enquire about feelings and how to deal with them positively – How did you feel about...?
- Confirm feelings as normal and feed this back to explicitly reassure.

    – Check they understand it is wrong to be unkind or disrespectful to other people.

    – Thank them for sharing and appreciate honesty of views and feelings.

– Encourage self-awareness and insight by sharing learning through talking
This enables teachers to become aware of what has been absorbed and learnt by students. This is the most effective learning strategy to transfer and apply learning. Of the information delivered in a lecture format, only 5% is retained – but 90% retention is possible if learning is shared or taught to others (Sage, 2020). Most of us are unaware of what we do not know, until we have to explain what we do know to others. Why? In British schools, students do not regularly give brief feedback on what they have learnt. This strategy exposes them to the different ideas of their peers in order to achieve a wider understanding. Sharing experience of learning broadens knowledge in a way that is impossible in just a teacher-transmission approach.

– Track progress and reward apparently minor but vital behaviours
Pay attention to tasks in order to develop insights on progress and discover motivation sources. All learners require emotional, collaborative and psychological as well as academic support. Understanding learning style as well as technological, disciplinary and nurturing needs is crucial. Challenges and progress markers must be suitable to assist progress.

– Develop a learning group by connecting with peers who help support and extend knowledge and abilities
Peers have similar experiences and communicate at a level that is understandable. Research at the University of Leicester (Sage, 2000) showed how communication with adults was the most difficult problem for students, because teachers talked in ways that were different to their own experiences and so they were unable to grasp information easily. Some teachers have strong, unfamiliar accents and use words and phrases which students have not heard before. Now that Standard English is discouraged as being "elitist" and so many varieties of English are accepted, the problem of understanding each other has grown. This is a particular problem in international exchanges, as people from other countries have been taught only Standard English. One is often flummoxed by what words mean today. Perusing a menu, on the starter list was, "Plant kitchen vegan duck croquettes". When the waitress came to take the order, we asked what this description meant, but even she was perplexed! Encourage links with others having similar interests, ambitions and approaches to life and who can comprehend each other easily.

6   Review

Learning is a communicative, collaborative and cooperative process and can be enhanced when it is given priority and opportunity. In Britain we do not value or promote this aspect in an active way, like in some other countries, and so have more learning and mental health issues. Our teacher-transmission style of giving information is not always understood, as students have less direct talk experiences in a world where technology dominates. Children regularly enter school with language and cognition capacities well below their chronological age and so are unable to grasp quantities of talk and text (Sage, 2020). The top 10 nations educationally put language, communication and relationships to the fore of learning, accepting that in life 80% of what we do is oral and only 20% is written (Sage, 2000, 2020). Improving these aspects pays off in better student performance. Above all, it is important to eat, sleep and exercise well for self-care and remember to talk with other people in a positive way that does not annoy them. Even if you strongly disagree with their views, do so in a pleasant manner that does not give offence. This issue is often ignored. Understanding the processes of learning is essential to achieve higher performances, which new job roles are requiring.

Notes

1   Haptic perception (Greek: *haptós* – palpable, *haptikós* – suitable for touch) is the ability to "grasp something". Perception comes from active exploration, as opposed to passive contact via tactile perception.
2   It is not surprising that smells affect memory, given that the brain's olfactory bulb is intimately linked to the hippocampus, which deals with learning and memory. Research shows that this increases communication between brain cells to explain how it improves brain function.
3   In Chapters 1 to 5, in "The Robots Are Here: Learning to Live with Them", Matteucci outlines how educational robotics are used in Italy. Students present projects to national and international Maker Fayre gatherings of inventors/creators and so are well prepared for a world dependent on intelligent machines.
4   "It is said that typical Americans listen [to] a book a day, speak a book a week, read a book a month, and write a book a year" (Loban, 1973, p. 687).
5   https://learningliftoff.com

References

Loban, W. (1973). Guest forum: The green pastures of English. *Elementary English,* 5(50), 683–690.

Matteucci, R. (2019). What is technology? In R. Sage & R. Matteucci (Eds.), *The robots are here: Learning to live with them*. Buckingham University Press.

Sage, R. (2000). *Class talk: Successful learning through effective communication*. Bloomsbury.

Sage, R. (2020). *Speechless: Understanding education*. Buckingham University Press.

Sage, R., & Matteucci, R. (Eds.). (2019). *The robots are here: Learning to live with them*. Buckingham University Press.

Treichler, D. (1967). Are you missing the boat in training aid? *Film and Audio-Visual Communication, 1*, 14–16.

CHAPTER 3

Why Technology Makes Learning Processes Difficult

Rosemary Sage

Abstract

Although e-learning has coped with the COVID-19 2020 pandemic, when face-to-face teaching has been impossible, it has illuminated inequality issues. This is not only that some students lack required technology and home support to access on-line materials, but a significant number are unable to learn without ongoing help. In Britain, we run a prescriptive education system focusing on what to learn rather than how. Students performing competently in supportive classrooms have found themselves floundering as they try to manage learning with less guidance. This has revealed their difficulties more acutely, resulting from language deficiencies that are rarely identified.

1 Introduction: Communication Issues

As a speech and language therapist, psychologist and teacher, I have worked in Health and Social Services, mainstream Education and latterly in Universities. Studies in a typical Leicester primary school over three years showed all entries had language and cognition below age level (Sage, 2000). At the feeder secondary school, 80% of students were found to operate at a 5–6 year level on psycho-linguistic tests when age 11–12, with the school continually in special measures. The Medical Research Council asked me to look at 300 children in this Midland area testing normally on intelligence (IQ) tests but failing in schools. This cohort all had problems with understanding and producing extended language, which component style IQ tests had not revealed. Therefore, a transmission learning style, with extended talk and texts, proved problematic. Individuals can appear chatty and deal with conversation successfully when able to control action, but have difficulty with lengthy language sequences in classroom situations where the role of the listener is predominately passive and not active. Their dialogue ability, observed outside class, means that teachers assume they are language proficient, but the monologue style of class discourse is a problem so they depend on direct or indirect help

© ROSEMARY SAGE AND RICCARDA MATTEUCCI, 2024 | DOI:10.1163/9789004688612_006

to complete tasks. During the pandemic period, students, at all levels, have talked about missing classmates and teachers, along with spontaneous conversations as well as relationships with them. The context of formal education makes them keen to learn, holds them accountable and motivates them to stay engaged, whilst acquiring much more from observing others, sharing information and gaining support and help when required.

Students, described above, would be viewed as having some degree of higher-level language problem and the pandemic has highlighted issues. This is not only a problem at primary but also at the tertiary end of education, as some students say they cannot cope with webinars and wander off. One suggested: "We'll pass courses anyway as universities don't allow us to fail". Transmitting information, in the way we might do so face-to-face, does not work for on-line presentations, which need material broken down into small chunks with more time to absorb visual or graphic input. On-line performances require training to be effective as they rely on auditory and visual material and exclude the haptic (touch, feeling, position in space) and non-verbal dimensions necessary for those learning best from real experience (Sage & Matteucci, 2022). This is important for people with subtle communication issues. Increasingly there are many instructed in a language other than mother-tongue, with the word nuances confusing. There has been press coverage of continual people misunderstandings. My neighbour left a note for a delivery of wood logs: "Empty sacks under the hall table", to find on returning home that her message was taken literally!

2   What Are the Problems Processing Quantities of Talk and Text?

The pandemic has highlighted students finding it difficult to work under their own steam and it is important to assess communicative competencies for their relevant support. One considers ability to *introspectively analyse* – (terms used in the literature – inner speech/talk, self-talk, sub-vocal speech, mental verbalisation, internal dialogue/monologue or self-statement). Alongside inner-talk is *external language dialogue and narrative monologues* (telling/re-telling, giving instructions, reporting, making an argument, etc.). However, the importance of inner-talk is not often recognised, but Vygotsky (1934/1986) suggested it was dependent on sequential narrative language and vital for making predictions. If students have problems with this, they are unlikely to carry out tasks alone and need prompting for each step of the way. Articulating each step, repeating, reviewing and recalling all the sequence builds mental verbalisation for completing tasks alone.

Hurlbert (2011) has made inner-talk a focus for study and found that there is only an average 20% frequency of use. External talk is necessary for developing internal self-statements. Is low frequency of inner-talk a result of technology as the preferred way of communicating? In countries, like Italy, Japan and Cuba, talk is the technology of learning and you do not find silent classrooms as students constantly verbalise to develop higher levels of speaking and thinking. Group work is more common than individual, so that participants constantly exchange ideas, reflect, review and refine performances, with Japanese students 4 years above UK counterparts in the Dialogue, Innovation, Achievement and Learning studies (DIAL – Sage, Rogers, & Cwenar, 2002–2010). One must take their approach seriously, as communication and relationships take precedence over subject learning in policy and practice. In Italy, the Roman traditions of Oratory and Rhetoric Schools are still seen today, with oral examinations important for judging performance, so reflecting their normal use in life.

3   E-learning

Many issues are involved with online education, but we cannot ignore the importance of it in times of a pandemic crisis. There are always solutions to fix problems. Technical difficulties can be solved through pre-recording video materials, testing content and having a reserve plan so that teaching–learning is not hindered. Online courses must be dynamic, interesting and interactive with information presented in small amounts, as it is not possible to judge audience understanding as in face-to-face contacts. Time limits (3 minutes is the maximum for attention – Sage, 2000), reminders and summaries of information keep students alert and attentive (especially important for those with language difficulties). Efforts should be made to humanise learning, so personal attention and initial face-to-face contact is vital for learners to easily adapt to this new environment. Social media and group forums help connect students and educators. Personal communication is key when texts, messaging apps, video calls, etc. prove difficult, as research indicates there is much miscommunication when non-verbal input is reduced (Sage, 2020). Deliver content with an applied task following, so students can practise and hone their abilities. Encourage review and reflection on experiences. Support sets of 6–8 students are more suitable for such exchanges, as some find a 30+ group intimidating in an on-line forum, although others prefer it to face-to-face experiences.

The quality of courses should be improved continually and designed to be creative, interactive, relevant, student-centred and group-based. Educators must produce clear, simple, effective online instructions which facilitate learner feedback and encourage them to question and expand course content. Institutions should focus on teaching issues and emphasise collaborative projects and case-based learning. Challenge is not only finding new technology and using it, but also reimagining approaches and helping students and staff wanting digital literacy guidance. This is important for students showing language problems, who find the on-line mode perplexing.

4   Equality: High Level Language Deficiency (HLLD)

People come across terms like articulation, stammering, voice disturbances and linguistic components, like sentence structure, vocabulary and grammar. These are problems of individuals seeking help from communication specialists. However, language can be affected outside ability to produce a sentence with correct structure, vocabulary, articulation and voice dynamics. Subtle communicative components, known as higher order/level language or executive function, can be impaired and more difficult to detect than distinctive limited grammar or defective speech sounds and voice quality. These individuals often score well on basic language (vocabulary) and visual reasoning intelligence tests (like Raven's Progressive Matrices) but struggle with verbal thinking, in depth explanations and storytelling. High level language includes:

– *Sequencing*: Sequencing impairment affects ability to organise and complete tasks and also impacts on telling/writing a narrative coherently or giving step-by-step instructions correctly. This might present as a difficulty in recounting an event without confusion. It also shows as a problem giving project steps to another person. These subtle skills are all underpinned by ability to correctly sequence within connected language activities. Typically difficulties in telling the time in early development are wrongly interpreted as being "dull".

– *Cause and Effect*: Cause and effect determines the reason for a specific outcome. Without this competence, an individual struggles to understand why something has happened, as they are unable to appreciate how an action leads to a certain outcome. If not understanding a sudden impact can cause a glass to break, you could not appreciate how knocking it off a table means buying a new one.

– *Inference & Predicting*: This is ability to use clues provided through verbal or visual contexts in order to infer further information and make a prediction based on it. Someone gives an instruction: "switch on the headlights". From this we deduce that the person is driving, as headlights are on vehicles. We also infer low lighting and vision, as the reason for the order. We can predict if lights were off an accident might occur. Although information is not explicit, connections must be made from experience to understand events, if no further facts are given.

– *Non-literal Language*: This refers to figurative language, including idioms, metaphors and similes, which do not directly convey a concrete meaning and are abstract in nature. This can make understanding jokes, humour and the nuances of language difficult. It makes reading material more of a problem to understand. An example of an idiom is "hit the sack" – meaning "go to sleep". Such phrases may confuse as people educated in the language tend to use idiomatic and metaphorical language frequently.

These difficulties arise in the amygdala – a small almond-shaped brain part. This limbic system area is below the brain lobes – consisting of the hippocampus, hypothalamus and amygdala. Both amygdala and hippocampus ensure memory processing. The amygdala encodes emotion and the hippocampus deals with event details: people, things, situations and where they take place. We are more likely to remember something if having a feeling or an emotion about it. Narrative processing or production and the capability to respond appropriately to significant visual or auditory stimuli are disrupted with problems in this area. Thus, the amygdala is primary for perception and expression of social and emotional nuances and mainly responsible for comprehension and expression of spoken and then written language. Parts of the auditory neocortex – from the anterior and medial temporal lobe and beyond the insula – to include the superior temporal lobe and inferior parietal lobule – are partly an evolution of the amygdala.

It is argued that the primary, secondary and auditory association areas, including Wernicke's visual zone, have evolved from the amygdala and are interconnected with this nuclei via the inferior portions of the arcuate fasciculus and claustrum. When neocortical auditory areas are impaired, the amygdala is sometimes disconnected and unable to extract or impart nuances to incoming or outgoing sounds and sights. Although the left and right amygdala are functionally lateralised, with the right larger than the left, both contribute to language perception and expression – helping to maintain the reliability of neocortical auditory areas in right and left temporal lobes. Through these interconnections, languages are hierarchically organized at the level of the temporal neocortex in this brain section.

Signs of Higher Level Language Deficiency (10+ suggest a diagnosis)

– Chatty but speaking, reading, writing and spelling not at expected level
– Average+ intelligence but achievements do not equate
– Oral components like vocabulary test well but not extended word sequences
– Lacks attention appears hyperactive or a dreamer

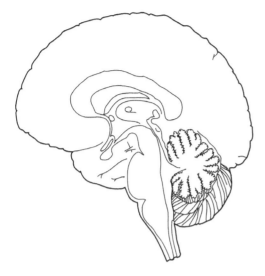

FIGURE 6
The amygdala within the brain –
the small almond shape in the middle

- Gains support from peers as not behind enough for special support
- Lacks self-esteem & hides weaknesses with clever strategies
- Easily upset, frustrated and emotional
- Loses sense of time & easily gets lost
- Viewed as lazy, dull, immature and disruptive
- Frequently good at art, music, drama, sports/sales, marketing, engineering, design
- Haptic[1] and visual abilities are strong
- Learns best from observation, demonstration, experimentation and experience

Vision, Reading, Spelling
- Complains of head/stomach aches or dizziness when reading
- Confused by letters, numbers, words, sequences or verbal explanations
- Repetitions/additions/transpositions/omissions etc. in reading and writing
- Letter, number, word reversals
- Visual problems seem evident but are not revealed on tests
- Sees/feels non-existent movements when reading/writing
- Keenly observant or lacks depth perception and peripheral vision
- Reads often with limited comprehension and attention
- Spells phonetically and inconsistently

Hearing, Listening, Speaking
- Distracted by noise and movements so fails to hear and listen
- Difficulty in putting thoughts into words – speaks in incomplete sentences
- Dysfluent when stressed – mispronounces/transposes words and phrases

Motor Skills, Writing
– Difficulty copying/writing – often illegible; odd pen/pencil grip
– Clumsy, uncoordinated; motion sickness in cars, trains, planes
– Difficulty executing gross/fine motor skills
– Ambidextrous – confuses left/right, over/under, etc.

Time Management, Mathematics
– Problems telling/managing time and with sequenced information/tasks
– Finger counts and uses tricks to reach answers – problems transcribing
– Counts slowly – objects/money, etc.
– Does arithmetic but not word problems; cannot grasp algebra/higher maths

Thinking, Memory
– Thinks with images and feelings, not sounds or words (little inner talk)
– Limited memory for sequences, facts and information not actively experienced
– Efficient long-term memory for experiences, faces, locations, etc.

Personality, Behaviour, Health, Development
– Sensitive; strong sense of justice; strives for perfection
– Can be class-clown, trouble-maker or too quiet/reserved
– Compulsive/disorderly in response to activities
– Prone to ear infections; sensitive to foods, additives, chemical products
– Light/deep sleeper; often wets the bed beyond appropriate age
– High/low pain threshold
– Symptoms/mistakes increase with stress/pressure/confusion/health problems
– Unusually early/late development stages (crawling/walking/talking)

This section is from a university course with permission for use.

Not all the above symptoms have to present for a HLLD diagnosis, but 10+ suggest further investigation. Generally there is little concern until starting school and required to read, write and calculate. Problems are labelled dyslexia,[2] when presenting with the secondary language areas of literacy and numeracy. In the UK, there are minimal checks of whether primary spoken levels are in place to support secondary language levels of literacy and numeracy. In some countries, language development is routinely assessed on entering formal education and they show less learning problems compared with Britain. Communication specialists see the above symptoms as in the cognitive-linguistic domains, with problems in integrating left verbal and right visual brain functions. Management targets brain integration (PACE system,

Sage, 2004/2007), as well as narrative language and thinking development. Learning activities with a creative, visual, active, hands-on approach are effective. Students with these problems often have above average intellectual ability and develop exceptional creative talents, with many historical geniuses showing HLLD difficulties. Sadly, issues are often not identified in the UK, which does not have high value for psycholinguistics compared with high-achieving nations and lacks a strong preventive health and education strategy. I have often written reports for courts, when adults with such problems suffer bullying at work and take employers to tribunals. These cases always win! The following strategies help all learners, using technology to enhance experiences:

Attract

3D domains and video presentations capture interest, making e-Learning stand out from Power-Point ones because they are processed more easily. Amaze and engage the audience and they will be more likely to learn.

Images

An image is said to represent 1000 words, but a video, with moving images, produces more understanding by introducing some *haptic* input. Thus, video conveys more than a still picture and helps to make a sequence of events active and meaningful.

Design

Multimedia must reflect learning goals. If the course is about *language development*, select a video showing the main stages of growth in a real person. Ensure multimedia does not distract from the learning message but enhances understanding.

Comedy

Humour gets a point across. An amusing presentation keeps attention to make the lesson memorable if a subject is dreary. However, avoid jokes if you think they will not work.

Interaction

Interaction breaks up the information and helps share ideas and views to broaden and assist understanding. Some learners find it frustrating when interactions with others spoil the information flow. Also, these can be hard to employ on mobile devices used to transmit content. As a general rule, use interactions to reinforce and apply learning in practical ways. This approach is vital to support personal and practical development which is marginalized in the exam rush.

Expectations

Set e-learning expectations at a higher level. This should follow the style of a documentary film. It uses sets, has video actors and is based in a 3D mode. The language should be clear, simple in structure, upbeat and amusing where appropriate. Study TV documentaries to review how they transmit messages. When presenting a story, with a beginning, middle and end, make it memorable!

Understanding

Audiences are diverse and a person's first language dictates how they think and interpret, so learning in another one requires great concentration and more time for information processing. Research shows that communication and language are problem areas in plural societies (Sage, 2020), so assume that any audience today will have listeners and viewers with additional linguistic and other needs. Check for information overload. Use short sentences, with good pausing between them and give important ideas suitable word-stress. English is a stress-timed language in contrast to many others with a syllable-timed rhythm, so this issue has to be brought to attention. Those, whose mother-tongue is not English, will speak it in the same rhythm as their first language and, therefore, be difficult to understand. Some will find it difficult to integrate visual with auditory input, so ensure the main messages separate these two mediums. Present the visual (picture/film/graphics) and make the explanation afterwards.

5   Review

E-learning has accelerated in education as a result of the COVID-19 pandemic and we are all reflecting on how to use more effectively to develop learning processes, with special attention for those not well-suited to the predominately auditory and visual input. With preferred processing through the haptic sense channel, some will find e-learning, as the major instruction mode frustrating, to turn them off formal learning.

   The Organisation for Economic Cooperation and Development (OECD) says that UK education is well supplied with technology, but staff are not trained sufficiently to deliver it effectively. The Director suggests Britain has made the slowest educational progress of the 38 OECD nations, because memorisation remains the dominant learning strategy in a narrow, exam driven culture (Schleicher, 2020). He reports that education today is not about teaching people something, but helping them develop a compass to integrate personal, practical and academic competencies. Education must rebalance to develop a more holistic, world approach for coping with life – fixing on real not abstract issues.

The OECD Educational Working Paper (Bertling, 2020) reports 25% of schools and colleges will never return to former teaching ways following the 2020 pandemic, with 50% preparing for a future of blended learning. There is an urgent need for ongoing professional development that monitors new teaching activities, using practitioner recording models to review evidence amongst colleagues. Since 60% of students worldwide do not reach required educational standards (Luckin, 2020), it is vital to review policies and practices at a time when education has been disrupted by pandemic lockdowns. The introduction of e-learning has thrown up communication and language-based issues. These have previously received minimal attention in traditional teaching models. Communication matters. Let us make it matter more so that less people struggle with e-learning!

Notes

1   Haptic is the non-linguistic communication subsystem through physical contact-touch, feeling, movement & proprioception. It is the basic sense and first to develop and last to be lost due to disease or injury. Although the easiest, most effective learning path, it is less used than auditory and visual modalities in education.
2   Dyslexia is a descriptive term meaning difficulty with reading, although it is often used as a diagnostic label.

References

Bertling, J. (2020). *Global crises models: OECD education working paper 232.* OECD Publishing.

Hurlburt, R., Heavey, C., & Kelsey, J. (2013). Towards a phenomenology of inner speech. *Consciousness & Cognition, 22,* 1477–1494.

Luckin, R. (2020). *I, teacher: AI and school transformation.* Newstateman.

Sage, R. (2000). *Communication & learning PG course.* School of Education, University of Leicester.

Sage, R. (2020). *Speechless. Issues for education.* Buckingham University Press.

Sage, R., & Mattueccci, R. (2022). *How world events are changing education.* Brill.

Sage, R., Rogers, J., & Cwenar, S. (2002–2010). *Dialogue, innovation, achievement & learning studies, 1, 2, 3. Preparing the 21st century citizen.* University of Leicester & The National Corporation of Universities/ University of Leicester.

Steil, A. (1991). Overlooked dimensions in language acquisition. *The Modern Language Journal, 75*(2), 173–180.

Schleicher, A. (2020). *Preparing the next generation for their future.* Newstatesman.

Vygotsky, L. (1986). *Thought and language.* MIT. (Original work published 1934)

PART 2

The Practices of Learning

∵

Introduction to Part 2

Rosemary Sage and Riccarda Matteucci

There is much agreement that formal education needs to change to prepare students to work with technology in groups as this will be common in work roles that have an interdisciplinary approach to enable solutions to complex world problems. Education for Robotics is a Europole initiative to assist new directions in educational practice and is examined to provide a model of practice. Following this are case studies giving teacher and student views of more technology input to learning. The part ends with a consideration of how false information is common practice on web platforms and students need to learn how to make judgements about content.

Chapter 4 – Teaching Practice for the New Industrial Age: The Europole System

The chapter presents a nation experienced and effective in using new technology to assist learning. It describes a visit to Italian schools, universities, robotic training courses and national competitions, where students present projects involving new technology in learning. Examining a successful model is the best way to learn and improve practice.

Chapter 5 – Technological Aids and Practice during the Pandemic and After: Training for Complexity

Complexity theory provides understanding of how systems, like economies, global corporations and government organisations, grow, adapt and evolve. Worldwide, we witness leaders, in various fields, adopting simplified, inadequate answers when attempting to solve complex issues. An interdisciplinary approach is needed in education, because philosophical, psychological and social factors come into play. Rather than applying the classic remedy of *best practice*, we must possess capacity to interpret the evolution of the context in which events take place, unfold and grow.

Chapter 6 – The False Practice of Web Information

False information is increasingly available on the World Wide Web. This misrepresentation leads to polarised views, anger and fear, to tear society apart. How to evaluate information sources for judgement about reliability and validity is crucial for impressionable students, who need a fair, unbiased perspective. Free speech has always been considered necessary for the learning progress, but is in danger from today's oppressive culture that cancels those whose views are not accepted.

© ROSEMARY SAGE AND RICCARDA MATTEUCCI, 2024 | DOI:10.1163/9789004688612_007

Reflection

Education for Robotics gives students control and creativity as they must use technology in innovative ways to assist their learning. Sharing their experiences with others assists understanding and memorizing and is the perfect practice model for later cooperative and collaborative workplace roles. Reliance on the web for research means that students must be aware of fake information and be taught how to spot this so they are not misinformed.

CHAPTER 4

Teaching Practice for the New Industrial Age

The Europole System

Rosemary Sage and Riccarda Matteucci

Abstract

This chapter provides an example of a nation experienced and effective in using new technology to enhance learning. It describes a visit to Italian schools, universities, robotic training courses and national competitions, where students present projects involving new technology in learning. The examination of a successful model of practice is the best way to learn and improve practice.

1   Introduction – Education for Robotics: The Context

Italy was chosen for investigation, as it has a recognized system for Educational Robotics to prepare students for dealing with intelligent machines (robots), now carrying out routine human tasks. The old Roman Grammar, Oratory and Rhetoric schools focused on public speaking to facilitate high-level creative thinking, underpinning Italian education with an emphasis on oral performances in learning and assessment. In a global world, with inter-discipline collaboration increasing, a value for effective communication is important to assist personal and practical development. A curriculum has been designed by engineers and information processing experts, such as psycholinguists, to assist personal, practical and academic abilities through integrated subject content, using robots. These are coded and programmed by students to support holistic development. Now that routine jobs are accomplished by machines, humans can concentrate on more complex issues, requiring creative, communicative engagement across disciplines.

The visit included:

Four School Groups – Verona (North Italy), Rome (Mid Italy) & Rieti (Mountain area) – across ages 3–18 years. These had Art and Robotics Laboratories, with teachers trained in robotics, such as engineers, teachers, psychologists and therapists with knowledge of brain information processing.

Three Universities – Rome (Mid Italy), Cassino (South Italy) for robotic research & Florence (North Italy) for the Education Robotic Challenge National Semi-Finals for Schools.

Two Training Courses (Verona & Rome) for Educational Robotics.

> *Verona*: attendance at Stage 1 of a 3-part course (total 6 hr.) 1) Background to Robotics 2) Psychological Aspects of Information Processing systems 3) Practical Demonstrations of Robotic Use.

> *Rome*: completion of a teacher training for robotics, including design, construction, coding and programming for use (Pre-courses +1 day for project presentation). A certificate was awarded following an oral presentation, robot design and construction.

Discussions with Experts: Europole and La Scuola di Robotica personnel; a CEO of industrial model-making firms in Italy and China; the owner of a world cooling apparatus company; a family magistrate; a political journalist, an ambassador for the United Nations, an education inclusion specialist, clinical psychologist and art expert. Talks also took place with university professors of engineering, psychology, sociology, philosophy, educational sciences and international relations. All professionals high-light an urgent need for a personal, practical as well as academic focus at all levels of education and training for smarter work roles, requiring effective communication and collaboration across disciplines. They also mention greater attention needed for cross-cultural communication issues in plural societies. The inclusion expert suggests that technology now replaces talk with a noticeable increase in speech and language problems affecting student well-being and learning. In the UK, the Department of Education is planning to ensure all children entering school can speak, as now many cannot string words together in narrative structures. There is concern that this communication issue results in inadequate thinking and disruptive behaviour, affecting mental health and academic performance.

2   The Robotic Approach

This integrates personal development and practical experience with cross-subject content relevant for real problem-solving issues. It is taught 1–2 hr. weekly, with older students (16–18) having options to develop robot building and programming. They enter projects in national/international Maker-Faire competitions. A recent national one held in Turin, organized by the R.A.I. (the

Italian BBC) saw Italian schools competing and the 'Nitti' group from Rome had second place (students 11–14).

At international level, two Italian schools, one from Vercelli (North) and the other from Livorno (Mid) were placed first and second at the N.A.S.A. American competition, where schools world-wide participated (*considered one of the most important robotic competitions for schools*).

3   Criteria for Development

1. *Personal Competencies*: communication, cooperation, collaboration – sharing ideas for problem-solving, inventing and constructing in group teams.
2. *Subject Knowledge*: languages, sciences, mathematics, history, geography, literature, philosophy, art, music, drama, design, computing, etc. are introduced in an integrated thematic project chosen by staff and students.

4   Project Implementation

Student groups (4–5) agree their project section with parts finally assembled and presented to others. This allows a greater range of knowledge to be exposed in a time period, showing various approaches. The method allows for personal observation and coaching which students say brings better learning than whole-class teaching. Older children act as teachers for younger ones, helping them learn how to code, programme and use robots for learning tasks. They all enjoy this opportunity and say sharing helps their understanding.

The 5 Fs for Project Development

1. Facilitate: engage and involve all students actively
2. Fun: produce a playful, happy atmosphere
3. Feature: use real-life situations for developing values, attitudes and abilities
4. Fit: select language and thinking levels for student needs (narrative structures)
5. Flow: produce experiences that match abilities to challenges

5   Lesson Structure

Context: explain aim and process outcomes. The why, what, when, how of events

Connection: use a communicative cross-modal input – sound, sight, action

Contemplation: share ideas/feelings for planning, action and completion

Comment: review and adjust for future activities

5.1   *Examples of Robot Projects in School Practice*

Scenario: The Pinocchio Story (Age 6+)

Aim: To use the story for personal, practical and cross-subject learning.

Tasks: Students make Pinocchio models (20 cm tall) with their parents. They paint scenes from the book at school, assembling these to form a large floor square (below).

Action:

Use 1: Teaching Non-Verbal Communication. A robot is coded to move in different directions over the squares – programmed to teach *non-verbal* communication. A player throws a large dice with the binary code *0* and *1* on the sides. If *0* is thrown – no action is taken, but if *1* appears the robot is programmed to move to the nearest *red disc*, scattered over the floor square, by a player pressing the correct button/s. The *disc* has a *scenario and instruction* on the reverse side for the player to respond. E.g. 1: A wooden piece in Geppetto's work-shop speaks and you are surprised. How would you look? E.g. 2: In Geppetto's house, Pinocchio is feeling hungry. How would he look? E.g. 3: Pinocchio has fallen over a stone and is annoyed. How does he show this?

The game continues with each group member taking turns until the story route is completed. This focuses on non-verbal behaviour, which research shows conveys 97% of word meaning in talk exchanges.

Use 2: Teaching Oracy into Literacy. The Pinocchio figures are photographed on cards and scattered across a large multi-squared board. The robot is coded to move in different directions and programmed by each player to walk to a character image, who then starts a story. The group takes turns, building the story as the robot moves to all the characters. This is then written up as a record. In a 30 minute lesson the group created the tale, "*Pinocchio Lies*". The moral of the narrative – if you start lying you may never stop!

Use 3: Teaching Geometry. Children use a robot coded to talk and instruct about shapes and respond to learner requests. The robot introduces a shape (e.g. triangle) which when programmed draws this on paper for the group to copy, repeating this in different orientations and giving instructions to measure sides, angles and area. Another child re-programmes for a different shape and finally the robot instructs the group to draw figures – *house, tree, fish etc.*, using the shapes for this. The group can ask the robot for information so creative interaction is established. (The group observed decided to 'I Spy' the different shapes in the laboratory – square box, Pinocchio's triangle-shaped hat, etc.).

Scenario: Alice's Adventures in Robotic land (Age 7+)
(Based on Alice in Wonderland)

Aim: Design and build a robot Alice/White Rabbit – code and programme to walk, meet and talk.

Tasks: Groups draw a character and create it from card/lego bricks, attaching this to a platform (WeDo 2.0), linked to a computer for coding. Symbols are selected for programming the robot to more forwards/backwards, etc. The time is decided for the walk. A STOP symbol is coded. Voice is recorded for meeting (Alice/Rabbit).

Action: Pair with a group producing a different character (Alice/Rabbit). The correct button/s on the platform are pressed to initiate the walk, meet and greet sequence.

Review: Possible adjustments to consider (e.g. Lengthen the walk time/ extend talk). What has been leant from the task?

The authors of this report used this story to develop in their workshop in Rome and have the materials as resources. The tale has a personal connection for Lewis Carroll, the author, as he was brought up in North Wales, on the West Shore of Llandudno. At the side of his house was the entrance to the old copper mines. This hole, which he saw from his bedroom window, caught his imagination and inspired the story of Alice disappearing down it to a magic land!

Scenario: A Pilgrim's Journey: Rome to Santiago Compostela (11+)
Aim: Plan a journey through 3 countries, introducing the language, culture, customs, history, art, architecture and landscape of different regions.

Tasks: From a route map each group decides on a place and researches this for interesting things to visit. They collaborate on a story-board, developing characters to meet up and question an *ancient pilgrim.* (e.g. A group chose Chartres cathedral, programming the robot to ask the pilgrim: *Why does the cathedral have so many high windows?'* Answer: *Gothic architecture was built tall to be nearer heaven and the divine presence*).

Action: Groups prepare their journey sequence and conversations along the way, using the computer programme – *Scratch* – to gather images. The sequences are assembled to present the pilgrimage and made into a film for public presentation. During the journey to Santiago the students programmed different language use in conversation according to the country they were crossing. They spoke Spanish in Spain and French in Chartres. This means the students ask questions in different languages to the old pilgrim who was leading the group to the sanctuary.

Review: What has been learnt? What went well? What could be adjusted?

Scenario: I Promessi Sposi Dei, 2019 (the Betrothed) (*Age 14+*)
This is an old story of 15th century peasant lovers near Milan. The local Lord was against their marriage, putting many obstacles in their way which they overcame.

Aim: To update the story for 2019 – examining problem-solving and personal character- determination, stamina and resilience – needed to overcome difficulty.

Tasks: Groups decide on the part of the story to develop its modern equivalent. A story-board is designed from rough drawings of events. Images are selected from the computer programme.

Scratch: Conversation is recorded for narrative sequences. All sections are assembled for oral presentation and a film of love overcoming opposition.

The Ecuadorian and Philippine students placed the story in Madrid as the teacher suggested they change the story setting for 2019. By choosing Madrid they acknowledged their Spanish language and cultures.

Review: What has been leant? (Below are comments from student interviews)

– Formal learning using robotics can be enjoyable and fun
– Communication varies across contexts: awareness avoids misunderstandings
– Talking together produces better thinking, ideas and consequences of actions
– The story teaches coping with others, flexibility and open-mindedness
– Helps imagination and problem-solving from the story difficulties presented
– Encourages attention and concentration with group control of the process
– Observing others helps learning and coaching from them develops abilities
– Learn more quickly from friends but teachers necessary to introduce knowledge

There was surprise at how aware students (age 14) were of what they had gained from this learning mode. Teachers direct them to learning outcomes – giving confidence by increasing observation, thinking and introducing relevant, interesting materials.

Scenario: Solving a Community Issue (Age 16+)

Students investigate local needs and groups select one for a project. The example below presents a Counting Robot to assess people usage of Rieti Town Parks.

Aim: To select a community problem – evaluating the challenges in solving it.

Tasks: Talk to local officials to appraise needs. Choose an issue that interests. Select a platform for building the robot (e.g. park counter). Code and programme necessary operations, using sensors to detect people and movement direction. The object (*person*) passes robot sensor, calculating numbers moving through in a selected time period. The counter is tried in situ to assess machine validity and reliability.

Review: Challenges: people might be accompanied by a dog, so must programme for human height. Weather changes (*wind, rain, snow*) could interfere with the mechanism.

(Note: one class group built a drone to carry equipment from home to school. Another assembled, coded and programmed a robot to clean floors!)

6   University Visits

6.1   *Università degli Studi di Cassino, South Italy*
Discussions took place with the Rector and Professors in the Faculties of Education Sciences, Sport Sciences, Human Sciences and Engineering. We watched students developing different exercise routines for the whole age range to promote physical and mental well-being. In the engineering faculty 20 PhD students were working on robots to assist the handicapped and elderly, with tasks like feeding or drinking, so that they could manage without help and have more independence. The problems of control and the ethics of using support machines were being addressed. Some students were developing drones for different purposes such as filming and carrying goods.

6.2   *La Sapienza University of Rome, Mid Italy*
We held discussions with Luca Iocchi, who runs a programme for schools, invited to send teams of 4 students each for a 60 hour course. This experience develops skills of coding and programming, which are vital for those in Technical institutions. The department also programmes humanoid robots on request from schools. A popular use is to assist the teaching of other languages, enabling students to hear words when they see the pictures on the screen. Students can attend Saturday courses to develop their robotic building competencies. The undergraduate/post-graduates were often commissioned to build robots for community uses as the chart below explains.

6.3   *Università Degli Studi di Firenze, North Italy*
We visited part of Florence University and talked with staff in the Engineering Faculty. The engineers engage with schools, planning and developing work

with students at different stages. They are all sure that robot use is essential for today's world.

These engineers judge the student challenge (below) and are inspiring people. One female civil engineer is working on materials for space rockets that will investigate other planets, using robots for this work to assess suitability for human life. Another works with medical experts producing 3-D images from MRI scans of individual patient brains needing surgery for tumour removal. This enables surgeons to operate more accurately for effective results. They are able to excise growths previously inaccessible and so save more lives. This engineer also does 3-D printing for other body parts needing treatment or operation. 3-D images enable serious limb breaks to be treated successfully. Recently, she has been working in Boston, USA, with speech pathologists and surgeons on cleft palate patients, to operate for improved accuracy of speech articulation and voice quality. Surgeons do not have the phonetic and linguistic expertise to understand sound articulatory requirements.

7   The Nao Robotic International Challenge

7.1   *Semi-finals for Italian Schools, February, 2019: The Faculty of Engineering, University of Florence*

This is an international, regular event when schools present robotic challenge projects. At the semi-final were 100 students in 10 teams from all over Italy. They had to present their project to three panels of 3 experts. On each panel were 2 engineers, assessing product construction and software applications for coding and programming. The third member was an educationalist evaluating humanistic perspectives, including content relevant for the challenge theme, the communicative, collaborative process, learning outcomes, performance and presentation (Dottaire Riccarda Matteucci, Visiting Professor on the Practitioner Doctorate at Buckingham, who arranged the Italian tour, was a panel judge).

Points were awarded for the above criteria with the top teams going forward to the finals in Rome during March 2019. The theme for the 2019 challenge is 'inclusion', with judges assessing content to demonstrate this, along with the use of appropriate coding and programming, showing effective group work. One project used a robot, dressed as Pinocchio, programmed to teach how to tell/write a series of happenings in a full narrative structure: context, characters, events, results, evaluation and conclusion. It was also able to ask and answer questions from the group of project participants. After a presentation, students were questioned by judges. Groups were asked what they had gained from their robot experience. They replied it was the novelty of coding and programming for a particular purpose, along with respect for each other and the ideas expressed. They came to realize that working with robots was how to change the world for the better – making life easier and solving difficult problems.

8   Comment

The experts involved with Education Robotics are passionate about equipping students more holistically for the future world. They all say that technology is fast overtaking many human activities, doing these more cheaply and effectively. The approach to learning now needs to be smarter with greater emphasis on improving communicative and cognitive human processes for higher-level activities. Developing better levels of speech and language are essential for this development. The university professors felt there had been a decline in educational standards due to technology replacing talk in child rearing. This had serious implication for independent learning, adding to the problems of well-being and mental illness seen in the world today. They were confident that robots, assisting new ways to learn, encouraged group communication, so making a difference. This needs stronger promotion to increase awareness.

9   Review

The Education for Robotics programme is widespread and has been well-established over the last 20 years in Italy, with Schools of Robotics in the main regions, offering teacher training to promote development work in schools. They are attached to universities carrying out research into robot use, with projects ranging from extracting plastics from oceans to producing technology for improved thinking and supporting cognitive differences/deficits. These projects are underpinned with the philosophy that all things are possible if one has the belief. There is a national drive to improve collaborative work between disciplines and encourage females to participate more in technology enterprises.

The universities also run courses for school students, which count towards their final leaving certificates.[1] For example, the engineering faculty at La Sapienza, Rome, runs a 60-hour course for students (16–18) with 8 meetings of 4 hours duration. During these they build a robot with a focus on developing coding and programming ability. The faculty also implements sessions in schools with a humanoid robot programmed, as requested by teachers, to support learning. This is useful for students needing extra input. All staff consulted (as well as students) suggested that the robot curriculum accelerated learning and engaged learners more actively and holistically than traditional teacher transmission lessons. An emphasis on personal development greatly enhances academic achievements, producing well-being. Noticeable were the significant gains of students with special needs, both educational and those from underprivileged backgrounds. The approach helps them achieve similar standards to other students and this was witnessed in the projects observed, when they were participating equally and successfully in all tasks.

As with all initiatives promoting changes, some teaching staff are unwilling to attend voluntary robot training or alter traditional, trans-missive approaches. The ER method follows the cognitive principles of the Communication Opportunity Group Strategy (COGS), commissioned by the UK Medical Research Council in the 1980s-1990s to cope with children not learning effectively at school, resulting in behaviour and mental health problems. This developed and researched a human-information processing way to teach. It was reviewed by Paul Cooper (Cambridge University) as one of the best teaching methods because of its research base showing a significant difference in student personal, practical, academic performances for all ages. This approach has received more interest from the top performing nations than the UK, as British teachers do not have the psycho-linguistic training for understanding the importance of narrative language and thinking and how to implement this within classwork.

At the time COGS was developed, robots were in their infancy and not available to researchers, but now can be purchased for as little as 20 euros (€) with Lego platform kits available for €120 and those used in university departments for €200. Thus robots, to support learning, are now easily affordable, but the world has yet to be convinced that this is not an educational gimmick that "throws the baby out with the bathwater" "Seeing is believing", as the robots are fun, acting as additional "teachers" to free human ones for other important roles, like individual coaching and attention to student-staff well-being. Teachers mentioned that the political, economic and social instabilities, now widely known through the media, unsettle society with consequence for child behaviour and mental health. An example is a boy of 10, bullied at school and consequently suffering from hysterical aphonia needing regular visits to a logopaedist (speech & language therapist). Such problems with student mental health are now more common, according to the clinical psychologists consulted, but they are well-supported with the robotic method of teaching, which has been noted to increase well-being and enjoyment, along with great communication and confidence.

10   Main Points from the Project

Robots are gaining popularity as teaching tools for 3 major reasons:
1.   All mundane jobs are rapidly being taken over by intelligent machines, so the traditional educational aim to produce compliant citizens for routine work is now redundant. We have a world where jobs require higher-level creative thinking, broader knowledge and greater inter-discipline communication and collaboration for complex problem-solving.
2.   Students must learn to code and programme machines – now as important as traditional 3Rs.
3.   Robots structure tasks for learners, enabling group work with minimal adult input. This increases confidence, control, creativity and collaboration with content integrating subjects.

Observing the robotic curriculum confirms that it encourages abilities wanted by employers, as the present system is not producing the personal, practical abilities for workplace demands.

The Italian teacher training system requires a subject degree plus education sciences, including psychology, psycho-linguistics, sociology, philosophy, pedagogy and the history of education. This makes training longer than in the UK. Many teachers met on the visit were qualified as practitioner doctors in their subject areas. Also, the Italian emphasis on oracy, which takes precedence over literacy, enables them to easily produce a robotic curriculum from a solid knowledge of psycho-linguistics in education courses. If the UK does not seek to change it will be left behind nations more proactive than reactive in facing new world challenges.

Finally, the tour of *Italian Education for Robotics* was inspiring, demonstrating a strong commitment of Government and Ministries to be proactive in changing the learning focus for the new industrial age. We found great interest in potential collaborations for sharing practice and research, which is important in achieving the quick dissemination of recent developments.

The exchange has meant much knowledge has been shared for mutual benefit and progress.

Note

1 The Italian system is divided into Elementary (6–11), Junior (11–14) and High School (14–19). From age 14 there are choices in subject direction in 3 types of Institute. The *academic*, specialist ones are for art, classics, languages, music, drama, dancing, mathematics, science, sport, human sciences and economics. The *technical* colleges include all types of engineering, surveying, business and finance. The *professional* institutes include specialisms like agriculture and rural crafts, nursing, construction, home economics and food technology, tourism, hospitality and commercial enterprises. Students can study at a school that specialises in any of these subject areas but must follow the National Curriculum that includes, Italian, a second language, Mathematics, Science, History, Geography and Philosophy. Formal assessments take place after elementary, junior and high school. These have a strong oral component, with students examined by an outside panel when they leave school. Those entering professional institutes may leave at 16, taking a professional diploma instead of the leaving certificate at age 19. These routes have equal status in society.

CHAPTER 5

Technological Aids and Practice during the Pandemic and After

Training for Complexity

Riccarda Matteucci

Abstract

Daily competencies and strategies used to govern uncertainty, to face trade-offs and unexpected events, are no longer suited to the actual organization of social reality. In fact, any variable, action or dynamic is related and interwoven with others and their effects are perceived locally and globally. Complexity theory provides an understanding of how systems – national economies, global corporations or government organisations, for example – grow, adapt and evolve. All around the world we witness leaders, in various fields, adopting simplified, inadequate answers when attempting to solve managerial issues in complex situations. An interdisciplinary approach is needed in education and elsewhere, because philosophical, psychological and social factors come into play. Rather than applying the classic remedy of best practice, we need to possess the capacity to interpret the evolution of the context in which events take place, unfold and grow. Organisations move from a complicated mode of handling day-to-day matters to a more complex mode of operation that evolves and adapts according to their internal characteristics and environment. To face future challenges, people must be trained to handle complexity, employing the tools needed to foresee the effects of their actions in order to evaluate the risks and opportunities that are involved in taking decisions as events unfold. As educators, our task is to teach new generations the skills they will need to help them live in this more complex environment. In 2016, the World Economic Forum (2016) published an interesting report, *The Future of Jobs*, where it foresaw that in 2020 more than a third of jobs in all sectors would require creative expertise in solving complex problems. Inadequate, obsolete abilities must be replaced by creative and critical thinking, to evaluate how processes develop with responsible decision-making. Data science and cultural competence are also added as tied to sustainability and ethics, necessary for any kind of job. Cognitive flexibility is the key to the whole process.

1   Introduction

> Does a flap of a butterfly's wing in Brazil set off a tornado in Texas?
> (Edward Norton Lorenz)

The basic premise of complex theory is that a multifaceted system obeys a hidden order in its behaviour and evolution, be it a national economy, an ecosystem, an organisation or a production line. According to David Berreby, author of *Us and Them: The Science of Identity* (2008), a system's organisation is no accident, but the result of laws of nature not fully understood.

Proponents of complexity theory believe specific traits are shared by most intricate systems, allowing independent actors to behave as a single unit. These actors respond to their environment, much as stock markets respond to news of changing economies, as genes respond to natural selection, or the human brain responds to sensory input. All these networks also act as a single system made up of many interacting components. Complexity theory tries to demonstrate that patterned behaviour and properties, while present in the overall system, are not present in the individual components.

Much complexity theory research has been generated at the Santa Fe Institute in New Mexico. George Cowan, associate director of research at Los Alamos National Laboratory, established the Santa Fe Institute in the mid-1980s. Stuart Kauffman, author of *At Home in the Universe: The Search for the Laws of Self-Organization and Complexity* (1996), and his colleagues, Howard J. Sherman and Ron Schultz, authors of *Open Boundaries: Creating Business Innovation through Complexity* (1998), all have a strong focus on the business side of complexity theory. They believe that business is fast moving and not linear (effects are not proportional to causes) and that experts cannot predict which products or companies will succeed. John Holland, a computer scientist and professor at the University of Michigan, designed the genetic algorithm, based on the idea that components of complex systems can be broken down into building blocks, with characteristics represented in code. In simulations, code units recombine to make offspring; the best of these are allowed to reproduce, while the worst are discarded. As the algorithm shows, better codes and results can be translated into real-world applications. Sherry Turkle, author of *Life on the Screen* (2021), professor of the social studies of science at the Massachusetts Institute of Technology (MIT), says that technology has brought issues of complexity theory to life. Computers have helped to persuade us that even knowing all the parts of a system cannot give anyone the ability to foresee how all components in the system will interact, due to the inherent complexity.

2   Interconnected Reality

Alessandro Cravera's *Allenarsi alla complessità* (Training for complexity, 2021) starts with a preface by Giuseppe Soda, dean of the SDA Bocconi School of Management at Bocconi University in Milan, and an introduction by Cravera. In these initial pages they question whether we are ready to govern complexity. We live in a complex world but we do not understand well what that may mean. Our educational models and institutions develop competencies and acquire strategies to face an interdependent reality, but they are no longer suited to dealing with the situation today.

The world is seen from an engineer's point of view, with an optimal, measurable strategy to reach objectives. We are convinced that the correct analysis will allow us to understand scenarios, foresee their evolution and plan actions to obtain the desired results. If this does not happen, we try to find the reason in an incorrect evaluation of the problem or in the strategy adopted. The truth is that we need to see the world as a complex system where any facets, variables or actions are correlated and interdependent. None of us can detect each and every connection.

Humanity, the internet, our economies and organisations are composite systems. In recent years we have improved technology enormously, AI and big data are opening up scenarios never imagined until recently. Unfortunately, our strategies and competencies have not enjoyed development at the same pace. We continue to focus on things rather than on their relationships and show more concern over a single aspect than on structural connections to our ecosystem.

We try to forecast the future instead of preparing ourselves to confront a variety of futures, aiming for efficiency and optimisation rather than relying on redundancy and exploration. Detailed plans are more trusted than emergent strategies and, worst of all, we are overloaded with knowledge but neither educated nor trained as to how to use it effectively.

Leaders worldwide set targets to reach objectives ignoring the costs involved. They plan the future without paying attention to the ways our present actions might mould the years to come. Humanity seems obsessed with controlling everything and misses the capacity to govern the system. Living in an interconnected reality requires new paradigms, cognitive schemes, competence training and strategies to recognise a phenomenon or a system. The growth of interconnection and interdependence generates complexity at an exponential growth and unpredictable speed.

In the last 20 years we have witnessed two historical moments and felt the effects of world complexity. The first was the economic-financial crisis during

2008–2012. Financial markets were strongly connected and banks behaved like single entities separated from each other. This shows how blind we are to understanding the implication of complexity and our thinking reveals we are still influenced by a reality that is linear, governable and predictable. The second was the pandemic crisis, due to the spread of COVID-19. Alarming news from China, concerning the spread of the virus and measures taken to control it, did not energise countries to act immediately. Failure in coordinating actions to combat the pandemic – from the diffusion of medical protocols to exchanges of information – was due to applying action schemes unsuited to a complex world event.

Twelve years passed between the financial crisis of 2008 and the 2020 pandemic, but many observers comment that governments have not improved in understanding and governing complex systems. To avoid being affected yet again by complexity, social and financial researchers advise acknowledging our ability limits. People must be trained to manage complexity and pass on their knowledge to future generations.

3   How Well Do We Know Reality?

The 20th-century scientific discoveries opened up knowledge that required acknowledgement of the circumstance/chance, disorder/chaos and uncertainty/vagueness of reality. Studies by Max Planck on particles, Albert Einstein on time and space, Werner Heisenberg on measuring the velocity of a particle, plus those of many other scientists, analysed the world around us in a different light. Laplace's theorem of predictability was turned upside down, regarding the law of causality. He states that when we know the present we can calculate/predict the future. What is wrong is the assumption, because we cannot know every detail of reality. To study a specific phenomenon or system, scientific knowledge was considered if it could account for behaviour at that precise moment or in the future.

Nowadays, we know this is not possible or correct, because the study of complex systems, elementary particles, human sciences and neurosciences, with the introduction of epigenetics in contemporary biology vs. classic genetics, have shown that knowing something scientifically does not mean we can predict its future accurately. Pre-vision requires that a linear system works and behaves in the same way every time we give it the same chances and conditions. Epigenetics studies cell properties that can be modified by their specific environment. It has been proved that lifestyle, climate, emotions and states of mind can change the behaviour of certain genes, which may function or not in a given circumstance. Fundamental for epigenetics is the relationship between genetics and the environment, as human beings are interdependent within their ecosystem.

New physics research, regarding the small and large, has discovered a reality that does not follow the linear principle of events. It is practically impossible to detect cause and effect for the same reason that we are unable to predict when a given phenomenon is going to take place. In his *Il Principio di Indeterminazione* (The uncertainty principle, 2020), Edoardo Boncinelli affirms science has changed from a deterministic vision to one based on probability and statistics.

4   Ordered and Unordered Systems

To understand the difference between ordered and unordered systems, Cravera (2021) says that we have to rely on the explanation put forward by Dave Snowden (2020) in his Cynefin sense-making framework. He offers a classification of the ordered and the unordered: the first are those where the relationship between variables is stable and linear, whereas the second are unstable and not linear. Among the ordered, we can list simple and complicated contexts, and in the unordered, complex and chaotic ones.

The word "simple" derives from the Latin words "*sine plica*", meaning without crease/wrinkle, referring to a problem/context that is easy to solve, as variables are known and its relationships are determined by cause and effect, so it is possible to govern their dynamics. For example, following a recipe step by step can achieve the desired result. A failure may depend on an inexperienced cook, or not following the procedure accordingly. Simple contexts are the domain of executors and precision, with reliability and accuracy as their characteristics.

The word "complicated" derives from the Latin words "*cum plica*", meaning with crease/wrinkles, referring to a problem/context that is difficult to solve. There are no recipes to be followed and yet unless the solution is unknown, there exists the certainty of reaching it. In a complex problem, it is impossible to know all the variables, or the relationships between them, but this is linear and stable. In fact, once detected it is possible to discover the solution. As examples, we can cite the challenges presented by a Rubik's Cube or a Sudoku puzzle. To reconstruct a car completely from its many pieces would be so problematic that few people could achieve this. We have an image of a car, so we know what the final product will look like, but to sort through the complex contexts, extensive knowledge and specialised abilities, closely related to the problem, are required. The domain of complicated systems is for experts whose competence is vertical.

The word "complex" derives from the Latin words *"cum plecto"*, meaning interwoven and refers to various parts that are interconnected and inter-dependent. In such a context the relationship between each variable is not known, nor is it stable or linear. This means that the problem is difficult to solve, just as in complicated systems, with the added factor that a difficult problem may have no optimal solution. Complex phenomena cannot be solved by using recipes and applying best practice. Best solutions are obtained if contextual-ised, meaning they function here and now. The same action repeated after five minutes could lead to different results. Every action enters a circle, where we find the principle of ecology of action, with inter-retroactions that can lead to consequences far from those expected by the decision-maker. Most social and organisational phenomena are, in this sense, complex. For example, the educa-tion of a child offers a complex context as well as requiring planning of a firm strategy, managing a project or organising a team.

In complex situations, vertical or specific knowledge does not guarantee the correct or desired results. As an example, what are the abilities or specific knowledge needed to educate a child or a government minister? Do we need a doctor to lead the Ministry of Health or a sports champion for the Ministry of Sport? Complex systems are the domain of merging phenomena. It is vital to grasp the patterns of variable interconnections to have foresight and manage the possible effects.

The word "chaos" derives from the Greek word meaning emptiness, abyss. In chaotic systems, as well as complex ones, the relation between variables is nei-ther linear nor stable. In complex systems, it is possible to detect recurrences of behavioural schemes that allow the decision-maker to learn continuously from the effects of actions taken, so that he can change or re-adapt the strategies pre-viously chosen. In chaotic systems this is not possible, because relationships are governed by chance and are unknown and not always traceable from subse-quent events. Chaotic situations are determined by unpredictability, as typified by a stock exchange or the science of meteorology. An example to explain this could be the well-known "butterfly effect", theorised by Edward Norton Lorenz (1963) in an article in the *Journal of the Atmospheric Sciences*. His research dem-onstrated that in chaotic systems minimal changes effected in initial conditions could provoke radical ones in the future. In 1972, he started to use the expression "butterfly effect" to describe the sensitivity of chaotic effects, asking: "Does the flap of a butterfly's wing in Brazil set off a tornado in Texas?" In chaotic, unpre-dictable systems it is impossible to learn how to manage precisely relationships between events, as they are not stable, with no binding ties, as everything is open and changeable in a domain characterised by speediness and fast reac-tions. The only possible answer to chaotic systems is an immediate answer.

5   What Strategies Are Suitable for Ordered and Unordered Systems?

In both systems, ordered and unordered, Cravera (2021) states that we need to understand the typology of events to choose the most suitable strategy for a given context.

In ordered systems, the best strategies to apply in a simple context are to follow best practice, because they are well defined, the relationship between variables is stable and the dynamics are fixed. The action scheme is based on implementation and monitoring. When following a protocol, for example, execution has to be precise and accurate, with a certain level of quality. Practically, it consists of just what is necessary to achieve the desired result: follow the instructions.

In complicated systems the scheme changes. In this case, the solution could be unknown and has to be detected. These systems are dynamic but linear and the strategy adopted is based on analysis, planning and implementation. The decision-maker studies diverse aspects of the situation, the relationship between variables and the major aspects before devising a plan. He implements it by monitoring effects on the decision taken to make necessary changes for getting the best solution.

To explain the best strategy for complex systems, we need to mention Heinz von Foerster and Bernhard Pörksen (2001), who synthesise the procedure, stating that if you want to learn, you need to always act in such a way as to increase the number of possibilities. According to Cravera (2021), the action scheme relies on action, learning and adaptation and these dynamic systems require a try and learn approach. The decision-maker must be aware that the situation evolves continuously and it is important to intervene even when uncertain. He has to manage the new possible course the variables might adopt. Decision-makers must observe the dynamic of the event to elicit novel patterns in its evolution and take new decisions to implement the next move.

For example, during the COVID-19 pandemic, the decision to implement a lockdown, taken in Italy as soon as news of the virus spread was clear, provoked sanitary, social and economic effects less critical than they would have been if adopted weeks later. When managing complexity, there are two major needs: tolerance towards uncertainty and audacity in taking action. Chaotic systems require a different action scheme, because they miss what it is called a learning phase. Their dynamic is unpredictable and they do not have stable patterns of behaviour tied in to systems. The only possible strategy is action-adaptation. Speed of response is the most important aspect, as the evolution of a chaotic system is continuous and fast. Decision-makers must tune into a rapidly changing system status and act accordingly. This strategy reacts exclusively to the evolution of the system status. Action will have consequences, but no schemes or patterns of behaviour will emerge, so there will not be any "learning" lesson.

To understand this better, we review child education. No parents will define their strategy of education on the basis of an ideal image of their child at 20 years old, as a model citizen with good principles. It is impossible to go backwards and define all the necessary steps to educate a child according to an ideal image. Parents can account for what is happening within the family and their relationship with their child at all times. Every action happening here and now will determine the impact on reality and indicate directions that will shape the good citizen.

The mistakes decision-makers often make reflect strategies adopted to solve problems. Ordered systems are easier to govern, but mostly belong to other categories, so governments, managers of firms and leaders waste precious time choosing the simplest way that is normally the wrong one.

6   What Is a Complex System in Education?

The educational system is a typical, complex system, because its properties are constant change, tightly coupled parts, feedback loops, nonlinearity, self-organisation, adaptation and emergence. In "Complexity Theory and Education", a 2006 paper by Keith Morrison, professor at the Macau Inter-University Institute, lists the central tenets of complexity theory and issues raised in the education system:
– The consequences of unpredictability for knowing, responsibility, morality and planning
– The significance of networking and connectedness
– Non-linear learning organisations
– Setting conditions for change by emergence and self-organisation
– Fostering feedback for learning
– Changing external and internal environments
– Schools and learners as open, complex adaptive systems
– Cooperation and competition
– Pedagogy
– The significance of context

These characteristics are common to all schools and their districts and it should also be noted that the systems are dynamic and affected by factors ranging from individual traits to political agendas. Educational interventions and reforms are commonplace, but only a limited number prove to be effective. Examples are as follows: The No Child Left Behind Act of 2001 (2002), adopted in the USA, and the distance learning and assessment policy adopted by Pearson Education Ltd. (2023) during the COVID-19 pandemic. Distance learning had to be applied worldwide soon after schools faced the lockdown in January–February 2020 (see Matteucci, 2022).

When thinking, planning and choosing a new pedagogical technique, it is difficult to measure the success of educational interventions and understand why some fail. The complexity of a school or learning system is easily underestimated, when viewed top-down. Failures in content, curricula and interventions are often the result of factors outside the school setting or copied from other institutions. Many factors have an impact on the outcome of an intervention, including the cognitive abilities of individual students, the courage and spirit of some teachers, the socio-economic status of the community, the principals' pedagogical beliefs, the standard testing policy, the school schedule, the level of parental involvement and so on.

In spite of system complexity, in the educational policy of the No Child Left Behind Act of 2001 (2002), reformers relied on quantitative models for more structured intervention decisions. Their objective was to develop a model framework that would help policymakers identify and understand barriers and trade-offs for educational interventions in different school settings. No single model was applicable across a broad spectrum of educational contexts, because of the numerous variables involved and unpredictable reactions. Nevertheless, a unified framework was developed to create models for particular contexts. By applying the framework to diverse schools, models were built, analysed and adjusted to identify common traits and relationships that helped to implement interventions.

John Adams High School, where I taught in New York City from 2001 to 2009, was located in the Queens District, where there was a large problem with Spanish as a subject in L2. Half of the student population spoke the language well, as they were Spaniards, but they had no writing competence in what was supposed to be their mother tongue. The other half of the population was of Indian origin and they were totally uninterested in learning Spanish, but all students needed to pass the subject to achieve their diploma. After talking with the students, analysing their interests and studying closely this national educational intervention plan, I organised a Spanish course based on watching films spoken in English, with Spanish subtitles, whose content was diversity and immigration. At the end of each movie, students wrote reviews of the film, expressing their ideas on diversity and how they would have proposed and solved certain problems in their family contexts. The language used for this task was Spanish. The result was a great success. Everybody came to class and students and families exchanged knowledge and experiences over the same problems and their cultural responses. The students passed the Regents, the final national exam in USA, with good marks. My model was adopted in other schools, but the results were different, as the major factor in its success was the enthusiasm of the students and the teachers involved.

The other example is the distance learning approach all stakeholders had to adopt the day following school lockdown, due to the 2020 pandemic. In this case, the system was chaos, where the actors – students, teachers, parents and community – were not locked into a particular position or role within the scheme, though they were never completely out of control. Every day there was a change of rules and procedures, so the context was not always helpful. Students in rural areas were the worst affected by the situation, as they were often unable to use the internet and lacked a tablet or personal computer. As Mitchell Waldrop states in *Complexity* (2021), the edge of chaos is shifting continuously between stagnation and anarchy. This is the only place, according to him, where a complex system can be spontaneous, adaptive and alive. There are no better words to explain distance learning during the COVID-19 pandemic. Everybody acted differently, each school chose a different way to intervene, especially in cases where access to the internet was not guaranteed. Some teachers made great efforts to reach students and there are endless examples of how knowledge was transmitted to enable the teaching and learning process to continue. With ups and downs, failures and successes, most students connected with their schoolmates and learned that schools were not only places to access knowledge and that their social connections were fundamental for growth. In most cases what they missed were daily encounters and contacts.

After the COVID-19 pandemic, remote learning experience and school-based reforms need to involve networking amongst teachers to monitor the success or failure of their intervention. Modelling teacher networks and examining their impact in different case studies could be a step forward, says Augwin et al. (2015). Any framework needs to be validated through the results of multiple, diverse case studies. All of these proposed frameworks are mere attempts; we are well aware that there is no single recipe for educational success.

7   How Can We Help New Generations to Move around inside
       Complex Systems?

Cravera (2008) recognises four meta-competences, at a higher hierarchical level compared to what is traditional, that we need to know and be trained to manage in order to govern complexity:

1. *Result orientation* – A typical managerial competence and mindset, allowing entry into action to reach an object even in presence of obstacles and trade-offs.

2. *Context reading* – The capacity to read the situation rapidly, to understand different variables and trade-offs, to develop knowledge of the dynamics between individuals, with the ability to confront different aspects at a precise moment.

3. *Complex thinking* – A mindset allowing the development of a systematic vision of the situation to show a strong capacity for understanding the consequences of the actions and decisions taken.

4. *Context generation* – The predisposition/capacity to build a context based on relationships leading to positive results. This competence is focused on the future and allows subjects to avoid decisions taken here and now that could destroy relations or assets fundamental to reaching further results.

Beau Lotto, in his *Deviate: The Science of Seeing Differently (Percezioni. Come il cervello costruisce il mondo*, 2017), affirms that the more connections with the world, the better able we are to possess a repertoire of answers for any given situation. Taking action is the starting point of any strategy: it develops the capacity to understand the world. It is the answer to uncertainty and by taking action we confront the unknown and transform it into something known and manageable. This process leads to adaptation to circumstances.

At this point, Cravera (2021) questions whether we can use these strategies in daily life. During lessons and seminars held by colleagues and himself, seminar students, post-university participants, managers and professionals learned about complexity and the strategies to govern these systems, but something was missing: a kind of gym where they could practise their new abilities. In 2016, they organised the Newton Factory, a centre of innovation, to facilitate immersive experiences.[1] Through a multidisciplinary working team, new technologies and learning experiences were born, defined as "novelty" on the job market.

One "novelty" is the "ROOM", a technological sound-proofed space in a physical version and platform digital one. This is simulative immersion that allows the development of a complex event, animated by digital technologies and by actors guided by a director. The user needs to manage a complex event, responding to the actors' incentives, guided by a director and coordinated by an educator. The participant task is to put into effect the course of events, choosing solutions that demonstrate knowledge of how we move in a complex system. In the ROOM there are no teachers explaining theoretical concepts, nor is the participant assigned a predefined role-play, in which to discover the best way to find the appropriate solution. Whoever enters the ROOM encounters a virtual business, with objectives to achieve, crises to solve and managers and colleagues (the actors) to deal with, in order to reach objectives through trade-offs. The complexity of reality is reproduced at each stage, every action determines a development in the situation that could improve or worsen it. The four meta-competences are constantly present and every five minutes a score appears to tell whether or not the strategy adopted is the best to arrive at a positive solution to the problem. The ROOM experiences reveal the attitudes, behaviours and skills deployed by the participant to solve problems, to manage relations and to take decisions under constant time pressure.

The other learning experience Cravera (2021) suggests is the "CAGE", an interactive movie that can be downloaded onto a personal computer or smartphone, or used in a live session. It is a psychological thriller, during which participants interact to evolve the story. At the end of each episode, each participant is asked to take the part of the protagonists and together decide what to do in order to solve the situation positively. Twelve people, who do not know one another, wake up in a bunker from which it is not possible to escape. The jailer proposes to the prisoners a series of challenging trials they must survive. The user interacts with the movie, deciding on the way to face them and if they surmount the trials, they are freed. In the expectation that none of the participants has ever encountered a situation like this before, the action scheme and decision-making process used by participants are authentic. Analysing the situation and context, the participant is trained to understand what mix of their capacities – positive and negative – will be most effective in finding the solution. Through whole episodes, participants develop the capacity to adopt complex thinking, to abandon automatic solutions and to learn constantly from the effect of their actions on the system. The CAGE is considered a gym where four meta-competencies and the interdependence process they share can be practiced.

Cravera (2021) and colleagues affirm that the ROOM and the CAGE are two experiences focused on the learner instead of the educator. Both have been devised to push people to reflect on the right questions to ask themselves in facing and solving complexity.

8   Review

Education for complexity is just starting. Besides formatting issues and single products, it requires the creation of learning situations that reproduce reality in its entire complexity, as in the Educational Robotics programme and Communication Opportunity Group Scheme, already discussed. People need to be trained to understand and assume responsibility for decisions and actions taken in their real contexts. We must encourage thinking that fosters processes that discover efficient solutions.

Planetary crises have increased the need for people to possess the knowledge and tools in order to understand the complexities of modern life and to have the commitment to improve our own capacity to have an overall view of reality. Without an appropriate widespread education to deal with complexity, our ignorance and short-sightedness in making personal choices may appear innocuous and banal, leading to consequences both local and global.

Everything is interconnected and, as the philosopher of complexity theory, Edgar Morin (2001, 2012) describes it, we live in a reality where we drink South American coffee or Asian tea every morning; take our exotic fruits from our German fridge; wear an Egyptian or Indian cotton T-shirt; switch on a Japanese television to watch international news; drive a Korean car, while we listen to a flamenco song on our Californian iPhone. What an amazing world we live in!

Note

1   For more details, visit https://www.newton.it/newton-factory/

References

Augwin, D., McGee, J., & Sammut-Bonnici, T. (2014). Turnaround strategy. In J. McGee & T. Sammut-Bonnici (Eds.), *Wiley encyclopedia of management, vol. 12: Strategic management*. John Wiley & Sons.

Baller, S., Dutta, B., & Lanvin, B. (2016). *The global information technology report 2016: Innovating in the digital economy*. World Economic Forum. https://formatresearch.com/img/file/varie/2016/WEF_GITR_Full_Report.pdf

Berreby, D. (2008). *Us and them: The science of identity*. University of Chicago Press.

Boncinelli, E. (2020). *Il principio di indeterminazione*. Il Mulino.

Cravera, A. (2008). *Competere nella complessità. Il Management tra ordine e chaos*. Etas.

Cravera, A. (2021). *Allenarsi alla Complessità. Schemi cognitvi per decidere e agire in un mondo non ordinate*. EGEA.

Damasio, A. (2021). *Feeling and knowing: Making minds conscious*. Pantheon.

Davis, B., & Sumara, D. (2009). Complexity as a theory of education. *Transnational Curriculum Inquiry, 5*(2).

Fairtlough, G. (2007). *The three ways of getting things done: Hierarchy, heterarchy & responsible autonomy in organizations.* Triarchy Press.

Kauffman, S. (1985). *At home in the universe: The search for the laws of self-organization and complexity.* Santa Fe Institute.

Laplace, P. S. (1799–1825). *Traité de mécanique céleste* (Vol. 5). Impr. de Crapelet.

Lorenz, E. N. (1963). Deterministic nonperiodic flow. *Journal of the Atmospheric Sciences, 20,* 130–141.

Lotto, B. (2017). *Deviate: The science of seeing differently.* Weidenfeld & Nicolson. (Translation of *Percezioni: Come il cervello costruisce il mondo*).

Morieux, Y., & Tollman, P. (2014). *Six simple rules: How to manage complexity without getting complicated.* Harvard Business Review Press.

Morin, E. (2001). *I sette saperi necessari all'educazione del futuro.* Raffaello Cortina.

Morin, E. (2012). *La via. Per l'avvenire dell'umanità.* Raffaello Cortina.

Morrison, K. (2006, November 28–30). *Complexity theory and education.* Paper presented at the APERA Conference, Hong Kong. http://edisdat.ied.edu.hk/pubarch/b15907314/full_paper/SYMPO-000004_Keith%20Morrison.pdf

Mulgan, G. (2017). *Big mind: How collective intelligence can change our world.* Princeton University Press.

No Child Left Behind Act of 2001. (2002). 107 P. L. 110 115 Stat. 1425, 2002, enacted H.R. 1. https://www.congress.gov/bill/107th-congress/house-bill/1

Pearson Education Ltd. (2023). Distance learning and assessment policy. https://qualifications.pearson.com/content/dam/pdf/Support/policies-for-centres-learners-and-employees/pearson-distance-assessment-and-learning-policy.pdf

Poli, R. (2019). *Lavorare con il futuro. Idee e strumenti per governare l'incertezza.* EGEA.

Sammut-Bonnici, T. (2014). Strategic drift. In J. McGee & T. Sammut-Bonnici (Eds.), *Wiley encyclopedia of management, vol. 12: Strategic management.* John Wiley & Sons.

Seddon, J. (2005). *Freedom from command and control: Rethinking management for lean service.* Productivity Press.

Sherman, H. J., & Schultz, R. (1998). *Open boundaries: Creating business innovation through complexity.* Perseus Books.

Snowden, D. J. (2020). *Cynefin: Weaving sense-making into the fabric of our world.* Cognitive Edge.

Snowden, D. J., & Boone, M. E. (2007, November). A leader's framework for decision making. *Harvard Business Review.* https://hbr.org/2007/11/a-leaders-framework-for-decision-making

Turkle, S. (2021). *Life on the screen: Identity in the age of the internet.* New Publishers. (Original work published 1995)

Von Foerster, H., & Pörksen, B. (2001). *La verità è l'invenzione di un bugiardo. Colloqui per scettici*. Meltemi.

Waldrop, M. (2021). *Complexity: The emerging science at the edge of order and chaos*. Simon & Schuster. (Original work published 1993)

World Economic Forum. (2016). *The future of jobs: Employment, skills and workforce strategy for the Fourth Industrial Revolution*. https://www3.weforum.org/docs/WEF_Future_of_Jobs.pdf

CHAPTER 6

The False Practice of Web Information

What to Consider When Accessing Internet Sources

Rosemary Sage and Riccarda Matteucci

Abstract

This chapter considers the practice of false information, which has been increasingly available on the World Wide Web, and is a danger to reliable, effective learning. This misrepresentation has engendered much distrust in populations, leading to polarised views, anger and fear, which is tearing society apart. How to evaluate information sources for judgement about their reliability and validity is crucial, particularly for students, who need a fair, unbiased, broad perspectives in their learning experiences, in order to develop proper judgements. The fact that universities have been cracking down on ideas and materials that are unpopular amongst certain sections of society is an issue that must be addressed if truth and knowledge is to be valued and supported. Free speech has always been considered necessary for the progression of societies, but is in danger from today's oppressive culture that cancels those whose views are not accepted by those in authority and control. This identity politics destroys democratic liberalism, which was fought for in previous generations and is now in danger of disappearing, due to narrow thinking and actions (Husain, 2021). Technology platforms are hastening this demise.

1   Introduction: The Background to Fake News

A teacher recently said a colleague switched on a Zoom lesson to find all the students hanging upside down! I then read about this happening elsewhere! What a relief! Students did not lose their sense of humour during the pandemic. They were demonstrating their digital literacy and able to press the right buttons to achieve this! Bats relax upside down because as flying mammals it is difficult to take off from the ground, so this orientation enables them to speed away quickly. Perhaps there is a hidden message here – the students will fly away (press leave) if the lesson becomes boring! This is regular behaviour, especially amongst university students, who often drop out of their lectures on Zoom, because a facility allows them to not reveal their personal image on screen.

Following the upside-down occurrence, there were many television interviews with people having no intention of taking the COVID-19 vaccine. Why? They had read on the web that it was designed to kill not cure. The pandemic exposes a gap between science and practice, showing the importance of educating about risk, prevention and treatment. Inferior experimental design and data interpretation or dubious ethical practices bring distrust, misinformation and vaccine refusal. The 2020 YouGov-Cambridge Globalism Project survey of around 26,000 people, in 25 countries, found widespread doubt about vaccine safety from popular web buzzwords or images, known as memes. These have become popular influencers across the world.

What is a "meme"? The word originated from Richard Dawkins's book: *The Selfish Gene* (1976), describing "a unit of cultural transmission" – passed between people and subject to selection pressures – similar to gene selection and transmission. Web memes include animated graphical interchange formats (GIFs), videos, images and words, offering humour whilst communicating ideas, which are often biased and inaccurate. Thus, a meme can produce "upside-down" thinking amongst us. To prevent this, digital literacy must evaluate internet sources for truth and credibility.

2   Evaluating Web Sources

Website numbers change constantly, with over a billion sites on the global internet (1,229,948,224 – Netcraft's November 2020 Web Server Survey). Many are protected by free speech and anti-censorship laws, so can print what they want (true or not) without legal consequences. This has changed ways for gathering and assessing information. Techjury.net presents 2020 statistics:
- 4.54 billion worldwide internet users
- 1.5 billion internet inactive websites
- 56.5 billion web pages indexed through Google
- 200 million active websites

Evaluating sources for their authority, accuracy and relevance is important for students acquiring knowledge, to enable them to become reliable citizens, speakers and writers. They must express information with integrity and to ethical standards for audiences to read and accept this reliably. It is said by academics that bad sources, like bad seeds, bear bitter fruit for those using them! Today, however, internet global connectivity makes verifying sources easy. Grammarly's Plagiarism Checker decides if content is original and the Online Writing Lab (OWL) gives advice on evaluating sources. Google's technology power is from big budget commercial websites, with social media ones often based on opinion not fact and so often biased. In order to evaluate credibility:

2.1   *Employ Trustworthy Sites*
If wanting world news go for *The Daily Telegraph* or *The Times* (or similar quality papers) rather than *The Wigston Spine* (a newspaper created by children from Wigston for hedgehog news). The same practice should be used for internet research. Choosing a reputable site is the first step. Type the topic into the search box and find related sites and links. For example, if you type in surveys on "inclusion" you will discover many possibilities. Look for reputable research organisations that carry out studies, like the respected Joseph Rowntree Foundation,[1] McKinsey and Company or a recognized government ministry found on the web.[2]

Type the URL into the search box. Click on "Get Details". Check links to them and other facts. The URL is the acronym for Uniform Resource Locator (web address) referring to an asset, specifying the computer network location and a mechanism for retrieving it. The common form starts with http:// followed by www and name. When visiting a specific site, type the link into the Google search box. Paste the URL after the colon with no spaces. If not discovering links, shorten the URL. Different search engines may show varying results, so it is worth re-trying. Alexa Internet Inc. provides web traffic data, global rankings and other information on over 30 million common websites to assist.

2.2   *Check Author Identity*
If searching for information about "Oral Communication" and the management strategies that could develop this process effectively, make sure the content author is appropriately qualified, with a background in human development, psychology, linguistics, phonetics and pragmatics to have the required knowledge breadth to provide accurate information and advice. Having a "Doctor" title may not indicate superior knowledge and application nowadays. This fact was pointed out by the Association of Chief Executives (ACE, 2018) in the public debate on whether new technology would reduce employment possibilities. A research doctorate can be gained with studies that do not follow significance level criteria, showing just one method of data collection (online survey with ambiguous questions).

Online data gathering is unreliable, because of unknown variables that are difficult to collect by this method. Also, it is problematic for checking authenticity of the respondents. These issues make such methods unreliable for making data judgements. Many theses, available for reading on the web, would not have been accepted in the past as of Level 8 content. I know of people who have bought their doctorates. A long debate on a Linked In web professional network provided further evidence on this matter! Also, many students buy their theses and assignments from the various websites offering such writing services.

Therefore, it is wise to be cautious and assess author credibility. A reputable academic has extensive research experience, is well-published and peer-reviewed with generally an ORCID ID. This is a non-proprietary alphanumeric code to identify scientific and academic authors and contributors. It enables an identity for people and connects their unique IDs with manuscript reviews undertaken for scholarly journals. Web authors should indicate their experience, with short biographies a vital check. Non-qualified writers must use professional sources and use properly referenced quotes for credibility. Always evaluate education and professional experience to decide if an author is competent to write about a subject.

2.3   *Appraise the Article*

Note the date of an article, along with the range of studies and resources presented. Topics, like "Teacher and Student Responses to Pandemic Lockdowns" require up-to-date sources – recent surveys, case studies and interviews. Other subjects, such as "Talk Matters", benefit from a historical approach. Literature in the 1980s fiercely debated the topic of talk, in line with public pressure to give it more attention in education and training at this time, for effective connections in an increasingly global world. This discussion was started by engineering professions, working in multidisciplinary teams internationally, who were dismayed at the limited abilities of British graduates to speak, write and communicate with colleagues from other discipline backgrounds. They noted the lack of expertise amongst teachers to develop such a complex process. (Shuman et al., 2005, Willmott & Colman, 2016 amongst many others). The number of articles on the web, from various parts of the world on the subject of communication, indicates that this is an important aspect of universal concern in both education and the business world.

2.4   *Look for Primary Source Evidence*

This is available from historical documents, personal interviews, author scientific experiments, works of literature, conference proceedings, etc. Secondary sources include: important thinkers' views on the problem, a review of topic studies, an interpretation, lead press articles, etc. These two source possibilities provide comprehensive understanding from a wide range of views.

Reliable information is vital. Many website articles include links for more data. If these do not go anywhere the article may not be recent information.

Ensure the reference list includes a wide range of material to give the content a proper perspective. Legitimate websites keep links updated for users to gain more material. Look for more articles on the site and those written by the same author to assess views on other topics and note particular bias. Is the writing consistent? Is opinion backed up by valid, reliable evidence? Are there a range of views expressed and explored? Academic content must have source data and be properly referenced and not just be opinion. If reproduced from another source, consult the original to ensure meaning has not altered. References show breadth of material consulted (Bailey, 2020). Effective research traces the history of the subject investigated to provide the context, so check for a spread of dates for work consulted in references.

The Facebook social-networking site often posts from fake news platforms like 'The Onion.com". The tagline of The Onion.com is: "America's finest news source". This is a popular internet news site used by many, but readers have been frequently hood-winked into thinking some stories are real/true when they are not. An example is an interview with Prince Harry and his wife, Megan Markle, with Oprah Winfrey on American television (March 2021) that was broadcast worldwide.

The interview berated the UK press for their racist treatment of the couple, but a third of examples shown on the programme were not from British sources. Those that were had titles taken out of context to appear racist, when the content actually presented an opposite view. The programme even altered titles, as in an example from the Daily Mail: "Yes, they're joyfully in love. So why do I have a niggling worry about this?" The headline had the word "niggling" removed in the programme, to appear bigoted, although the article contained no racist or colonial negative views. Associated Newspapers (AN) stressed that an impartial researcher would know the term "niggling" was not offensive, suggesting that the idea was constantly coming to mind. By blanking out the word, and including the item prominently in the montage, audiences were invited to speculate what word had been used and, in the programme context, to reach a false, damaging racist conclusion. A statement went to Viacom CBS, the US Television giant airing the 2 hour programme. In AN's view, the programme made a "deliberate distortion and doctoring of newspaper headlines".

Domain Tools a Washington security analyst company, in the United States of America, says the internet proliferates with fake news sites, used by the media. Research shows how *typo squatting* and *spoofing* on domains are normal. *Typo squatting* involves deliberately registering internet domain names to redirect users to unintended destinations, or stealing traffic for economic gain. Christopher Elliott, a senior contributor at Forbes, the global media company, focusing on business, investing, technology, entrepreneurship, leadership and lifestyle, presents the Domain Tools Survey (2019) of the top USA news sites to examine the tricks done to them: *Newsday, New York Times, Washington Post, New York Post, Los Angeles Times, New York Daily News, USA Today, Boston Globe, CSO* and *Chicago Tribune* are all papers internationally that have been seduced by typo squatting techniques. This is a dreadful discovery leading to distrust and dismay!

Typo squatting (URL hijacking) relies on internet user mistakes when typing an address into the browser. *Spoofing* is when a scammer pretends to be a premium publisher. Such criminal acts can extract personally identifiable information, download malware, or spoof news sites to spread information. Organisations with high readerships are lucrative for scammers seeking spoof domain names.

2.5   *Evaluate the Top Level Domain (TLD)*

The site address (domain) ending assesses its purpose for deciding online resource reliability. This part is known as the *Top Level Domain*. Lastminute.com and Booking.com are websites showing hotel availability and savings in world destinations. The ending .com indicates a commercial website. If researching something, .com sites require more inspection, because of a commercial bias, as they aim to sell a product or service. If requiring a frank comparison between Android and iOS, a bias towards the latter will be found on Apple.com. The .org TLD was originally intended for non-profit organisations, but now anybody can use this tag. Just like .com websites, you can expect what you read on the location to incline towards the specific goal or mission of the organization.

A .mil TLD denotes a military site, whereas TLD .edu belongs to an educational institution, normally referring to a Higher Education (HE) one, with .ac indicating a university. A reputable institution has academic staff credentials. Look at their research profile, major research grants and leadership of international projects to assess trustworthiness and credibility. As students contribute to .edu sites, it is important to look for citations when dealing with their writing. If researching a paper or study assignment, it is vital to look for peer-reviewed articles. If a professor publishes something on an .edu website it may not be peer reviewed, but their record and reviews may lead you to find the information dependable. An address ending with .gov is a government website. If looking for reliable information on topics like health or education, etc. these are places to start as having updated information. The tag .net is open to anyone but originally intended for use by domains indicating a distributed computer network, or "umbrella" sites as gateway to smaller ones.

The .int TLD is limited to organisations, offices, projects and programmes endorsed by a treaty between two or more nations. However, a few "grandfathered domains" do not meet these criteria. This term refers to the first registration phase of Top Level Domains, which were developed after their particular Second Level Domain (SLD) was already active. Grandfathering allows SLDs to apply for their name under the newly launched TLD before anyone else.

In June 2020, there were 1,514 current TLDs, according to the Internet Corporation for Assigned Names and Numbers (ICANN). This organisation regulates and coordinates the internet domain. TLDs are useful for looking at specific information, but offer no guarantee of content credibility, so evaluate material carefully and make a judgement across a range of the criteria discussed. The internet is a quick information source, but libraries are best for accurate content, as research databases require subscription and are not available from traditional search engines. Resources are peer reviewed by professionals in their field to ensure quality and credibility, although many requirement payment and so cut corners to destroy validity and reliability.

3   The Background to False Information

The increasing power of technical companies is tearing societies apart, by making them more divided and fragile from the fads of those who think they know better than the majority and enjoy exerting their powerful influence over others. They dare to dictate what we should say, know or do. *The Wall Street Journal* reported in December 2020 that millions of celebrities are being exempted from rules monitoring content by Cross Check, which makes a second layer review to ensure policies are applied. As a result, inflammatory postings were made 16.4 billion times that year. Influence is focused in the Silicon Valley, an area of California, USA, developing advanced technology. Experts working there on intelligent machine systems represent the most radically Left-wing views in the present world. Their biases have made web platforms become the enemy of enlightenment, respect for diverse views and proper thinking. These people are powerful worldwide, because technology dominates present life and has taken over many routine procedures. The present "Woke philosophy is encouraged by these limited ideas and promotes an identity culture which dismisses views that do not align". This is destroying and dismaying society and promoting anger and anxiety.

As a result of this trend, impartiality shows a growing, worrying loss of trust. A 2020 report, produced by the Centre for the Future of Democracy, University of Cambridge, involved more than 4 million respondents from 154 nations and 3,500 surveys. It showed that 58% of the population felt that governments were abandoning commitments to justice and human rights. Voters were being misinformed and misled, seen in accounts promoting state-backed political opinions not based in fact.[3] Unless democracies, like the UK, forge a stronger common national purpose, conflicting cultural identities will pull them apart and destroy their nations.

Thus, it is vital to regulate social media, so that diverse views are heard, instead of a continual stream of assertions that strengthen prejudices to divide and rule. The French philosopher, Bernard-Henri Levy (2021) warns that our "cancel" culture, which ostracizes others who do not agree with us, is "churning out imbeciles". He says it is essential to acknowledge that all human relationships are both welcoming and worrying. Both are vital, as convictions must be challenged and imperiled by others. Cancel culture thus goes against the contract of life as it is the opposite of life and living. This was predicted by the 20th century philosopher, Alexandre Kojeve, who said that humanity would regress to an animalistic, vegetative state – everyone in their own burrow. Ed Husain, a Muslim, in his book: *A Journey Across Muslim Britain* (2021), warns of the quick spread of the "quiet caliphate" in Britain, because the internet has distributed a radical version of the religion producing a communal identity that sees others as enemies. He sees a rapidly increasing generation growing up in the UK who are utterly detached from British culture. The internet contributes to this rapid growth and Husain predicts the loss of liberal values and free speech. It is significant that he has recently chosen to leave Britain.

4   The Danger to Universities

Nowhere is this more important than in the university and college systems. *Civitas*, the Institute for the Study of Civil Society, is a British think tank focusing on democracy and social policy issues. It suggests that UK universities banning free speech can be placed into categories – red (35%), amber (51%) and green (14%). The top ten Russell group universities had the worst record for free speech according to Civitas studies in: "Why Academic Freedom Matters" (2020). Researchers found that speech could be curbed by perceived "transphobic episodes" in around 70% of red universities and 50% of green ones. Also, around one third of staff had experienced serious bullying and harassment and even been "cancelled" (removed from their posts) for their views. Many UK highly qualified and experienced experts have left the university system, because of disrespectful treatment and are pursuing their intellectual interests in other directions.

Freedom of speech, understanding and respect for all positions is fundamental to the pursuit of *truth* and academic excellence. Herbert Maruse (1969) in: *An Essay on Liberalism* said: "Society cannot be indiscriminate in its tolerance of speech, where freedom and happiness are at stake". The modern, educated mind and its pretentious rationalism nods in agreement! Rationalism, in this context, refers to the practice or principle of basing opinions and actions on reason and knowledge rather than on religious belief or emotional response.

The Chopper's Podcast suggests that 50% of Britons do not feel they are free to speak their minds.[4] There are many examples of controversies regarding free speech. Gonville and Caius, one of Cambridge University's oldest colleges intends to remove a commemorative window to the eugenicist, Sir Ronald Fisher, the President of Caius who died in 1962. Winston Churchill, an English Prime Minister (1940–1945 and 1950–1955) has become to symbolize the old world versus the new, with attempts to remove his statue and rename the college, supported and founded in his name at Cambridge University in 1960. He has been deemed "a white supremacist", promoted by the "CharitySoWhite", which is devoted to attack white dominance. Churchill fought to protect the hundreds of millions of non-white people in the British Empire. Andrew Roberts, author of *Churchill: Walking with Destiny* (2018), said:

> Churchill did his best in the exigencies of wartime to alleviate the Bengal famine. In his political career, he fought again and again against slavery and for the rights of non-whites within the British Empire. Churchill was moreover instrumental in destroying the worst racist in history, Adolf Hitler. (p. 48)

As the last globally powerful Englishman, Churchill is blamed that Western nations have dominated the world for 200 years, with undoubtedly a history of exploitation, but also the positive spread of Christian principles, the rule of law, modern medicine and education. People should be judged for character not skin colour. It is a general understanding about human nature that people who dominate tend to exploit the rest to some extent. However, sadly the response of many UK universities is to decolonise the curriculum and wipe out white culture. This is in response to movements like "Black Lives Matter", which take action to dismantle systemic racism, racial discrimination and social and criminal injustices, in order to create fairer, just systems. The UK "should be regarded as a model for other white-majority countries" although it cannot be considered "a post racial society", a government-ordered review has found (March 2021). The independent Commission on Race and Ethnic Disparities - which was appointed by the then Prime Minister, Boris Johnson, following "Back Lives Matter" violent protests, in which buildings were burnt and ruined as well as many people severely injured.

5   Modern Hypocrisy

An example of the hypocrisy now rife in modern life is seen at Jesus College, Cambridge. Students are reluctant to attend chapel services because they feel offended or intimidated by the stunning Baroque memorial to Tobias Rustat, the 17th century philanthropist. The plaque is attributed to the studio of Grindling Gibbons, the famous Anglo-Dutch sculptor and woodcarver and regarded as artistically important. Until an activist started digging, most students and staff were unaware of Rustat's life. What has been revealed is unconvincing. Rustat had a tiny investment in the Royal Africa Company, with some if its business linked with slavery, but the money he gave to develop Jesus College is said to be before this outlay. He is commemorated because his large gift has enabled many students to attain a degree to enhance their lives. How the Archbishop of Canterbury, Justin Welby, a Cambridge-educated historian, can describe the Gibbons monument as "a memorial to slavery" has no logic, as it was to acknowledge the College greatest benefactor. Today, the College is happy to receive large funds from the People's Republic of China, which is enslaving many of its citizens in factories that produce our technology equipment, such as computers and mobile phones. This fact seems to have eluded those who find the memorial distressing, as they tweet their messages, or are they unmoved by the plight of human beings alive today? This lays the College Master and Fellows open to the same condemnation they apply to Rustat. Some wrongs are clearly more emotive than others. The company producing Volkswagen cars has used slave labour within living memory. No one has suggested this car boycott. Archbishop Welby's own cathedral was built on the coerced labour of Anglo-Saxon serfs following Norman conquests. Studies show that people with this heritage are economically disadvantaged compared with Norman descendants today. Has the world gone crazy with this twisting of the real facts?

The Rustat plaque is one more ugly skirmish in a bruising campaign to recast British history as centred on slavery and colonial oppression. In Wales, the steam train built in 1804 is now cancelled. The National Museum of Wales had steam-powered technology displays, which have been removed over claims it was linked to the slave trade. Richard Trevithick, who invented steam trains, had no links with slavery, but the museum asserts they empowered an imperial British economy. "How Slavery Built Modern Britain" is the content of an academic monograph discussed in Cambridge. Critical Race Theory – neither critical nor theoretical, builds on this to accuse British society of systematic racism to sweep evidence and truth aside, with arrogant demands of victimhood and a continual outpouring of self-described emotion.

Confident, thoughtful, reasonable people should not be seeking ways to denigrate their ancestors for doing things in the past that were not considered crimes at the time, although we would not necessarily repeat all their actions today. The relentless focus on supposed negative associations of progress is taking us backwards, with science, philosophy and now industry all being renounced. This shows a desperation to attack every part of British history and one feels there is more to this movement than meets the eye and an attack on the very basis of democracy. Technology for all its positive powers is exposing the negative side of enhanced connectivity with the relentless brain washing of users.

6 Two Opposing Groups of People

People tend to fall into 2 opposing groups. There are those who accept that movements have legitimate reasons for rejecting the status quo that does not work for them and are dismissive of concerns about preserving their valued national traditions, culture and ways of life. The second one dismisses the other as reprehensible racists, who have been manipulated by distant elites and so are unable to make their own judgements and choices.

Evidence shows hardliners are winning by exploiting liberal principles. These are dangerous times for the rights and safety of the individual. Social media now acts as judge, jury and executioner. In 2020, a social media campaign led to the beheading of Samuel Paty, a teacher in Paris, France. His killer was incensed by on-line posts and denounced him publicly for showing pictures of the Prophet Mohammed in a lesson on free speech. The parent of a girl, in Samuel Paty's class, published the teacher's name and address on Facebook and YouTube, demanding his sacking and urging others to act against him. Later, it emerged from investigation, that this 13 year-old student had admitted to lying about the incident and, because of her suspension for truancy, was not even in school to attend the lesson.

Quick as a flash, in a few clicks, the teacher's famed reputation for fairness, respect and understanding of different views in a plural society, was brutally destroyed. In March 2021, a British teacher produced the same picture in a lesson on blasphemy and has had to go into hiding, because of vicious media, school-gate attacks and harassment at home. People are using the norms, rules and fashions of a liberal democracy to attack its principles. Fear, naivety and cynical complicity mean we are failing to deal with such incidents. Extremist beliefs control public thought and conscience and use pluralistic values to destroy the unity and community of society.

The world is built on a blend of post-modern philosophy and its critical theory developments on the one hand and self-indulgent narcissism on the other. Liberal elites appear to accept that discourse is oppressive, so admitting that language, customs, values, institutions and traditions abuse the weak and maintain the power and prestige of the strong. They use traditional narratives and social roles to keep them in their place. In this "woke world" alert to issues of social and racial justice, it is suggested that exploited people take part in their own oppression by using language and stories. Words and reality do not need to correspond, as the teacher examples above suggest. Scrutiny is dismissed as racially charged and misogynistic.

Today, UK universities are driven by the expectations and demands of fee-paying students, who presume instant satisfaction from their higher education experience. Also, university leaders are expected to comply with the bureaucratic demands of the Research Excellence Framework (REF) and its latest off-shoot, the Teaching Excellence Framework (TEF). In this rapidly changing higher education setting, the belief that academic freedom matters, represents an important continuity with the past. This historical link, even if its existence is only rhetorical, makes possible evaluation of change.

Truth matters and has become twisted and dangerous. In a "woke world", alert to issues of social and racial justice, words and reality do not have to correspond. Across, academia, business, sport, the arts and public life this new, woke paradigm holds sway. Truth (or mistruth) is a commodity to be bought, manipulated and sold for profit. Until recently, the successful in society, sought to prove they earned their place through hard work, resulting in intellectual brilliance and superiority. Now many are seeing themselves as victims and place themselves above others by teaching the masses about social justice. Technology giants, with huge social influence, are failing to control fake news and hate messaging and have spread the word of woke warriors world-wide. We must act now if we wish to prevent society destroying itself.

7   Review

As the Internet is open to everyone, it is easy to access false information or opinions instead of fact. This review considers *accuracy* (reliability); *authority* (expertise); *coverage* (analysis); *currency* (relevance) and *objectivity* (impartiality). There are links: the author's authority and sources often predict accuracy (Tate, 2010). Skill in making a content analysis is needed, as Beck (2009) points out. Another issue about Internet-based sources is URL changes to the accessing link. Also, web pages alter or disappear, so it is possible that the page cited may be gone by the time a reader tries to find it. This has happened to me! Beck's (2009) title in the web article: "The Good, the Bad & the Ugly: Or, why it's a good idea to evaluate web sources" is entirely appropriate here! The consequences of not reflecting on the information we receive is disastrous for everybody and leads to the most awful consequences.

People will always diverge on social issues, but compromise and taking the middle ground, brings a chance of reconciliation and understanding. There are signs that this possibility is vanishing fast. Hatred and hostile behaviour has become our mode of operation, so that there are very few matters which we are unable to fall out about. Instead of proper dialogue, we have memes, putdowns and dismissals of those who do not think in our way.

The fact that universities are following this agenda, means we are producing students with strong bias and prejudice built into their psyche. Suppressing views gives no opportunity to study and understand other standpoints and learn how they have come about in people's thinking and actions. Research and evidence have been trumped. Unless we are prepared to reverse this grave situation the world will become an increasingly unpleasant place to live and work.

When students complain that they are offended, many universities opt for the easiest solution, which is to give in to their demands. Universities are under continual pressure to encourage student applications, so they have become risk adverse when it comes to free speech, because of a fear of damaging their reputations. Winston Churchill has come to symbolise the old world versus the new. This generational clash, in which each side is seemingly less able to see eye to eye than ever before is disturbing. It means by reducing issues to misrepresentations, we fail to articulate positions developed from a place of genuine concern. Education has an important role to play here. The sooner we get our heads around this matter, the better!

Notes

1   http://www.jrf.org.uk
2   http://www.yougov.co.uk
3   telegraph.co.uk/front-bench
4   telegraph.co.uk/choppers-politics

References

Bailey, R. (2020). *Quickly evaluate a website.* WCC Library Research Guide. Retrieved December 12, 2020, from https://libguides.wccnet.edu/researchtoolkit/evaluatewebsite

Beck, S. (2009). *The good, the bad & the ugly: Or, why it's a good idea to evaluate web sources.*

Elliott, S. (2020). Here are the real fake news sites. Retrieved December, 12, 2022, from https://www.forbes.com/sites/christopherelliott/2019/02/21/these-are-the-real-fake-news-sites/?sh=215003cb3c3e

Husain, E. (2021). *Among the Mosques: A journey across Muslim Britain.* Bloomsbury.

Levey, J. (1968). *Differential perceptual capacities in major and minor hemispheres.* Proceedings of the National Academy of Science, *61*, 1151.

Marcuse, H. (1969). An essay on liberation. http://libgen.org/search.php; Transcribed by A. Thamm; PDF version. https://news.netcraft.com/archives/category/web-server-survey/

Roberts, A. (2018). *Churchill: Walking with destiny.* Allen Lane.

Shuman, L., Besterfield-Sacre, M., & McGourty, J. (2005, January). The ABET "Professional skills" – Can they be taught? Can they be assessed? *Journal of Engineering Education.* ASEE.

Tate, M. (2010). *Web wisdom: How to evaluate and create information quality on the web* (2nd ed.). Taylor and Francis Group.

Techjury Statistics. (2020). *The Internet.* Retrieved December 12, 2020, from Techjury.net

UK-SPEC. (2014). *The UK standard for professional engineering competence* (3rd ed.). The Engineering Council.

Web Server Survey. (2020, November). *Web Server Survey.* Retrieved December 12, 2022 from www.netcraft.com/resources

Willmot, P., & Colman, B. (2016). *Interpersonal skills in engineering education.* AAEE2016 Conference, Coffs Harbour, Australia.

Hudson, E. C., & Williams, J. (2016). Civitas: Why freedom matters. In J. Williams & C. Hudson (Eds.), *pub. Civitas* https://www.civitas.org.uk/reports_articles/on-academic-and-other-freedoms/

YouGov-Cambridge. (2020). *Globalism 2020 tech use working age only all.*

PART 3

Performance in Learning

∵

Introduction to Part 3

Rosemary Sage and Riccarda Matteucci

The fact that only 8% of students from world studies deem on-line learning satisfactory has broached discussion on how information via technology is given in a different way to the traditional face-to-face experience. Thus, the principles of performance are important for all to grasp and knowledge of communication is vital for all disciplines to know how to present both face-to-face and remotely more effectively. Teachers and students give their experiences to illuminate the communicative and performance aspects of teaching and learning, which technology must adjust for the fact that information transmitted remotely loses the non-verbal input of real contexts.

Chapter 7 – Perfect Performance with Technology!

The Top Hat Survey (2020) of 3,500 Higher Education American and Canadian students finds only 8% deem on-line learning satisfactory for them. Informal discussions with British students show a similar result. They miss the bonding coming from learning together in the same space, but suggest that the way content is communicated is a big factor. The chapter considers how technology supports both learning of content and the development of communication competencies. It defines and locates these before looking at how to present information via audio-visual technology.

Chapter 8 – Teacher and Student Experiences of Learning Performance

The modern, global, connected world depends on advanced technology for communication and progress, so it is important that teachers and learners are adept at using tools for acquiring and applying knowledge in life and work. The information discussed shows the different reactions people have to technology and learning styles. A mix of face-to-face and online experiences, called *blended learning,* appears acceptable and suitable for most individuals, as long as support (*on-line and face-to-face*) is continual, consistent and easily available when required. The chapter presents the views of students in Italy as well as in the UK, with also experiences of teachers.

Chapter 9 – Communication Performance in a Technology World

Evidence suggests that recent world changes, particularly in technology, have altered the way we communicate. This has positive effects for greater connectivity but is negative for face-to-face experiences and non-verbal interaction,

© ROSEMARY SAGE AND RICCARDA MATTEUCCI, 2024 | DOI:10.1163/9789004688612_011

which have the advantage of transmitting paralinguistic information more effectively for enhanced understanding. The chapter considers the principles of effective communicative performance in both face-to-face and remote learning situations.

Reflection

Communication training is not a priority in professional preparation courses but is essential for giving an effective presentation of information. The European Distance E-learning Network has established communities who are collaborating on successful performances through technology.

CHAPTER 7

Perfect Performance with Technology

Rosemary Sage and Riccarda Matteucci

Abstract

The Top Hat Survey (2020, https://tophat.com/teaching-resources) of 3,500 Higher Education American and Canadian students finds only 8% deem online learning satisfactory for them. Informal discussions with British students show a similar result. They miss the bonding coming from learning together in the same space, but suggest that the way content is communicated is a big factor. A survey carried out by the Association for Project Management (2020) identifies communication, engagement and management as the vital workplace competencies to survive and thrive. Professor Steven Pinker (September 2021) has also been tweeting this message in response to the Woke movement silencing people. However, communication is rarely a subject for formal study as there are few people trained in its use. This chapter considers how technology supports both learning of content and the development of communication competencies. It defines and locates these before looking at how to present information via technology in ways that are effective. The problems that people have with online learning are mostly to do with how content is presented and delivered.

1   Introduction: What Is the Communication Process?

Communication is the verbal and non-verbal process of transmitting information and common understanding from one person to another. It is the exchange and creation of thoughts, ideas, emotions and comprehension between sender(s) and receiver(s) to build and maintain relationships. In educational settings, most of the time is spent communicating, but one cannot assume that meaningful messages occur in all exchanges. There are many reasons why a message may not be received, including: the language form and level are not appropriate; the receiver does not like the giver and so is not inclined to accept it; and context effects, like noise distractions, take attention away from the process. A receiver may hear but not listen to legitimize a message. Being constantly engaged in encoding and decoding information does not ensure one is an expert communicator.

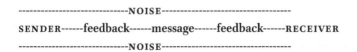

FIGURE 7   A simple communication model (Note: "Noise" refers to anything that might interfere with the message exchange, including environmental distractions and personal animosities that might exist between participants).

Actors spend much time and effort learning how to communicate effectively in the many stage roles they have to undertake. It is strange that teachers have very little training in this process, even though they are on the "class stage" for much of the school day. Thus, it is not surprising they are the largest professional group in voice clinics, suffering from vocal strain problems.

Understanding is a personal matter between people, who interpret messages differently according to their abilities, knowledge and experiences. Misunderstandings happen because meanings are in people, not in words. Communication does not occur until information and understanding have passed between the sender and the receiver with feedback regulating the process. With only 15% of the brain needed to process language, there are plenty of opportunities for interference (Sage, 2000).

2   What Are the Communication Competencies?

2.1   *Knowledge of Informal and Formal Communication*
Informal conversational moves are needed before managing extended formal narratives. These include:
– Follows conversation thread
– Asks questions
– Answers questions
– Assembles and contributes ideas
– Shows maintenance behaviour (eye contact, smile, head nod, etc.)

In conversation, one can control the action by asking to slow proceedings for information to be repeated if misunderstood, as relations are equal. However, this is not easy in formal presentations when power dynamics are different, with a speaker transmitting prepared information to an audience expected to listen quietly. To cope with a formal style you must be able to concentrate and deal with a sequence of ideas which develops in stages called the seven narrative levels:

1. *Record*: produce ideas
2. *Recite*: arrange ideas
3. *Refer*: compare ideas
4. *Replay*: sequence ideas in time
5. *Recount*: introduce, describe and discuss ideas
6. *Report*: introduce, describe, discuss, review ideas
7. *Relate*: setting, characters, actions, results, reactions (Sage, 2000)

Studies suggest that many students leave education without achieving levels 5 to 7, so simple language is needed – one idea per sentence with pauses between. Students complain that presentations (particularly remote learning ones) are too rapid, because of difficulties coping with narrative reference, inference, coherence aspects, especially if not in their mother tongue (Sage, 2020).

2.2   *Self-awareness*
Self-awareness is the ability to focus on yourself and how your thoughts, emotions and actions align with internal and external standards. If self-aware, you can objectively evaluate, manage emotions and align communication behaviour with values, attitudes and situational requirements, competencies and the standards expected. Therefore, you can understand how others perceive you. A communication questionnaire can achieve this insight (see Sage, 2000).

2.3   *Audience Awareness*
Knowing your audience (listeners/readers) helps determine what information to include in a presentation or document, as well as how to convey it effectively. You should consider the audience when selecting the content, language level and tone, or the information may come over as unfocused or inappropriate. This aspect is often referred to as "emotional intelligence", but is an important component of the communicative process to indicate self-awareness, self-management, social awareness and relationship management. With presentations via technology, monitoring the audience and their ongoing needs is more difficult without seeing them, so chat facilities should be used to provide audience members with instructions or alert them about problem issues.

2.4   *Manner*
A confident, friendly, affable manner is essential to show respect, non-judgement, equality and integrity when dealing with people. Successful communicators require an open mind and commitment to understand other people's needs and view points. If you disagree with your audience, it is important to

reach a middle ground that everyone accepts. Trust is crucial and charm helps to form the relationship that you want for cooperation and collaboration.

2.5   *Connection*

Connection is made initially through *phatic communication* – the non-referential use of language to establish a mood of sociability and share feelings. This begins with a smile and a greeting to establish enjoyment and enthusiasm for the message to be given. Research shows that if the connection is not made, the audience feels cheated and will fail to listen (Sage, 2020). It has been noted that since the UK National Curriculum came on board, in the last two decades of the 20th century, that teachers in their rush to get through lesson requirements dropped the phatic part of the process, which experts deem vital to achieve audience attention and control. The disruptive behaviour of children, which is now common in schools, is rooted in communication failures (Sage, 2000, 2020). Online presenters must keep acknowledging the audience and encouraging their feedback through chat facilities to reinforce the interactive nature of the experience.

2.6   *Structure*

Formal communication needs a brief overview with an indication of the structure to follow. We all process information differently – either top-down or bottom-up, with a 50-50 split in audiences (Wallach & Miller, 1988). Top-downers will only be able to grasp content with a clear outline, and bottom-uppers need details, stories and personal anecdotes to process properly. We tend to produce information in the way we prefer and Wallach and Miller's research shows that students perform better with teachers having the same information-processing style as themselves. If teaching remotely, a short overview of content is important before the lesson, so that students can think about what they are going to study with questions to consider (see below).

2.7   *Verbal Ability*

The term " verbal" relates to spoken or written words and not just speaking (which is defined as "oral"). "Competency" means the ability to use words, both in their choice and in their arrangement. Vocabulary knowledge is important as well as a familiarity with standard word forms if normally speaking a dialect. Organising words into sentences has many rules to convey meaning ("grammar"), such as noun and verb agreement. The grammar elements are:

– *Sentence parts*: subject, predicate, object, direct object (receives action)
– *Morphology*: word structure (prefixes, suffices, plurals, etc.)
– *Phonology*: word sounds

– *Semantics*: word meanings and relationships, which vary according to context
– *Syntax* (Greek, meaning "arrange together"): sentence word structure

The syntax elements are as follows:
– *Sentence parts*: subject, predicate (modifies subject), object, direct object (receives verb action)
– *Phrases*: word groups without subject or predicate
– *Clauses*: word groups with subject and verb
– *Sentence structure*: simple, compound, complex or compound-complex word arrangements

Example: Mum went to the shop. *Grammar*: 3rd-person singular noun (Mum) agrees with past tense (went). The preposition (to) connects action to a definite article (the) and another noun (shop). *Syntax*: Simple sentence of one independent subject, one subject (Mum) and one predicate (went to the shop), with one direct object (shop). Technology is changing grammar rules, so beware!

2.8   *Non-verbal Ability*
Mehrabian (1971) calculated that total message impact owes 7% to words, 38% to voice and 55% to gestures. Non-verbal input informs about a person's feelings, intentions, motivations and more. People speak with vocal organs but communicate with their bodies. Sage (2020), in a student survey, found *voice tone* was the top feature to assist lecture listening. Note that in online presentations it is easy for voice tone to become monotonous, without the audience in front to maintain interpersonal dynamics.

2.9   *Listening*
Four types of listening determine the listener's goal – *appreciative* (to enjoy), *empathetic* (to show mutual concern), *comprehensive* (to achieve understanding) and *critical* (to evaluate). Note taking aids attention, retention and recall. Remind students of this when the lesson is online.
– *Body language*: way you situate your body in response to a situation (crossed arms when defensive)
– *Movement*: quick or slow moves; standing, sitting or fidgeting convey different messages
– *Posture:* the way you sit or stand conveys confidence, professionalism and disposition to others
– *Gestures*: vary across cultures, so need to be considered carefully so as not to cause distress

– *Space*: views about the appropriate distance between people varies across cultures
– *Para-language*: voice pitch, power, pace, pause must show variety and passion
– *Facial expressions*: mouth, eyes, eyebrows and face muscles convey feeling and emotion
– *Eye contact*: communicates interest and attention but varies across cultures
– *Touch*: shows support or comfort but only use positively and if receiver accepts it
– *Context:* helps establish meaning and can influence what is said and how it is said

2.10   *Feedback*

This aspect is last but not least because unless feedback is given and accepted the communication is unlikely to be effective. In communication that is informal this is easier to establish, but formal presentation has to make this explicit, with the speaker checking that they can be heard by everyone and the signal (e.g. waving a hand) to indicate a need to stop for adjustments or comment etc. Online presentations can do this through a chat facility. Therefore, understanding the communicative process is essential for creating an effective performance in three stages.

2.11   *Planning: The Time for Questions*

– *Goal*: What is the purpose? What outcome is needed? What does the audience need?
– *Cross-curricular issues*: How does the input connect with other subject studies?
– *Transferable competencies:* How will the presentation encourage these? (communication, problem-solving, cultural awareness, leadership, data analysis, time management, ethics).
– *Multi-modal*: How will auditory, visual and haptic (feeling/space) input be provided?
– *Differentiation of tasks*: How are tasks provided for the student cognitive-linguistic range?
– *Evolution*: How does this input connect with past and future learning requirements?
– *Assessment*: What is an appropriate test of input understanding? (Retelling?)

These questions are important to pose for effective input. If queries reflect a holistic learning approach, not only will students engage but they will also remember the content. The mantra – see, hear, say and learn – follows how the brain processes information. However, learning activities generally exclude the "saying" element. Unless students have the opportunity to speak about what they have learnt, chances are the information will be soon forgotten.

2.12 *Presentation: The Structure of the Teaching Session*
– *Overview*: With online presentations a session summary must be provided, as reduced face-to-face opportunities make orientation more important. Questions must be posed. A platform facility can check that students have accessed the session summary before the online input. This feedback can be made a small percentage of an assessment grade. (An example is provided in Appendix A.)
– *Modelling*: Demonstrating information is vital and brief video clips are useful for this.
– *Direct instruction*: In face-to-face situations, PowerPoint inputs accompany direct instruction with the presenter judging reception from verbal and non-verbal audience feedback. This is not easy to do in a web-based module. Make sure written input is presented first, with time to absorb before speaking. Make the explanation, with a five-minute maximum, before a break, which could be a question with a video clip illustrating an answer.
– *Paraphrase*: Provide the main points after each section, asking what listeners have learnt (different for everyone).
– *Assessment*: In some nations (e.g. Italy/Japan), oral as well as written assessments are seen as important. In the UK College of Teachers online courses, students produced short videos (three minutes long) explaining what had been gained from teaching and assessment. These were screened for clarity, content, conventions and conduct and with practice are quickly examined. The IDIAL European project (2009–2012) demonstrated the importance of this (Sage et al., 2012).

2.13 *Performance*
A consistent finding of student attention span studies is that variability arises from differences in teacher performance (Bradbury, 2016). Certainly, the most interesting material, if performed in a dry, dull manner, is a turn off for any listener. What is different between an online and a face-to-face presentation is the emotional commitment. A lively, inspiring teacher motivates students to delve more deeply into the content and provides a more satisfying experience than can be gained from passive materials. When presenting online the following issues need addressing to help overcome the problem.

2.14   Camera Angle

This must be at the same level or above the face. Raising the computer will be necessary. A laptop stand, a box or book stack will enable the camera to be directed right into the face. The light source should be located in front of you as back illumination produces a scary silhouette. A ring light is ideal, as it enhances facial features and highlights eyes by casting a flattering beam. Choose a suitable background – people do not want to see piles of washing up, an unmade bed or even a row of books as these distract. Choose a neutral background that does not fight with your face.

2.15   Consider the Audience

Take time to imagine you are talking individually to those tiny squares – think of them as "friends" and not "foes"!

2.16   Smile and Make Eye Contact

Keep smiling as it is easy to present a panicked face as you worry about software and whether it will let you down. Assigning someone to deal with glitches can take the anxious look away, but this may not be possible, so make sure you are familiar with web functions. When looking at the black dot (the eye of the camera) over the computer screen, the audience will feel that you are viewing them. You will need to gaze at the computer or elsewhere on occasions, but make sure that you regularly look at the camera. This helps you to make contact and establish a connection with the audience in order to keep them engaged.

2.17   Posture and Appearance

Dress up rather than down, as a web presentation is a formal occasion and how you look supports this. Wearing something that flatters you is important as it improves posture and presence. If sitting, ensure your back is straight and you stretch up from the waist so that your lungs take in the maximum quantity of air in order to sustain speaking – otherwise your voice will tail off at the end of a sentence and be difficult to hear. If standing, check that your legs are about 20 centimetres apart with your weight over the balls of your feet to release the muscles that control your volume and speech rate. Keep your neck straight in order to project your voice well. Remember not to cross your legs as this puts tension on your voice muscles and interferes with production.

2.18   Grab Attention

Smile and make a strong phatic introduction of welcome and pleasure at the opportunity to share and enjoy knowledge. Show an outline of the presentation, giving time for the audience to read it before making any explanatory comments. This includes the topic, purpose, central idea and main points. Starting with: "Today I am talking about X" is not arresting. Use a startling statistic, anecdote or quotation to focus interest. Check that everyone is comfortable about seeing and hearing you and mention that the chat function should be used for feedback. A host can be appointed to monitor this. Try to promote active discussion with questions.

2.19 *Voice*

Make sure you vary the pace, pitch and power of your voice, so that your speech sounds lively and interesting. The same sentence can have a very different meaning depending on which words are emphasised and the voice tone used. With age our voice range decreases without vocal exercise and actors do warm-ups to ensure their words are striking. Find your high and low note and work at extending the range (see Sage, 2000). It is easy to lose vibrancy in your voice without a face-to-face audience that constantly gives non-verbal feedback to monitor performance. Personality comes through voice, so ensure you sound real by telling stories, anecdotes and jokes (if appropriate) in order to enliven the material. Non-verbal communication carries most of the affective message. Good delivery conveys ideas clearly without distraction. Lack of clarity and cohesion results in poor decisions and confusion.

2.20 *Delivery*

Reading from a script fractures the interpersonal connection. Maintaining eye contact with the audience keeps the focus on yourself and the message. A brief topic outline at the level of your face prevents bending down and losing audience attention. Gestures are important to reinforce points, but they can dominate in the small screen space, so use sparingly. Check the rate of delivery and speak more slowly than in a face-to-face context, as without the real situation the processing cues are reduced. Short sentences and regular pausing help the message to transmit effectively. Use audio-visuals sparingly as too many break the direct connection to the audience. They should clarify and enhance the content, or capture and maintain attention. Give time for them to be scanned before expanding on them with comments. The presentation should have limited periods of talking, with continual summaries of main points with reflective questions in between to give listeners the opportunity to take stock and review what has been said. Video clips are useful illustrations to make the material real. Finish with a final review of main points and a discussion of the questions asked.

2.21   *Questions*

During a presentation pose open-ended queries, which encourage further points and details. Probing questions require more thoughtful responses, such as "Think about the process of...". A mixture of questions, including the clarification of "what if" and open-ended scenarios, help to make sure that the goal of the presentation is achieved. On a webinar, these can be posed and responded to on the chat function to then be discussed before the summary.

Communication is never perfect, but putting effort into preparing a presentation and thinking about making a good performance pays off with a positive impact for students. People seem more nervous about online activity and you cannot shake this off entirely, but aim to minimise this to maximise the occasion!

3   Review

Technology can foster improved communication in online presentations, as it gives speakers the opportunity to assess their performances from recordings and hopefully learn from these for the future. Technology critics claim that the use of digital technology is ruining interpersonal communication. It is certainly changing it and it can be for the better by making us more aware of issues that help or hinder exchanges. Effective web presentations that are recorded give audiences a chance to review (for as many times as needed) the content so that they can comprehend it effectively. It is a skill to learn how to use the different types of technology for communicating and learning. Usually this ability is picked up haphazardly, so there is a need for continual training. As technology becomes more integrated into life, the ability to use it well becomes essential. Employers are now calling for e-portfolios of personal evidence of experience rather than examination results. They find numbers and grades unreliable predictors of personal, practical and academic performance. Reviews and reflections on achievements are a better indication of individual potential and provide a holistic view of a person and their development (Sage, 2020). Portfolios enable short video or audio clips to provide real performance evidence.

The COVID-19 pandemic has relied on teaching through technology and blended learning has advantages in enabling flexible learning. It has the means to teach communication to varied audiences. People have always had communication apprehension and anxiety about talking to others, particularly in large group settings. Some students show this in classrooms but are fine outside in more informal contexts. Anxiety is fear of the unknown. When interacting face-to-face, the feedback that a sender gets from the receiver is uncertain. In order to reduce uncertainty, people stereotype to reduce worry. With technology it is easier to communicate because people do not have to cope with that initial face-to-face reaction when they are remote. Although technology has its downsides, because of the rise of cyberbullying, respect for others and responsible use must be continually emphasised in all learning contexts. Undoubtedly, teachers will be relying on blended learning in the future to cope with a continuing rise of students and this can support face-to-face learning if effectively used. Good luck with all your efforts!

References

Association for Project Management. (2020). *Salary and market trends survey 2020: APM research report.* https://www.apm.org.uk/media/44073/apm_salary_and_market_trends_survey_2020_report.pdf

Bradbury, N. A. (2016). Attention span during lectures: 8 seconds, 10 minutes, or more? *Advanced Physiological Education, 40*(1), 509–513. https://doi.org/10.1152/advan.00109.2016

Keyton, J. (2002). *Communicating in groups: Building relationships for effective decision making* (2nd ed.). McGraw-Hill.

Keyton, J. (2010). *Case studies for organizational communication: Understanding communication processes.* Oxford University Press.

Keyton, J. (2011). *Communication and organizational culture: A key to understanding work experience.* Sage.

Mehrabian, A. (1971). *Silent messages.* Wadsworth.

Sage, R. (2000). *Class talk: Successful learning through effective communication.* Bloomsbury.

Sage, R. (2020). *Speechless: Understanding education.* Buckingham University Press.

Sage, R., Rogers, J., & Cwenar, S. (2012). *A communication course for teachers: Research on the impact on practice.* IDIAL EU Project 2009–2012.

Schaffhauser, D. (2020, November 16). Survey: Interactive, in-class engagement makes a difference to students. *Campus Technology.* https://campustechnology.com/articles/2020/11/16/survey-interactive-in-class-engagement-makes-a-difference-to-students.aspx

Wallach, G. P., & Miller, L. (1988). *Language intervention and academic success.* Little, Brown.

APPENDIX A

Example of a Pre-lecture Information Sheet

This is an example from a speech and language therapy course but should be part of all formal instruction, as research shows that since the implementation of the National Curriculum the use of phatics has declined in teaching to the detriment of interactions and behaviour (Sage, 2000, 2020).

Course: Understanding Communication

Module: Phatic Communication

Phatic language is used for general social interaction, rather than conveying information or asking questions. Utterances like: "Hello, how are you?" and, "Nice day, isn't it?" are phatic. Although seeming to have little purpose, this small talk helps people to bond, define relationships and categorise social positions. It lubricates interactions, relating to a need to maintain positive face and to form a bond before information is exchanged.

The session has three topic sections
1. *Conversational patterns*: Introducing Grices's Maxim of Quantity
2. *Gender differences*: Collaborative styles of women v. competitive ones of men
3. *Culture differences*: Small talk rules and topics vary widely across the world

Module Aim

To understand the importance of phatic communication and how it can be improved to establish effective relationships in culturally diverse communities.

Questions to Answer

– Why is phatic communication important?
– What are your observations from real-life situations on the use of phatic communication?
– What makes phatic communication effective?
– Has knowledge of this process changed your views about communication?
– How will you improve your phatic use?

Useful Reference Texts for the Three Areas

- Grice, H. (1975). Logic and conversation. In P. Cole & J. Morgan (Eds.), *Syntax & semantics: Speech acts* (Vol. 3). Academic.
- Tannen, D. (1991, June 19). Teachers' classroom strategies should recognize that men and women use language differently. *Chronicle of Higher Education, 37*(40), B1, B3.
- Ventola, E. (1979). The structure of casual conversation in English. *Journal of Pragmatics, 3*, 267–298.

Assessment

Choose one of the three topics above that interests you. Review the literature and provide a practical example from a real-life situation to illustrate. Produce a final reflection on what you have learnt from your topic study and the competencies you have gained. Prepare to share this information with your class group.

Pre-lecture Task

Get in touch with your lecture "buddy" and exchange thoughts about the session topic. Briefly report the conversation on your reflection log.

Post-lecture Task

Prepare a three-minute presentation on your assessment task for your personal learning group and also for the whole class.

Competencies

Knowledge of part of the communicative process, transferable competencies, observation studies, literature reviews, reflection, spoken and written reporting.

Source: BSc, Medical & Communication Sciences, Dr. R. Sage, Head of Clinical & Educational Studies.

CHAPTER 8

Experiences of Learning Performance

Riccarda Matteucci and Rosemary Sage

Abstract

This chapter has two sections to illustrate issues of those involved in education. Section 1 presents institutions from Italy and Section 2 from England for comparisons.

Students from Rome – Liceo Scientifico Aristotele (School 1) – and Rieti* – Istituto di Istruziione Superiore I.I.s Celestino Rosatelli (School 2), completed a questionnaire on their learning post-pandemic. Data reveals student preference for active learning and some control over the process. Technology screen visual information dominates, so the auditory modality is less preferred for processing meaning, which must be recognized within instructional methods. Auditory processing is required for narrative language and higher level thinking, so must be monitored to ensure expert teaching. Concentration is a problem for many students, so may reflect verbal and visual domination of educational presentations – on-line technology or face-to-face. A small data set is reported, but is in line with world evidence.

Section 2 considers technology and learning views in schools, colleges and universities. Respondents value on-going support to transition from traditional to new teaching styles. They show insight and understanding of the world and volunteered to talk rather than chosen at random. Information discussed shows the different reactions people have to technology and learning styles. A mix of face-to-face and on-line experiences (blended learning) is acceptable and suitable for most people, as long as support (on-line & face-to-face) is continual, consistent and available when required. Comparisons reveal a need for active learning with some student control over the process for them to fully benefit from education. In a global world, which puts institutions into league tables, this proves difficult, leading to narrower learning that is test-based rather than focused on individual needs and personal development .

1 **Student Survey – Italian Student Reflections on Their Post-Pandemic Learning Experiences (Riccarda Matteucci)**

1.1 *Background and Methodology*

In making educational change, the views of those receiving instruction are paramount for understanding how to plan effectively for required outcomes.

© ROSEMARY SAGE AND RICCARDA MATTEUCCI, 2024 | DOI:10.1163/9789004688612_013

In the Italian school system, the cohort of students in the age bracket from 14 to 19 is divided into the *biennio* (the first two years of secondary school) and the *triennio* (the final three years). Students in the latter have had a longer experience of learning in mainstream contexts and so are able to review and reflect on a variety of instructional modes.

Students aged 14 to 19 at two schools in Italy – the Liceo Scientifico Aristotele (School 1) in Rome and the Istituto di Istruzione Superiore I.I.S. Celestino Rosatelli (School 2) in Rieti[1] – were asked to complete a short questionnaire on their learning experiences post-pandemic. Questionnaire I, consisting of 12 questions to elicit data on learning preferences, difficulties and needs, was devised in consultation with educators and given to the *biennio* students. Questionnaire II was a more sophisticated version that was created for the older *triennio* students to answer. Both questionnaires are reproduced in Appendix A. The level and accuracy of the English language used by students to answer the questions was not considered, as this was an unnecessary measure for the study. The survey was reviewed by both schools and piloted on a small group, with the purpose explained to staff and students. School 1 (Rome) produced 49 responses and School 2 (Rieti) gave 50, thus making both groups statistically viable for analysis.

The data was collected from a range of classes within the schools: In Rome, it was the 1st and 2nd year stream I; the 3rd year stream D; the 4th year stream I and the 1st Cambridge course. The questionnaire was delivered by Professor Loredana Adamo. In Rieti, the classes involved were the 5th AEE (ITT Elettronica and Elettrotecnica); the 3rd MA and the 3rd MB (ITT Meccanica, Meccanotromica and Energia) and the 4th SQ Liceo Scientifico Quadriennale. The questionnaire was carried out by Professors Gabriella Gallo, Alessandra Giovannelli and Anna Crisostomo.

I was present on the day of the submission in Rieti and able to tell respondents that they had to view me as if I was the minister of education asking for advice to improve student needs and school benefits, to adapt learning to the requirements of the third millennium. The students felt empowered and delivered interesting and significant suggestions.

1.2   *The Results*

The data in Table 1 show a great difference between the participant working preferences of both institutions, with School 1 having 100% of respondents favouring studying with others, whereas School 2 had only 36% choosing this approach. This may suggest there are school differences in the learning methods employed. Learning with active engagement is favoured by both cohorts and in line with knowledge of the development that the haptic sense

TABLE 1   Learning preferences

		School 1% N = 49	School 2% N = 50	Comments
Working practices	Alone	0	64	
	Others	100	36	
Preferred processing	Hearing	12.1	10	Active learning is the largest preference.
	Seeing	21.2	16	Similar across both schools.
	Doing	66.1	66	
	Hearing/seeing	3	4	
	Hearing/doing		4	
Working method	Mixed – computer + face-to-face	75.8	42	Large difference within and across schools.
	Not mixed – one or other	24.2	58	

Note: Not all figures add up to 100% because some questions were not answered.

(touch, movement, sense of position in space) is the fundamental and preferred method of learning in the population, supported by studies of students by the UK Medical Research Council (Sage, 2000). The decreasing ability of students to cope with large quantities of verbal information and assemble their meaning has also been noted in research by Sage (2021) over many years. This is attributed to television and screens supplanting talk as today's common connective mode between people. The working methods show variance between both institutions, with School 1 (Rome) much preferring a mixture of computer and face-to-face experiences, whilst School 2 (Rieti) liked the input to be one or the other, noting that some academic subjects lend themselves to different methods of input according to the topic studied. For example, learning how to pronounce English was easier to acquire from online input while working alone, whereas reviewing constitutional history required face-to-face discussion to achieve a thorough understanding of the many political views expressed in today's plural communities.

As seen in Table 2, concentration for learning content is a major issue for three-quarters of students in both schools. Examining comments, there are

TABLE 2   Learning difficulties

		School 1% N = 49	School 2% N = 50	Comments
Differences – school	Concentration	75.8	76	Concentration problems due to attention.
	None	24.2	24	Understanding and lack of motivation.
Differences – home	Concentration	90.9	89.1	Lack of interest in the subject or method of delivery.
	None	9.1	10.9	

clearly problems in assembling verbal information, keeping attention focused on a task and being constantly distracted by surrounding circumstances. This is an age when information overload is a problem for everyone – constantly coming from every direction. When learning from home, in the pandemic lockdown periods, the distractions (dads and pets were especially mentioned!) were more evident for students. Approximately a quarter of students, in both cohorts, felt they did not have problems in learning at school, but these increased when working at home for the reasons mentioned.

Table 3 shows that the majority of students in both schools wanted additional support for learning, which ranged from more personalised approaches; teaching opportunities when they could share knowledge with peers and articulate their understanding; study buddies; and the introduction of new

TABLE 3   Learning needs

	School 1% N = 49	School 2% N = 50	Comments
Support required	84.9	86	Support required; individual, study buddies, time, new ways to learn.
No support needed	15.1	14	Similar number require no additional help for learning than what is presently provided.

TABLE 4   Benefits of home learning

	School 1% N = 49	School 2% N = 50	Comments
Control over learning	66.7	64	Chance to work how and when preferred.
No benefits	33.3	36	Some students mentioned interference from parents.

instruction methods. This evidence is in line with problems of concentration and attention and the need for greater assistance with learning for positive outcomes.

Table 4 shows that there is a clear preference for some student control over learning. Comments mentioned a liking for group projects. The Educational Robotics programme, adopted in some Italian schools and operating for around two hours weekly, is obviously much enjoyed by students as then they have opportunities to think about options and make decisions. It is interesting that a third of students, in both schools, see no benefit to working at home; they mentioned a need for physical contact with others to make learning meaningful and interesting. They valued being exposed to many views in group contexts, as well as the consistent support of their fellow peers and teachers. Question 6, concerning the choice of music listened to, did not show a significant difference during and after the pandemic, whereas some studies curried out in the USA have underlined different choices according to the mood of listeners, especially when connected to the time they had spent at home without seeing their peers.

Students were aware of Elon Musk's "magic chip", either by hearing or reading about it (Table 5). A small number in both schools viewed that brain insertion might make learning easier and help their concentration and understanding. By far the larger group were suspicious of this technological invention, as exerting some control over them or being dangerous to their health in some way (further explanations will be in the Epilogue, p. 239)

1.3   Discussion

In examining the data and the comments made on their answers, one is impressed by the articulateness of students recording the information in English as their second language, which is a tribute to their expert teaching. Words mean different things to us all and what is indicated by them should always be

TABLE 5   Knowledge of Elon Musk's Brain-Machine Interface (BMI) "Magic Chip"

	School 1% N = 49	School 2% N = 50	Comments
Wanting chip inserted to benefit learning	6.1	16	View that inserting the chip would make learning easier and help concentration.
Not wanting chip as dangerous	93.9	84	Felt chip could be dangerous to health and would take control away from themselves.

treated with caution. The data were examined by experienced linguistic specialists, so the analysis is as accurate as possible when dealing with qualitative information.

It is evident in the data that students across the sample age range commonly experienced concentration and attention problems in the learning context. Thus, it is important to further examine this aspect to fully understand the issue. The fact that much information, at all educational stages, is transmitted verbally and is factual in type, would appear to be against the information-processing capacity of most students today. We have moved from a verbal to a visual world, messaging through text rather than talk and with screen images the priority for information processing. It is important that in offering information to learners that the visual input is presented first, with time to absorb this before verbal explanation/discussion follows in the input sequence. This rarely happens, but the fact that only a few students, from the present studies, coped well with the online involvement, suggests that the presentation of information is not in line with their needs, capacities and opportunities. Undoubtedly, some students have better technology access than others, although schools are diligent in arranging equal opportunities for everyone. These issues are enlarged by Peter Chatterton in his chapter in the book *How World Events Are Changing Education* (2022).

1.4   *Summary of Student Comments*
- Present education is not for this modern age and school does not work well for many students.
- Assessment marks/grades are outdated – portfolio evidence gives a broader view of performance.

– Transmissive teaching is not always an effective or an appropriate learning
  method for all subjects.
– Control over learning is important to help develop thinking and expressive
  capacity.
– Time is needed for student to be able to follow passions and learn about
  what is personally interesting and rewarding.
– Teachers are often not familiar with computers and how they can be best
  used in education.
– Learning alone is important but group projects bring together thinking and
  extend it.
– Subjects easier to learn alone are the favourite ones as they are intrinsically
  interesting and motivating.
– Teachers talk too much and are often not understood properly as attention
  to speech is a problem.
– Teacher's communication/explanation is not clear, especially if they speak
  differently to students.
– Since the pandemic, many students feel more nervous in a group context.
– There is a need to explore new study methods to suit a range of learning
  styles.
– Many subjects studied are not relevant for the modern world.
– More personalised programmes would be welcome, with a choice of areas
  to study.
– Students only like computer learning if the technology works.
– Practice is more important than theory – learning application is required in
  all study areas.
– Students value teaching others in class (e.g. educational robotics) to con-
  firm understanding.
– Students have difficulty understanding information delivered via videos or
  online lectures because of presentation.
– Summaries are needed more frequently to help focus on the topic presented.
– Students need to learn to listen better, with an emphasis on this and how to
  communicate.
– Study buddies are helpful in creating learning communities and establish-
  ing a circle of interest.

1.5   *Recommendations*

1.5.1   Concentration

This is a major issue for students, indicating their inability to process large
chunks of verbal information. How to address this is outlined in Rosemary
Sage's *Class Talk* (2000), which evaluated this problem in a major project

assessing why students, deemed intelligent by teachers, failed to make progress in school. They all showed problems in processing verbal information to affect narrative understanding, expression and thinking.

1.5.2 Active Learning
Active learning is promoted in some systems, such as in the Educational Robotics programme that is coordinated internationally by Dr. Stefano Cobello (see Cobello & Milli, 2022).

1.5.3 The Flipped Classroom
If structured on an information-processing model, the flipped classroom would be a way to learn that incorporates technology and face-to-face learning that can suit all students as it enables flexible learning (see Matteucci, 2022).

1.5.4 Assessment
Assessment needs to reflect a broader range of personal and practical as well as academic abilities. This check on performance is better suited to an ongoing portfolio of evidence encompassing different recording modes to suit the present capabilities of students, which are now less verbal and more visual and haptic in processing and performance (see Frath, 2022).

1.5.5 Training
Suitable training is required for appropriate use of technology for learning and more in-depth knowledge of information processing (see Chatterton, 2022).

2 Case Studies – Experiences of Learning (Rosemary Sage)

2.1 *Teacher Experiences, Part 1*
As a speech therapist, psychologist and teacher (in English, mathematics and sciences), I have frequently been summoned into schools to observe struggling students and offer help. There are many children in schools who find the prescriptive, one-size-fits-all system, which encourages transmissive teaching, a learning barrier for them. Once, I visited a class of 7- to 8-year-olds, using iPads in a mathematics lesson. I observed a lad, with a downturned mouth, looking very fed up and defeated. The iPad asked him to "Combine 10 and 5". He eventually pressed "Help", but remained puzzled and scribbled busily on the iPad screen instead. I asked if I could help, receiving a vigorous nod: "Do you know what 'combine' means?" I queried. He answered, "No", so I explained it meant "add". His problem was instantly solved and the answer easily provided.

On another occasion, a girl stared at a screen question, with tears in her eyes: "What number comes after 43?" She tried 42, then 41 and 40, with repeated error messages. She had confused the word "after" with "before". I myself have often muddled left and right as a cross-lateral information-processor. In my driving test I turned left, when told to go right, and so I failed the test, of course! Opposite words are often a problem for people, like me, having brain sides that are not well differentiated for processing. I have frequently come across directional difficulties with students and so can sympathise with their particular challenges, which others laugh about and can inspire bullying.

These experiences stimulated me to look at other students in learning contexts with screens displaying statements like these:
– "Find the *odd* numbers in the series".
– "What is this *times* table called?"
– "How many *digits* come before 20?"
– "What *operations* are there in this multiplication?"
– "*Round* 99 to the nearest ten".
– "Write a series with each number the sum of the two *preceding* ones, starting from 0 and 1". (This relate to Fibonacci sequences.[2])

The vocabulary highlighted in these statements has been regularly observed as appearing on screens when visiting schools and also been discussed in conversations with teachers as proving difficult for (or even unknown to) students. Unfortunately, in Britain, we put less emphasis on communication and language issues in education than found in other countries (Cuba, Finland, Italy, Japan or Poland, for example) and therefore encounter many more students experiencing difficulties that are rooted in language rather than in mathematics itself. As teachers, we must be aware that the programmes accessed by students may have come from other countries and use language in a different way to us in Britain.

The fact is that mathematical terms, experienced and learnt in other contexts, like *odd*, *after*, *times*, *digits*, *operations*, *round* and *preceding*, are often problematic for students with undeveloped English language knowledge of structure, content and use (Sage, 2000, 2020). After all, the 500 common words in use have over 15,000 different meanings. This needs to be discussed with students and explained with examples of their various uses. When considering Fibonacci sequences, we collected examples, like a pineapple fruit, fern plants and pine cones to provide relevance and a purpose for studying them for real-life reasons. Medical Research Council studies on children testing as normal on psychological tests, but failing at school, showed consistent higher-level language problems not identified in commonly used assessments, which focus on components rather than the assembly of overall meaning of talk or text. Many subjects showed an inability to assemble quantities of words as well as exhibited terminology confusions. The particular ones discussed above have been observed in many contexts and been reported in various research studies on education, language and employment (Sage, 2000, 2020).

When students chat happily and show adequate use of informal language, they are not identified as having linguistic difficulties in formal connected sequences. Teachers have to cope with large groups and it is not easy to spot subtle problems. Moreover, children are adept at hiding their difficulties and depend on their friends to sort them out if they are in trouble with tasks.

2.2 *What Do International Reports Indicate?*

The UK has the most Microsoft Showcase Schools in Europe announced the software firm in 2021. Head teachers drive schools through digital transformation, with Microsoft experts supporting them. Classes often use the Microsoft Teams platform, with teachers sharing learning materials and homework. Use of digital technology is highlighted in class with a "bring your own device" policy. Schools are encouraged by hardware and software companies to introduce technology into daily teaching. However, reform strategies, like school choice and efforts to improve teacher quality, have not resulted in increased student performance across all development areas. The UK has climbed up the tables of the 2018 Programme for International Student Assessment (PISA) for 15-year-olds, but at the expense of making progress in other areas, according to the Organisation for Economic Co-operation and Development (OECD).

- Reading: 14th, up from 22nd (from tests three years ago)
- Science: 14th, up from 15th
- Maths: 18th, up from 27th

Moreover, the OECD study found just 53% of UK students are satisfied with life, compared to 67% in the 38 member countries.[3] They attribute this to the narrow academic approach to education, one dominated by testing (Schleicher, 2020). This marginalises personal and practical growth, which builds communication, resilience and adaptability. The UK teaching unions say tests are tarnished by this data. Recommended strategies to deal with well-being, like mindfulness, are useful but do not get to the core of problem, which include higher-level language difficulties.

Educators place confidence in instructional software to narrow the large test score gap between students at the top and bottom of the socio-economic scale. The OECD found that technology is limited in bridging the performance divide between these students, with a similar effect for "flipped" classes (OECD, 2016). Students watch lectures at home via technology and use class time for discussion and problem-solving. Consult Matteucci (2019) for the effective use of this method, demonstrating that both teacher and student expertise is needed, such as effective communication abilities.

A 2019 report from the National Education Policy Center at the University of Colorado on "personalised learning", a term corresponding with "education technology", expressed some strong views. It found "questionable educational assumptions embedded in influential programs, self-interested advocacy by the technology industry, serious threats to student privacy, and a lack of research support" (Boninger et al., 2019, p. 3). Vulnerable students spend more time on digital devices than advantaged ones and experience the dangers of relying on technology in early literacy education. Much of the primary school day is spent on reading and mathematics, if there are low test scores for these subjects, so other areas tend to be sidelined. Students often work alone on reading and mathematics with digital devices, while the teacher assists a small group. Recently, I was asked for help by a parent who had a child who spoke in monosyllables only. The school had advised the child use an iPad to encourage listening to talk in stories. However, the child needed one-to-one speaking experience with an adult, who was aware of the strategies to promote speaking abilities. I advised talking through home activities while doing them, such as dressing/undressing, preparing a meal, making a bed etc. The parent had never thought of doing this and the idea is working well, with the child beginning to contribute to the talk sequences in sentences of their own.

2.3   *Why Do Devices Hinder Learning?*

When students read from screens, they absorb less information than from paper, because of the more restricted viewing angle and the less haptic, three-dimensional, feeling experience (Sage, 2020). Another issue is the distraction that devices bring – the primary student doodling on the screen instead of doing mathematics, or a senior one checking their Instagram constantly. However, there are serious reasons regarding learning progress (Sage, 2012–2015).

– *Motivation:* When intervening with the mathematics student, the language problem was spotted and a relationship formed to boost a correct response. Technology conveys information but cannot show social use. Teachers and classmates help make knowledge meaningful, so technology may lessen motivation and depress group learning. Experts support students at screens that deliver lessons for ability, interests and choice. Learners must swap ideas to extend understanding. Allowing topic choice may lead to knowledge gaps (Sage, 2012–2015).

– *Understanding*: In regard to student problems with mathematics instructions, learners should take pretests to select software at the appropriate cognitive-linguistic level, but they may find this makes false assumptions about understanding. It can supply instruction better than a human in some ways, but if the content is faulty, inadequate or not presented at a level to suit students, learning is ineffective.

In only a few cases are there defined concepts or standard learning sequences to chart progress. Secondary language literacy and numeracy activities have developmental stages, when brains are ready to think about whole (4 to 7 years) and parts (7 to 9 years). If teaching tables in mathematics or sound analysis for reading, learning will be difficult before maturation (Sage, 2020). Progress cannot happen unless students have acquired spoken language narrative levels that enable them to assemble sequences coherently. Otherwise, we do not know *what* must be taught or the order for this to occur effectively.

Technology is often used for reading comprehension. Even in classes with no technology, learners are asked to find the main idea and make inferences before having acquired narrative thinking and language to make this possible. Thus, content may lack meaning for them, which encourages disruptive behaviour to avoid tasks (Sage, 2000, 2020). Teachers choose texts to illuminate topics and students read them for reinforcement. When computers/tablets are used, the material takes the same approach, but subject background knowledge and vocabulary are more important than components. For reading comprehension, learners must examine the topic carefully and talk about it together in order to construct knowledge and vocabulary. This is crucial for those from less educated backgrounds, who are unlikely to pick this up at home and may lack knowledge of basic terms, as in the student examples above. You will find learners who can read fluently because of an educational focus on analytic phonics to aid mechanical literacy, but who are unable to retell information because they have not developed narrative abilities to assemble and express ideas.

Studies on the use of e-readers for students produce mixed messages, with researchers acknowledging their motivational aspects and the fact that people of all ages read continually from various screen devices today. However, the importance of teachers and others in interpreting and comprehending text is widely acknowledged. Also, the lack of haptic experience is crucial for some readers in making meaning (Picton & Clark, 2014; Reid, 2016; Long & Szabo, 2016; Kaynar et al., 2020; Sage, 2020).

2.4 *Can Technology Help Build Knowledge?*

Software based on brain science can assist creative and critical thinking, retention and recall. However, if used for just support it may not work effectively. "What are the education aspects that a computer can do instead of a human being?" "How can technology assist learning aims?" To answer such questions, teachers need an understanding of learning that enables them to deal with problems effectively.

Classes have an ability range amongst students, but instead of providing them with different content, they are given the same information in an inclusive, one-size-fits-all philosophy. However, for this to be effective, learners must have different tasks that take account of their thinking and narrative development.[4] Older students might study the history of language, but the more advanced ones could compose a discursive essay, produce a poster, create a set of comparisons or instructions, write a report on a key aspect or carry out other tasks at their narrative level of development. For teachers, this differentiation is challenging without psycho-linguistic knowledge and understanding. Technology assists grouping students by ability, with appropriate tasks and means to assess performance. Video and audio recordings bring topics to life, offer real pictorial contexts and give access to texts. Digitalised books are easily updated for those who struggle to read them, as the Top Hat Company does well. Mathematics software facilitates student debates, when they give different answers to the same problem. Also, technology enables gifted students to study content not taught in their context and caters for those with learning problems, delivering programmes designed by experts.

2.5   *Comment*

Educators wanting learning equity must consider technology hindrances as well as the help it affords learning performances. Research highlights a digital divide – the lack of access that low-income citizens have to technology and the internet. Students, in the chapter examples, must learn computer use to benefit from online information, but content language issues must also be considered. Software developed in other cultures may use different language expressions and vocabulary for instructions and information that users find unfamiliar in their particular country. This possibility must be checked by teachers. There is a danger of creating a digital divide of the opposite kind by outsourcing learning to devices for building competencies, while advantaged students have the benefits of being taught by expert teachers, who can adjust learning to suit their individual needs.

2.6   *Introduction: Student Experiences*

We may think that all students are happy having technology as their learning companion. In fact, students in Britain, together with Chile, spends more time on screens compared to those in other nations (Sage & Matteucci, 2019). In a study of a hundred students at the University of Leicester, three spent 14 hours daily on their devices – watching sport in bed for half the night! (Sage, 2000). No wonder teachers complain about class yawners! However, parents are now more aware of these negative issues and some provide rules about technology use, so students can learn to deal with the downsides of devices. This is necessary to regularly reinforce, as schools report that the majority of primary students are on social media accessing questionable content (Sage & Matteucci, 2019). This fact is constantly communicated when working on the Magistrates in the Community (MIC) project,[5] which aims to develop activities with students to help them look at the consequences of their actions. The huge surge in crime committed by 5- to 15-year-olds demonstrates the importance of this learning for students.

An American study (Lepp et al., 2015) looked at mobile phone use for learning. Participating anonymously, students identified drawbacks: cheating, communication face-to-face reduced, competence for writing declines, cyberbullying, distractions, disruption of routines, inappropriate content, ringtone nuisance and sexting. However, they recognised benefits that included creativity, improved attendance, increased engagement, motivation and productivity. Although there was a high level of support for phone use in classes or lectures, around one-third of students felt phones should be banned, but 90% said that they used them for course work and they were invaluable for researching information on the web.

A Swedish study (Olofsson et al., 2020) reported that mobile phones were both useful tools but also annoying distractions. The aim is to maximise the benefits of classroom technology and minimise learning barriers. These studies help instructors to become aware of technology useful for learning, as well as to reflect on, refine and review classroom experiences to improve overall ongoing performance. Students from primary, secondary and tertiary education were asked how they best learnt and how technology helps their studies. Answers are reported with names and some identifying details changed to make the data anonymous. The responders were interviewed face-to-face in an informal context and notes were taken by me and then written up and checked for authenticity by the subjects.

Molly: Age 10 years, at a village primary school in middle England
I learn best with my mum and dad at home. At school, I have to do things that are difficult for me. The teachers do not know my problems. I do badly and my friends do better than me. This makes me feel stupid! I do good things when they mean something and I understand why I have to know them. Mum had me tested by a lady and my ability to work out things that I could see was really, really good. My problem is putting words together. I get in a muddle

listening to teachers talking non-stop. My dad told me that brains grow at different rates and mine is slow like his was at my age. He said that he had troubles at school but his mum fought to get help. He told me we have a seeing brain on the right side and a hearing brain on the left one. Sometimes they don't like talking with each other or take time to learn how to do so. He is a doctor, so there's hope for me yet. My family always support my school activities and keep me going.

My worst things at school are spelling and maths. If we have to do exercises on the iPad I sometimes have to ask what the instructions mean. I am not afraid to do so. Others in the class are frightened of doing this in case they are made to feel stupid. They muck about to avoid doing the work! I find videos good, as they are moving and tell a story that I can see and follow. I do not like screen tasks that are mostly words. I am not on WhatsApp yet, as my parents think it is not good for me. My brother, who is 13, uses a WhatsApp group to discuss homework and says it is a good way to swap ideas with friends. He is always texting his friends and my parents check this! They do not like us spending all our time on screens and make sure we do sport and other things. I play the violin and have swimming lessons and go to Beavers, so I get to do real things, like cooking and forest tracking. I am a good dancer and gymnast so often perform at concerts.

Comment: Molly is aware she has learning issues but seems adjusted to these and has home support. As 85% of what we learn is outside formal classrooms this is crucial for progress (Sage, 2000). As Mollie knows about her problem areas she is in a position to manage learning that works for her, but clearly feels that school does not recognize her problems.

Ajay: Age 15 years at a London secondary school

I am afraid of new things, so was worried about using technology in lessons, when moving to secondary school. My parents are not tech savvy and we do not have a computer at home, but the school provided iPads for those of us who did not own them. The school has had a big technology drive, so I have learnt about apps that keep me interested. These make the lessons more fun. A favourite one of mine is Nearpod. This is a shared presentation and assessment tool and quite easy to use. You can create presentations like PowerPoint and include quizzes, surveys, videos, images, drawing boards and web content. The presentation is interactive and shared with others in the class on their devices. The teachers like it because they can insert material they already have or use one of the many lessons available on the website for a change. Slideshows are more fun with surveys, quizzes, virtual reality trips (such as to the Egyptian pyramids), drawing boards, fill-in-the-blank questions, web content and 3D objects – good for biology lessons and help to make the content real.

We follow lessons on screens and answer questions, so we take an active part. When we answer questions, the teachers can see them and support us with things not understood. They sometimes share model answers on our devices, which help us with what to aim for. There is an issue with some students being more used to technology from home devices. This annoys some students as the lessons are held up trying to sort out techy problems. Nothing is perfect!

My preferred learning is from doing things in an active way and my friends are the same. One problem about lessons is that teachers talk for a long time, often too fast for some of us who do not speak English as our first language and need a slower pace. Some teachers have strong accents, which make it a problem to understand and they use words we don't know as well, without explaining them. Technology improves visual presentations and gives me a clue on how to take notes or arrange information. Things like pictures, diagrams and film are slotted into the lesson text. This makes for interest and impact with visual examples of the topic. An advantage of things like PowerPoint is that drawings and diagrams, which are a big part of my science course, are better in colour and clearer than blackboard or whiteboard sketches, which depend on the teacher's artistic talent. Bad drawings can be very distracting.

One big problem is that teachers go through things like PowerPoint presentations quickly, as they have to get through a lot of information in lessons, so slides vanish before points get noted. When recordings are available online, we can look at them again in our own time. This takes off pressure, so I can concentrate on looking at slides and listening to the teacher and not bother about taking notes, which can be done later. We have a quiz after each lesson, which makes us think about what has been understood. These can be quite fun.

Problems do come from using technology, as bugs are common. Sometimes, the pictures wobble or do not show up and the screen freezes. The picture and sound may not match. On the whole, the teachers are good at sorting out problems, so they do not hold up lessons too much. I don't think that all teachers should use technology in lessons, as a few are good, lively speakers and nice to listen to. We learn when information is clear and easily understood. It helps to repeat content differently, which some teachers do well. As we do not seem to learn in the same way, new technologies have tools to help us all. Technology connects the teacher, lesson and students in ways that can suit everyone. Most of us do not cope well when having to listen to a teacher just talking for all of the lesson. Technology can motivate us, if we know how best to use it and take the trouble to learn.

Comment: Ajay has a good grasp of his learning preferences and takes his lessons seriously. He makes a strong point about repetition of material in different ways and the importance of interaction between teachers and learners. He does acknowledge the disadvantages that students have who do not have access to technology in their homes.

Mattia: Age 18 years, in the last year of a secondary school in a city in the north of England

I learn best by seeing things presented in different ways and then going over them again in my own time, as well as discussing things with friends. I don't think I would learn well if I had to listen to an audio of someone going on and on about something in a boring voice. This is what gets me about normal lessons. Some teachers sweep in, deliver the topic, give the homework and then rush out to the next lesson. Visual information keeps me interested and helps me remember things better, as I can picture them in my head.

Technology is a cool learning aid. Not only does it help the teacher and students to communicate knowledge and ideas in new, interesting ways, but it allows us to access the information later when it suits us. For example, a group can plan and present a PowerPoint presentation and the teacher streams it from the subject web site, which we can access at home. (My group recently did a presentation on river life from observing the one running through our city on an out-of-school trip.) This is a good way to support lessons, without needing more teacher time and resources. Also, new technologies appeal to us younger ones, as we are into them in a big way. Look at the number of mobile phones, iPads and laptops that students now have. This makes technology easy in class, because the teacher does not have to tell us how to use it. As many own devices (phones/iPads) less class ones are needed. School only has to provide devices if these are not available at home. This shows how learning is improved by new technology use.

As said earlier, learning is an exchange of ideas and views between everyone in a class. Teachers and students must interact constantly to get the most out of an experience. Technology helps the move into the future digital world. The jobs we go into will demand tech skills. There are downsides, as technology can let you down, but we can learn to cope with this and know the infrastructure will get better as the present problems get sorted out.

Comment: Mattia is sold on technology and appreciates the versatility and variety it brings to learning as he obviously does not warm to the traditional lecture-style approach. He understands the importance of becoming skilled in technology use for later working roles.

Vicky: A second-year undergraduate psychology student from East Anglia

I am a visual-haptic learner, which I found out about in course lectures on cognition. This means I learn best when seeing real things with tasks that apply new knowledge and understanding. In this way, I get the best from class experience. I have no problem reading books/articles for information, providing my housemates keep quiet! However, this does not make up for regular discussion about our topic work with other students, who widen and stimulate thinking from their many different takes on things. That is why I need active involvement with the lecturer and the rest of the group, in order to get my head around the subject. Personally, I do not wait for this to happen as I don't mind speaking up! I come from a family who really highlight this ability and it has been my best achievement. I am not afraid to question or introduce my ideas in a group! I begin discussions or continue ones which others have started.

The reason that I am so keen about all this is because I know that learning is an exchange of ideas, beliefs and knowledge, as my studies of psychology make clear. You only get what others want to give. The way to really learn is to facilitate talk in class, which makes your brain buzz with the many different thoughts that race around inside it. We have a Japanese student who is brilliant at group talk. He says that in Japan the teachers focus on communication and relationships for effective teamwork in present and future working roles. He understands the rules of group talk and so knows how to apply them to teach us all! Most of us have not learnt these in British schools. It is interesting to know about experiences of international students.

I do find technology useful and like the flipped classroom, where you have the material online to study, with questions and tasks to then bring results to seminars with tutors. I have had boring lectures to put up with and the move to blended learning suits me fine! However, I do want chances to hear inspiring professors, who have done international research and can put us in touch with what the wider world is thinking and doing! This could be done with a short series of key lectures at the beginning or end of term. We have a great WhatsApp group going with psychology second years and this keeps us in contact, as many of us are scattered over the city now that we have left campus halls of residence. I think the flipped class has kept us going during the 2020 pandemic. Even the simulated lab work has been useful, although I must say the real is best, as I like to touch things and feel them in space (haptic sense). There are problems with technology, when the screen freezes and the sound disappears. Sometimes it is difficult to enter Zoom events and download materials, when the internet speed is low. Nothing is perfect and one has to get on with things and cope with difficulties!

However, one thing bothers me and that is the popularity of internet essay mills,[6] where you buy your assignments and theses for a price. I know of students who do this and get away with it. Although my parents did not go to university, I have an uncle who did and is now a lecturer. He thinks standards have gone down, which is not surprising as many more are now entering higher education. Universities are big business and this mentality may affect quality. There are good staff, but we are also taught by those who lack the experience and research knowledge that my uncle has acquired and so do not have much to offer us.

Comment: Vicky is a keen, active student who appreciates real experience to help her learn best. She sees the flexible benefits of online learning and is a fan of the flipped classroom, which seems to suit many students. Her ability to cope with technology let-downs means she is a good model to follow!

Donald: A post-graduate student at a university in the south of England

My research subject is andragogy, the art and science of adult learning. My mum is a further education lecturer, teaching many foreign students learning in English, which is not their first language. I have heard about the challenges of their formal educational experiences, as they find problems with names and nuances. Therefore, it is interesting to work out how I learn, as no one has made me aware of this in my own education, even though I am a qualified mainstream science teacher! As a post-graduate student in my thirties, I value continual professional development opportunities. I have always been an achiever and like to find out new things. I question, search for answers and get on with things. I have a nosy nature and queries inspire and motivate me to go on learning. The best teachers have pushed me to follow my passions, while providing support and help when needed. I have found the higher education journey a huge test of independence, will power and determination! However, I have noticed how many students (even at my post-graduate level) need support and have problems thinking, making decisions and using their initiative. The number with mental health issues astonishes me and makes me wonder where we are going wrong. Education has mainly an academic, exam focus with practical and personal talents having less status and attention.

Many students go to universities who would be better suited to technical or practical training linked with the industries to which they aspire. UK education steers students in just the academic direction. If you don't get to university, society thinks you are a failure. My dad is a builder and when challenging an architect recently about implementing some plan was shouted at and told: "You f****** builders are all thick as sh**!" This just shows the views and values held by our society, as Dad talks about the public attitude that people who do his job are judged as society's failures. The young generation aim to become lawyers, medical doctors or accountants so that they earn big bucks and have social approval and status. We don't have value for people with practical and personal intelligences. I do try to inculcate in my students a value for all talents and interests, so they do not acquire a view that one ability is better than another.

Technology has been a blessing and a curse for me. My research shows only 8% of students are happy with technology. Fortunately, I took a tech course last year, which improved my confidence and skills. I found that I couldn't ruin my computer, unless in a fit of temper I threw it out of the window! Now, I'm happy to try out things. A course learning contract kept us up to the mark and on track. We all had to learn a new technology or improve a skill in using it for our work activities. People produced web sites, instructional programmes, video conferences and digital photography, as well as creating PowerPoints with sound and movement for presentations. Choice of possibilities in the contract was good to suit interests and work roles.

We have learned to create online curricula and use a chat room for discussions about articles and required readings. Group exchanges were paperless except for project handouts. It was a good experience for reluctant and eager tech learners alike! Technology gives many opportunities to explore, create and cooperate. I see an increase in communication and confidence amongst course mates on the tech course, which should be a must for everyone in all faculty areas.

Tutors are often frustrated with technology, as the tools do not always work properly and the ongoing training received is erratic or non-existent. I was in tech hell when my research presentation went wrong and the screen continually froze! Luckily, it has not affected my assessment, as the tutor assured us that dealing with problems calmly is what matters. Machines fail just like humans! However, it puts one off stride, but others were willing to help out and give support. Technology is constantly changing and differs in each setting. Patience and willingness to learn allows technology to extend the world for students at every level. It also helps to personalize learning so that everyone can benefit.

However, technology has dangers for academia, as not all online information is correct and fake news is constantly bandied around. Also, some students are inclined to cheat, buying assignments and theses from website essay mills. There are academics willing to write these for large fees. The media reported this in March 2019. Professors were compiling theses for students, charging over £6,000, according to journalists. This service is easy to find on the web and should be stopped. Someone I heard about bought an essay for £60, saying he could earn more than that in an evening working at a city bar, so saving time for socialising! This mentality seems to be growing. I spoke to a friend who works in a university, who confirmed that cheating is rife amongst students, as many are not up to the mark and find it difficult to speak and write in good English, especially if it is not the common, everyday language for them. Cancelling obligations to speak/write in correct English is not helping them for future career success. When you go about the campus, it is surprising how many different languages you hear spoken nowadays. Sometimes, I feel in the minority!

I like the idea of research being more practice-based within the actual workplace of participants, to broaden their knowledge and understanding of issues as well as sharing this with colleagues for real impact on practice and progress. As I am investigating my own learning, recording this and then comparing my journey with other adult students, I feel that outcomes will be worthwhile for everyone. I understand Harvard University now focuses on PhD research degrees and practitioner doctorates, which are global developments. These are not as popular in the UK, because some think investigations within one's own practice are not credible research goals. I have heard academics say they Americanise and cannibalise the UK system! This is not my view as you have gathered! I think a personal record for assessment is more useful to take back into the workplace and introduce to colleagues for comment and review. It is difficult to cheat with this method, so it must be a favoured assessment to give a broader and wider view of a person's performance.

Comment: Donald is a "goer" and determination has helped him succeed. He has a love-hate relationship with technology because of its unreliability, but is able to cope with this. The learning contract is a sound idea to encourage the use of technology for creative purposes and is one that all courses should adopt as mandatory. Donald's research topic has led him to support practice-based inquiries for its impact on workplaces.

2.7   *Summary Comment*

Polarised views of classroom technology are common. Some think they distract and result in lower performance. Others suggest learning experience is improved and banning technology prevents student progress, especially for those with specific needs. Many views are based on anecdotes and not scientific data. The case study samples presented here may not reflect an overall view of technology and learning, but do give some interesting opinions to reflect on with colleagues. Recommendations must be based on research regarding how students process, retain and retrieve information.

When students use mobile phones in class, their performance might be less. Psychologists explain this as multitasking and divided experience. Students believe they can attend to many things at once, but this can harm the user and other classmates (Lepp et al., 2015). Students do better on tests when taking written notes rather than relying on laptop records (Mueller & Oppenheimer, 2014). It is not a question of distraction in these studies, but the computer process that harms learning. Taking notes by hand is slower and has to keep up with the pace of speech. Students must interpret quickly and think actively about information received, which depends on retention and recall. Some students prefer laptop records and only re-read these for exams, but unless followed by written notes to deepen thinking, this is less effective. Also, hand movements for writing help ideas to form and flow, as seen in COGS studies (Sage, 2020). However, those with writing problems, like dyspraxia, benefit from processing/producing work on computer and so must be allowed to do so.

2.8   *Review*

Limits and strengths of classroom technology must be acknowledged. Studies show that multimedia-sensory learning increases retention-recall processes. This occurs when learners encode visual, auditory and haptic information into memory, as when they listen to a topic presentation (auditory), then watch a display (visual) before carrying out practical tasks (haptic) to implement understanding. Studies show the efficiency of this mode of learning (Newman et al., 2019). Sharing information learnt greatly enhances retention and recall (Sage, 2020).

There are cognitive benefits to using certain technological aids, especially quiz tools. Quizlet, an online app, can improve study strategies and retention-recall of material. It allows students to make flash cards, view those of other students and use gamification for courses. The app also enables self-testing, determining how and what to study through metacognition (167 – Students' perspective and experience on higher education – YouTube).

Technology enhances other goals as well. Students do not always check teacher emails! It may be possible to text them, although staff might not want to disclose phone numbers. However, I have found texting a helpful way of keeping in touch with tutees. Apps, like Google Voice, work without revealing personal codes. These tools are multipurpose, enabling a dialogue on course content or notification of arrangement changes.

2.9   *Recommendations*

Technology can produce effective learning, but must fulfil ethical educational goals:

- Ensure devices in class minimize distraction with solutions suiting students and context requirements.
- Deliver multifaceted, multimodal learning, enabling students to use all sense modalities if possible (hearing, sight, feeling, smell, taste) and explain technology pros and cons to manage these effectively.
- Use an e-reader (£50+) for texts if possible. This device reads e-books and is like a computer tablet, but without a screen. It uses electronic paper, reflecting light like the normal type, but is easier to read with a wider viewing angle and is, therefore, much better for eyes, which can easily become short-sighted from too much screen use. Electronic paper is a portable, reusable store-and-display medium, looking like paper but can be written on repeatedly. The e-reader downloads e-books from a computer or reads them from a memory card, to hear how they sound and assist changing writing style for student needs. This technology is adaptable for many purposes and useful for those with specific needs.
- Use captions for showing videos, to help process information for inclusive learning. These help gain attention, with a longer viewing time for the message, vital for students with word-processing problems. They make content perform better on search engines.
- Make sure support is always available as using technology can make learning a more complex business and this can stress students who are not technically minded.

Although it might seem tedious to set up tech systems, they are easily updated for reuse. Tools are constantly changing so ongoing training for everyone is a priority, but not regularly available in many institutions (Chatterton, 2022).

The five students were brave to talk about learning and are impressive for their awareness and acceptance of events. Their views are echoed in the 2020 student webinars of the OECD, EDEN, Top Hat and world rankings. The overall opinion suggests that blended learning is the future, as people must be tech-savvy for jobs, with tools providing flexibility and choice and the opportunity to study and achieve understanding at their leisure. However, the downsides must be addressed, such as unreliable infrastructure, easy access to unsuitable materials and opportunities to cheat and pass courses without engagement. A strong view has been expressed that assessment must change to become a personal online record that can be updated for a job passport. Employers are aware of dubious practices and prioritise jobseekers from institutions with ethical principles. They now offer positions to non-graduates showing high-level personal and practical competencies, which are often regarded as more important than qualifications of dubious standard.

In 2012, the UK laws were relaxed, allowing non-qualified teachers to be employed in schools. Although bringing valuable life experience, it is vital that unqualified staff have understanding of psycho-linguistic learning processes. Education is a complex business in a diverse society. It is common for around 250 different languages and dialects to be spoken by students in UK city schools. Therefore, the linguistic content of computer programs must be of concern to ensure learners can access the content successfully. When these are produced in other countries with a different vocabulary and way of expression to the students who are asked to use them, this hinders rather than helps learning.

Finally, a quote from Bill Gates, the software billionaire: "Technology is just a tool. In terms of getting the kids working together and motivating them, the teacher is the most important" (Gates, 2016). If wisely implemented, technology improves engagement, knowledge retention, individual learning and collaboration, with innovation and inequality the defining global and educational issues of the 2020s.

Notes

1 Rieti is a mountain town outside the capital.
2 In mathematics, these are known as *Fibonacci* numbers (e.g. 0, 1, 2, 3, 5, 8, 13, 21). Fibonacci was a famous Italian mathematician. His book, *Liber Abaci*, introduced the sequence to Europe although it was discussed in 200 BC by Pingala, in India, regarding patterns of Sanskrit poetry formed from syllables of two lengths. The journal *Fibonacci Quarterly* provides studies of these numbers, for example, addressing how they appear in biology and building construction.
3 The 38 OECD member states are: Austria, Australia, Belgium, Canada, Chile, Columbia, Costa Rica, Czech Republic, Denmark, Estonia, Finland, France, Germany, Greece, Hungary, Iceland, Ireland, Israel, Italy, Japan, Korea, Latvia, Lithuania, Luxembourg, Mexico, the Netherlands, New Zealand, Norway, Poland, Portugal, Slovak Republic, Slovenia, Spain, Sweden, Switzerland, Turkey, the United Kingdom and the United States of America.
4 See Sage (2020) for examples of how to introduce tasks at different narrative levels.
5 For more information, see https://www.magistrates-association.org.uk/get-involved/help-educate-your-community/
6 Chris Skidmore brought the Essay Mills Prohibition Bill to the British Parliament on February 10, 2021. An ex-university lecturer reported: "My latter years of lecturing were blighted by constant attempts by students to hoodwink me into believing that the work they had submitted was a true reflection of their ability. [...] Year after year they purchased essays by companies that promised excellent grades" (Letters to the Editor, 2021). The bill is available on Hansard (https://hansard.parliament.uk/).

References

Boninger, F., Molnar, A., & Saldaña, C. M. (2019, April 30). *Personalized learning and the digital privatization of curriculum and teaching*. National Education Policy Center. https://nepc.colorado.edu/publication/personalized-learning

Chatterton, P. (2022). The rise and rise of digital learning in higher education. In R. Sage & R. Matteucci (Eds.), *How world events are changing education: Politics, education, social, technology* (pp. 177–196). Brill.

Cobello, S., & Milli, E. (2022). Sociological aspects of educational robotics. In R. Sage & R. Matteucci (Eds.), *How world events are changing education: Politics, education, social, technology* (pp. 150–158). Brill.

Frath, P. (2022). Imaginative alternatives to the "macabre constant". In R. Sage & R. Matteucci (Eds.), *How world events are changing education: Politics, education, social, technology* (pp. 90–103). Brill.

Gates, B. (2016). Technology is just a tool…. In S. Ratcliffe (Ed.), *Oxford essential quotations* (4th ed.). Oxford University Press.

Iskandar, A., Rizal, M., Kurniasih, N., Sutiksno, D. U., & Purnomo, A. (2018). The effects of multimedia learning on students achievement in terms of cognitive test results. *Journal of Physics: Conference Series, 1114*(012019). https://doi.org/10.1088/1742-6596/1114/1/012019

Kaynar, N., Sadik, O., & Boichuk, E. (2020). Technology in early childhood education: Electronic books for improving student's literacy skills. *TechTrends, 64*(6), 911–921.

Lepp, A., Barkley, J. E., & Karpinski, A. C. (2015). The relationship between cell phone use and academic performance in a sample of US college students. *SAGE Open, 5*(1). https://doi.org/10.1177/2158244015573169

Letters to the Editor. (2021, February 10). Letters: Focus on getting the country vaccinated – not going after travellers [J. S. Keighley Oakham, No more essay mills]. *Daily Telegraph*. https://telegraph.co.uk/opinion/2021/02/10/lettersfocus-getting-country-vaccinated-not-going-travellers/

Long, D., & Szabo, S. (2016). E-readers and the effects on students' reading motivation, attitude and comprehension during guided reading. *Cogent Education, 3*(1). https://doi.org/10.1080/2331186X.2016.1197818

Matteucci, R. (2019). What is technology? In R. Sage & R. Matteucci (Eds.), *The robots are here: Learning to live with them*. Buckingham University Press.

Matteucci, R. (2022). Technology and COVID-19: Remote learning and flipped classes to maintain live education. In R. Sage & R. Matteucci (Eds.), *How world events are changing education: Politics, education, social, technology* (pp. 197–222). Brill.

Molner, A., Miron, G., Elgeberi, N., Barbour, M. K., Huerta, L., Shafer, S. R., & Rice, J. K. (2019). *Virtual schools in the US 2019*. National Education Policy Center. https://nepc.colorado.edu/publication/virtual-schools-annual-2019

Mueller, P. A., & Oppenheimer, D. M. (2014). The pen is mightier than the keyboard: Advantages of longhand over laptop note taking, *Psychological Science, 25*(6), 1159–1168. https://doi.org/10.1177/0956797614524581

Newman, T., Beetham, H., Langer-Crame, M., Killen, C., & Knight, S. (2019). *Digital experience insights survey 2019: Findings from students in UK further and higher education.* Jisc. https://www.jisc.ac.uk/reports/digital-experience-insights-survey-2019-findings-from-students-in-uk-further-and-higher-education

OECD. (2016). *Science, technology & innovation: 2016 report.* Organisation for Economic Co-operation and Development. https://www.oecd-ilibrary.org/science-and-technology/oecd-science-technology-and-innovation-outlook-2016_sti_in_outlook-2016-en

Olofsson, A. D., Fransson, G., & Lindberg, J. O. (2020). A study of the use of digital technology and its conditions with a view to understanding what "adequate digital competence" may mean in a national policy initiative. *Educational Studies, 46*(6), 727–743. https://doi.org/10.1080/03055698.2019.1651694

Picton, I., & Clark, C. (2014). *The impact of ebooks on the reading motivation and reading skills of children and young people: A study of schools using RM Books.* National Literacy Trust and RM Books. https://nlt.cdn.ngo/media/documents/2015_12_09_free_research_-_impact_of_ebooks_2015_8uTEZVb.pdf

Reid, C. (2016). *Ebooks and print books can have different effects on literacy comprehension.* MS thesis, St. John Fisher University. https://fisherpub.sjf.edu/cgi/viewcontent.cgi?article=1329&context=education_ETD_masters

Sage, L. (2012–2015). Motivational effects on attention project [includes practitioner report and lesson plan examples for primary and secondary schools]. https://www.nuffieldfoundation.org/project/motivational-effects-on-attention

Sage, R. (2000). *Class talk: Successful learning through effective communication.* Bloomsbury.

Sage, R. (2020). *Speechless: Understanding education.* Buckingham University Press.

Sage, R., & Matteucci, R. (2019). *The robots are here: Learning to live with them.* Buckingham University Press.

Schleicher, A. (2020, February 4). Preparing the next generation for their future, not our past. *New Statesman.* https://www.newstatesman.com/politics/2020/02/preparing-the-next-generation-for-their-future-not-our-past

APPENDIX A

Questionnaire I (for *biennio* Students)

WHAT CAN YOU SAY ABOUT YOUR LEARNING?

1. How do you learn best? (Tick)
    Alone_____ With others_____

2. Do you like to HEAR things, SEE things or DO things to learn them best?
    _____

3. Do you like learning from computer or in a classroom with others around?
    _____

4. Do you like a mix of computer and class learning?
    _____
    WHY?
    _____

5. List any problems that you have with learning.
    _____
    _____
    _____

6. Is a quiet space or music playing helpful for learning? What music did you listen to during lockdown? And now?
    _____
    _____

7. What is your best and worst subject you acquire using technology?
    _____
    WHY?_____

8. What was difficult for you learning at home in lockdown? _____

9. What was easy for you learning at home? _____ WHY?_____
    _____
    _____

10. Is there something that could help you learn better?

_____

_____

_____

11. Have you heard about Elon Musk's BMI "magic chip"? _____

12. Would you like to install it inside your body? _____
If YES, explain why.

_____

If NO, explain why.

_____

_____

Comments: Write down anything you would like to say about learning and how you might have changed your ways since the pandemic.

_____

_____

_____

_____

_____

Thank you for completing the questions.

Name.. Age.................. Date............

Questionnaire II (for *triennio* Students)

THINK ABOUT YOUR LEARNING

Thinking about learning makes it more successful. Answer honestly.

1. What was difficult about your learning in the pandemic?

_____

_____

_____

2. Using technology to learn has increased recently. List ways this has helped your learning.

_____

_____

3.   List ways that it has made learning more difficult.

_____

_____

4.   Education gives knowledge and abilities as below:
      a.   Speaking, reading, writing and numbers
      b.   How to learn alone and in a group
      c.   Sciences – ways to study the natural world (physics, chemistry, biology, etc.)
      d.   Arts – ways to express thinking (drawing, painting, music, etc.)
      e.   How to help others
      f.   Designing, organising and running activities – alone or in a group.

      Which of the areas are you good at? Which need more attention?
      Strengths (give letters a, b, c) _____
      More attention (give letters d, e, f) _____

5.   How could your learning be improved?

_____

6.   How do you take in information best? (Tick)
      Hearing it _____ Seeing it _____ Doing it _____

7.   On a scale of 1/2/3 – How do you *feel* about your learning experiences?
      Put X by your preferred statement below – a, b or c
      a.   Learning meets my needs and interests....
      b.   Learning does not meet my interests or needs....
      c.   I am often anxious about doing what the teacher wants....

8.   Have you heard about Elon Musk's BMI "magic chip"? _____
      Would you like to install it inside your body? _____

9.   If YES, explain why.

_____

10.   If NO, explain why.

_____

11.   What music did you listen to during the lockdown?

_____

12.   What music do you listen to now?

_____

Comments: Write down anything you would like to say about learning and how you might have changed your ways since the pandemic.

_____
_____
_____

Thank you for completing the questions to help improve experiences.

Name... Age........................ Date.....................

CHAPTER 9

Communication Performance in a Technology World

Rosemary Sage

Abstract

Evidence suggests that recent world changes, particularly in technology, have altered the way we communicate. This has positive effects for greater connectivity but is negative for face-to-face experiences and non-verbal interaction, which have the advantage of transmitting paralinguistic information more effectively for enhanced understanding. The chapter considers the principles of effective performance in both face-to-face and remote learning situations.

1 Introduction

In a terrifying way, the COVID-19 2020 pandemic revealed limitations in knowledge application that clinicians, educators, scientists and government ministers faced in publicly communicating and managing this lingering, cruel illness. For those who have received training in evidence-based methods to communicate, these situations are common. Delivering important information and giving clear instructions, without engendering apprehension, uncertainty and fear, requires skill, not only in providing understandable content, but also in presentation dynamics. For those prepared with a thorough understanding of communicating processes, production, performances and principles, with a flexible range of competencies, this know-how is helping them to adapt, innovate and avoid misspeak (Back et al, 2020, Merrill, 2020). Speech and Language therapists played an important role, in the pandemic, passing on their expertise in this domain, according to Health Service colleagues.

2 Issues about Speaking

Speaking is our primary representational system and required at narrative levels for processing and producing information accurately and easily. Reduced human interaction from continuing coronavirus threats is affecting communication competence according to sources (Sage & Matteucci, 2022). Communication problems are always with us as words are so easily misconstrued. Speech and language studies (Sage, 1996) found that misdiagnosis of human disorders was due to ineffective human communication between patient and doctor as well as amongst medical professionals themselves. Gaining and explaining information requires expert teaching for listening, talking, understanding, thinking, problem-solving, effective judgements and decision-making, so needing attention in learning. Gawande (2011), a surgeon, says around 50% of British patients receive inappropriate management because of scientific complexity and a struggle to process, because knowledge is not properly understood or correctly applied. Communication blunders account for £220 million medication claims alone over the last 15 years, estimated to have killed 22,000 UK patients annually. Pay-outs have doubled since 2014, indicating the importance of prioritizing spoken communication in education and training (Statistics-NHS England). This surely reflects a reign of error which the pandemic situation has highlighted (Sage, 1996).

3   Problems of Communicating in an Age of Increasing Technology

Sending information in the way we might do face-to-face does not work for communications via technology, which have vastly increased during the pandemic. Our greater use of machine devices to communicate requires a different transmission style to ensure effectiveness. Information should be delivered in small chunks with more time to process outputs. On-line performances must be modified to be effective, as they rely on auditory and visual material, excluding haptic[1] (touch, feeling, position in space/context) and non-verbal dimensions necessary for those learning best from real experience (Sage & Matteucci, 2022). This is vital for people with subtle communication issues, like being exposed to communication that is different from their mother-tongue, so finding nuanced information confusing. Fisher & Adams (1994) reported studies showing that 75% of people struggle with listening, understanding and recall of information. More diversity in 21st Century societies make this a greater issue today. It is estimated that we need 15% of brain capacity to process language which leaves 85% free to day-dream. We only attend to 20% of what we hear, with 20% of time preoccupied with erotic thoughts (Goldhaber, 1970). Who is admitting to these?

    Thus, the pandemic highlighted communication difficulties from reduced sensory input. It is important to analyse issues - like ability to *introspectively*

TABLE 6   A comparison of teaching time for spoken and written development

Steil 1991	Listening	Speaking	Reading	Writing
Percentage of life use	60%	20%	12%	8%
Learnt	First	Second	Third	Fourth
Used	Most	Next to most	Next to least	Least
Taught	Least	Nest to least	Nest to most	Most

analyse – (literature terms - inner talk/speech, self-talk, sub-vocal speech, mental verbalisation, internal dialogue/monologue or self-statement). Alongside *inner-talk* is *external language dialogues and monologues* (telling/re-telling, giving instructions, reporting, making an argument, etc.). The importance of *inner-talk* is rarely recognised, but Vygotsky (1934/1986) suggested it depends on sequential language - vital for processing, production, predictive thinking and action. If people have problems with *inner-talk*, they need an approach accounting for *time* and *content* factors (topic route with staged summaries) as well as psychological factors that are barriers to attention (Sage, 2000, 2020). Articulating each step while doing it - repeating, recalling and stating the whole sequence is necessary to build mental verbalisation and understanding. This is rarely recognised in practice.

Hurlbert (2011) has made *inner-talk* a focus for study and found only an average 20% frequency of use. *External talk* is necessary for developing internal self-statements. Is low *inner-talk* frequency a result of technology as the preferred way of communicating? In countries, like Italy, Japan and Cuba, *talk* is the technology of learning and you do not find silent classrooms, as students constantly verbalise to develop higher thinking and speaking levels. Group work is more common than individual, so participants constantly exchange ideas, reflect, review and refine performances. With students 4 years above UK counterparts in the Dialogue, Innovation, Achievement & Learning Studies (DIAL, Sage, Rogers, & Cwenar, 2002–2010), one takes their approach seriously, as communication and relationships take precedence over subject learning. In Italy, the Roman tradition of Oratory and Rhetoric Schools is still seen today, with oral examinations important for judging performance, so reflecting speaking and listening use in normal life, seen in Table 6.

One can easily see that primary language competencies get less attention than secondary ones in education which have life consequences. Experts suggest this analysis has not changed in the last 30 years (Sage, 2020).

4   Organising Strategies for Information

In discovering what the figure represents we engage in our preferred goodness-of-fit analysis. Some people attempt to find an outline for achieving the big picture, searching for an overall form as a guide to insert detail. This is called the *"top-down"* process - wanting to find the general pattern (gestalt) before moving to component parts. This outline might suggest face, eyes and other body parts not shown. This is analogous to *deductive thinking* when a hypotheses infers specific outcomes on the basis of a general principle. However, other people favour starting with *details* in order to achieve the big picture. This is *"bottom-up"*, data driven processing (Miller, 1984). These learners like details to fall into place before deciding a good fit at the more general level. Thus, they might find an ear as a part, leading to a search on a more general level for the rest of the *head of a horse*. Bottom-up processing corresponds to *inductive* reasoning and involves accumulating examples until a goodness-of-fit analysis draws a general conclusion from detail.

Although, having a preferred style we need to use both for many tasks. Take reading - we must get the gist of the content and focus on detail for synthesizing phonemes into whole words for coping with the text. The communication issue is that we produce information in our preferred style. A top-down processor gives an overview and the structure of their presentation, with a final review of main points. A bottom-up processor moves straight into the content and uses personal stories and experiences along the way to illustrate points. The distribution of learning styles is about 50-50 amongst the population according to Miller's research.

I shall never forget a post-graduate lecture by a famous neurologist, who had moved into the arts world. He bounced into the theatre, sat on the edge of the stage and told his life-story. Afterwards, half the audience said how marvellous he was and the other half ruminated that they really did not grasp the content! The moral is that we need to acknowledge both thinking styles, by giving a concise overview and clear structure but supporting data with real stories and experience. Wallach & Miller (1988) found that students did well with teachers who had the same processing style as themselves. We all have experienced presentations that suited us and others that have been difficult to fathom. The thinking-style behind the performance may have contributed to this reaction.

5   Principles When Communicating Information

There are principles to observe when imparting information for whatever purpose:

- Smile and make audience eye contact, connecting with a brief, friendly comment before conveying important information. This phatic[1] (social) part of the exchange is vital to engage those receiving spoken/written messages. If appropriate, make this amusing as a good joke helps difficult concepts and removes fear! In our dash for facts we forget to make this vital connection.
- Be aware of the feelings and emotions of those receiving information. This is vital and influences how messages are received and interpreted.
- Deliver information in small chunks. We only have capacity to listen for about 3 minutes and need a breather to absorb material (Sage, 2000). A pause, question or comment, is an effective break-up strategy. Long, technical narratives mean listeners lose the thread and miss important points.
- Divide information with a memorable headline for each new part. After each one, ask listeners to paraphrase (What have I just said?). Pause and summarize main ideas at intervals along the way.
- Top-down processors need an overview, structure and review, but stories of real experiences help bottom-up processors to engage with content.
- Deliver content with a lively voice. 300+ students listed and ranked what helped them attend to lectures. 97% said *voice tone* was the top essential for listening. If information is delivered with passion and vocal variation, this sustains attention and interest (Sage, 2020).

6   Pandemic Issues

During the pandemic, with people on lockdown and unable to meet face-to-face, technology has been a life-line for enabling connectivity. Email, social media and video conferencing have become normal for both work and social exchanges. My family have Zoom crossword sessions once weekly to keep updated with group gossip! Communication might be verbal, written and electronic, like texts, emails, telephone calls, teleconferencing, voicemails and occasionally hand-written notes/reports. These communications have varying impacts than do face-to-face meetings and are permanent, recorded and easily searchable.

I know a student teacher who put on face-book that he was having a tough time at school on a group post. A staff member heard about it and he was sacked from his placement and university course. This was a misunderstanding, as nothing negative was said about the school or blame made, but a suggestion he was personally finding teaching difficult. In a university faculty, we collected 3,000 emails in a term that had been misunderstood. As a result, a student session took place on contextualising messages for understanding, when immediate, on-going clarification is impossible. We have all sent emails as a joke, which were taken literally by the recipient. Imagine if this happens in a work situation! In today's sensitive environment, communications get continually misinterpreted with negative results.

Messages must be introduced with a phatic[1] comment. On a communication course, I had a surgeon moaning that his emails were often ignored. Viewing them, they were bald messages with no humanity conveyed. I suggested he prefaced them with a friendly comment. Meeting 6 months later, he fed back that this had made all the difference with now very few non-responses. Reviewing a message for *context* and *content*, think about tone. Is there a chance the communication seems out of touch given present economic and social conditions? Research in "Class Talk" (Sage, 2000) showed how *phatic communion* has flown out of the window now life has "speeded-up". Without this pleasantry we feel cheated and react negatively to communication. A PhD student researched the topic, finding 80% of communications lacked phatic content.

A Third Age Trust survey (2019) discovered that over-60s face a constant barrage of name-calling, insults and patronizing language, with 63% saying this happens publicly to embarrass them. Youngsters consider such language "banter" but the words are received as "insults". This shows the importance of awareness of how language and communication can exclude people. Sharing and creating ideas, refining social capacity, respecting different ages, cultures, beliefs and interests, are primary to effective communicative experiences in plural societies.

7   Implications for Underdeveloped Communication

Profound psychological implications result from underdeveloped communication. Conversely, effective communication brings a higher life quality and is basic to effective relations. Communicating well enables people to know and ask for needs, resulting in self-efficacy and lower instances of bullying, self-destructive and depressive behaviours (Matteucci, 2022). Those suffering hearing impairment reveal depression and loneliness, because of communication difficulties. These are now common, resulting from stress producing high cortisol levels that interfere with hearing development (Sage, 2020; McGregor, 2022). Communication deficits hinder human need to engage – resulting in social and emotional problems. We are hard-wired to connect with fellow humans (Ryan & Deci, 2000).

If a child cannot communicate needs, a tantrum is likely. An older one shows frustration and a teenager produces a tornado! When adults cannot understand or state needs their lives can easily fall apart, as happens after strokes or brain injuries. Everyone benefits from taking communication seriously and presently we desperately need effective contact with those around us. It is a habit that must start young. Effective communication equips children with ability to have needs met. As they grow, these must increase to cope with difficult situations. In school and social contexts, peers play a vital role in how communication competencies develop relationships. It is essential to model effective talk strategies, but sadly these are not always experienced in life or on-line events, as people can confront and be rude. Communication ability is needed for survival. However, something as important as eye-contact, enabling people to connect and maintain discourse, can be difficult, especially in cultures where this is not appropriate. In the West, eye-contact makes social connection and demonstrates good manners. When communicating well, people pursue opportunities with confidence and self-efficacy. It is never too late to learn effective communication.

Technology is now deeply integrated into life and we cannot escape it (Bertling, 2020). Doctors conduct virtual appointments online and even three-year-olds handle phones, iPads and open apps. Despite technology immersion in all life spheres, there is evidence of it contributing to a decline in communicating pleasantly and well. World studies of bullying behaviour show how this has increased and exacerbated, demonstrating limited communication strategies of abusers and victims (Matteucci, 2022; Cobello & Milli, 2022) explain how robots improve communication. As this approach brings miles of smiles it is effective for diminishing bullying and enabling positive interactions.

Some adults retain social and communication competencies acquired before the rapid rise of technology. However, it has been shown that devices inhibit development of these crucial abilities, needed to learn successfully, obtain and keep jobs as well as become contributing members of society. Popularity of technology communication, in various mediums, has escalated during the pandemic, making it vital to highlight this trend. The technology rise will continue to escalate and increase its negative effects on communication and society. We need to be aware of these to mitigate bad effects.

8   Review

The pandemic has shown up the challenges of interacting responsibly. It is important to encourage people to ask questions and maintain open lines of communications with each other. Implementing best communication practices helps everyone connect more effectively, maturely and respectfully, not only during a pandemic, but also in normal times. We need to take communication processes, presentations and performances more seriously if intent on improving relationships and seeking a more peaceful world. The importance of understanding different cultures and their communicative customs is vital and Negus (2022) shows how increasing the literature range in educational contexts assists understanding of others and the world we live in. It is notable that geniuses have a strong arts and science background, as this is required to become effective 21st century citizens.

There is concern that social media negatively impacts on society and communication. A psychology study by The University of California, Los Angeles (UCLA), validates this. Scientists discovered that 6th graders having 5 days without smart phones, television, or other digital screens, did considerably better at reading human emotions than classmates spending hours on electronic devices daily (Wolpert 2014). Findings indicated fewer errors from children attending camp after 5 days were the same across genders. The groups tested, both ones attending camp and those not - reported spending an average of 4.5 hours daily watching television, playing video games and texting (Wolport, 2014). This research indicates that the less time spent participating in face-to-face communication, the more social issues that children develop. Stressing the importance of developing communication abilities helps them to respect others and behave appropriately in interactions. Rising crime, learning difficulties and mental health crises are to a large extent influenced by limited communication and the social and economic problems caused. While many people are excited about digital media benefits in education, not all are looking at risks that come with it.

Patricia Greenfield, UCLA Professor of Psychology, believes:

> Decreased sensitivity to emotional cues, losing the ability to understand the emotions of other people, is one of the costs. The displacement of in-person social interaction by screen interaction seems to be reducing social skills. (Wolpert, 2014, p. 14)

Social competence is part of the communicative process although often viewed separately to linguistic abilities in enabling interaction. David Shariatmadari (2020) suggests it is nonsense to complain that English is deteriorating under the influence of new technology, adolescent fads and loose grammar. He quotes Douglas Adams (2005, p. 2) on technology.
– Anything in life when born is normal and ordinary and the natural way the world works.

– Anything invented between when one is 15–35 is new, exciting and
  revolutionary.
– Anything invented after you are 35 is against the natural order of things.

Although there is truth in this, Shariamdari's discussion revolves around the
structure of language not its social *use*. Undoubtedly, this has transformed.
The Queen recalls changes over her long reign. At the beginning, when exit-
ing her car on a visit, the crowd would clap, cheer – shouting pleasantries and
words of welcome. Now, when this happens, there is complete silence, because
everyone is using phones to record the occasion. This is understandable but
demonstrates behaviour variations. Older people interpret this as rudeness
and discourtesy – ignoring the Queen and failing to ask if a picture/video is in
order. Change is natural and brings benefits, but we must be aware of what is
lost in the process. At school, I was told every positive has a negative and the
latter must be dealt with appropriately. Communication is our most important
human development, but in some respects changes have brought terror and
error, which must be examined and eliminated. A recent YouGov Poll (September 2021)[2] demonstrates the problems of intergenerational and cultural
language and thinking differences which they fear will grow and grow because
of the lack of interest in the real issues that divide us.

Notes

1 Phatics denotes speech used to express or create an atmosphere of shared feelings, goodwill,
   or sociability rather than to impart specific information.
2 https://www.yougov.co.uk

References

Adams, D. (2005). *The Salmon doubt*. Del Rey Books.
Back, A., Tulsky, J., & Arnold, R. (2020, April 2) Communication skills in the age of
   COVID-19. https://doi.org/10.7326/M20-1376
Bertling, J. (2020). Global crises models. OECD *Education Working Paper 232*. OECD.
Cobello, S., & Milli, E. (2022). The social impact of educational robotics. In R. Sage & R.
   Mattueccci (Eds.), *How world events are changing education*. Brill.
Fisher, B., & Adams, K. (1994). *Interpersonal communication: Programatics of human
   relationships* (2nd ed.). Random House.
Frey, C., & Osborne, A. (2013). *The future of employment*. Oxfordmartin.ox.ac.e

Gawande, A. (2011). *The checklist: How to get things right.* Profile Books Ltd.

Goldlhaber, G. (1970). Listener comprehension of compressed speech as a function of the academic grade level of subjects. *Journal of Communication, 20,* 167–173.

Hurlburt, R., Heavey, C., & Kelsey, J. (2013). Towards a phenomenology of inner speech. *Consciousness & Cognition, 22,* 1477–1494.

Luckin, R. (2020). *I, teacher: AI and school transformation. Spotlight.* Newstateman.

Matteucci, R. (2022). Theories and management of bullying behaviour. In R. Sage & R. Mattueccci (Eds.), *How world events are changing education.* Brill.

McGregor, G. (2022). Additional learning needs: Hearing development. In R. Sage & R. Mattueccci (Eds.), *How world events are changing education.* Brill.

Merrill, S. (2020). *In schools, are we measuring what matters.* Edutopia.org/article/teaching-communication-skills

Miller, L. (1984). Problem solving, hypothesis testing and language disorders. In G. Wallach & K. Butler (Eds.), *Language learning disabilities in school-age children.* Williams & Wilkins.

Nørgaard, B., Ammentorp, J., Ohm Kyvik, K., & Kofoed, P.-E. (2012). Communication skills training increases self-efficacy of health care professionals. *Journal of Continuing Education in the Health Professions, 32*(2), 90–97.

Negus, E. (2022). Conversational intelligence: Learning for others. In R. Sage & R. Mattueccci (Eds.), *How world events are changing education.* Brill.

OECD Report. (2018). Educating 21st century children and young people: Well-being in the digital age. www.oecd.org>els>heathsystems>children-and-young-people

Ryan, R., & Deci, E. (2002). Intrinsic and extrinsic motivations: Classic definitions and new directions. *Contemporary Educational Psychology, 25,* 54–67. https://doi.org/10.1006/ceps.1999.1020

Sackstem, S. (2015). *Hacking assessment.* Times 10 Publishing.

Sage, R. (1996). *An investigation of misdiagnosis of human problems.* RCSSD 47 P.

Sage, R. (2000). *Class talk: Successful learning through effective communication.* Bloomsbury.

Sage, R. (2020). *Speechless. Issues for education.* Buckingham University Press.

Sage, R., & Mattueccci, R. (2022). *How world events are changing education.* Brill.

Sage, R., Rogers, J., & Cwenar, S. (2002–2010). *Dialogue, innovation, achievement & learning studies, 1, 2, 3. Preparing the 21st century citizen.* University of Leicester & The National Corporation of Universities. University of Leicester.

Schleicher, A. (2020). Preparing the next generation for their future. *New Statesman.*

Shariamdari, D. (2020). *Don't believe a word: The surprising truth about language.* W&N.

Statistics-NHS England. (2020). *Statistics NHS England.* www.england.nhs.uk

Steil, A. (1991). Overlooked dimensions in language acquisition (C. Feyten). *The Modern Language Journal, 75*(2), 173–180.

Third Age Trust. (2019). *Survey of views regarding language use.* https://www.u3a.org.uk

Wallace-Stephens, F., & Morgante, E. (2020). *Who is at risk: Work & automation in the time of COVID-19.* RSA. www.thersa.org

Wallach, G., & Miller, L. (1988). *Language intervention & academic success.* College-Hill Publication.

Wolpert, S. (2015). In our digital world, are young people losing the ability to read emotions? *UCLA Newsroom.* UCLA. 21 Aug. 2014. Web. 17 Nov. 2015.

Vygotsky, L (1986). *Thought and language.* MIT. (Original work published 1934)

PART 4

Predictions for the Future

∵

Introduction to Part 4

Rosemary Sage and Riccarda Matteucci

There is discussion that the focus on academic development and assessment directs people in a specialist direction. However, the new world of technology with its rapid changes requires a more generalist approach so that persons can be flexible and creative. The specialist mode leads to narrow views that can lead to the loss of other views. The generalist has a broader more balanced view and copes with misinformation and malign influences more effectively and is likely to work with machines in a sensible way. This has to be considered for the future along with how we going to evolve with machines and the support now required to cope with the rapid changes in life.

Chapter 10 – Predicting Generalist Not Specialist Routes for Education and Technology

The generation heading into further/higher education and workplaces today is one of the first to have grown up entirely online. The chapter presents concerns about free speech in the context of educational policy, which encourages a narrow specialist rather than a broad generalist direction in goals for learning. Online platforms support particular viewpoints at the expense of other ideas, to produce a society that dismisses a balanced approach to their evaluation, so hindering critical and creative thinking processes.

Chapter 11 – Predicting How Humans and Machines Will Evolve?

Throughout the intelligent machine system cycle – from design, development, dissecting and distribution, we must ensure safe use now technology devices are acting as teachers, coaches and companions. With unprecedented roles in life aspects, questions arise about personal agency, autonomy, privacy, identity, authenticity and responsibility – who are we and what do we want to be? Technology is rapidly changing lives and we must be abreast of this process.

Chapter 12 – Predictive Protocols for Teachers and Students Support

Without time for proper preparation, educators adapted to a new way of teaching because of the COVID-19 pandemic (2020 onwards). Educators are still stressed as they have to constantly manage the anxiety associated with threats to health, wellbeing, and livelihood. The chapter gives ideas for support.

© ROSEMARY SAGE AND RICCARDA MATTEUCCI, 2024 | DOI:10.1163/9789004688612_015

Reflection

Our future life will be more and more involved with machine systems and we have to make sure they are our servants and not our masters. An intelligent approach is required and education must radically change to focus more on how to manage this complex technology, so that the negatives do not overcome the positive uses it can contribute to our lives.

CHAPTER 10

Predicting Generalist Not Specialist Routes for Education and Technology

Rosemary Sage

Abstract

Learning assessments for national and international comparisons incur a specialist, academic approach to restrict thinking and learning. Increased reliance on technology in the pandemic now means many learning assignments and assessments happen on-line and are marked by machines, which encourage tick-box responses and less opportunity to think and express creatively. Moreover, a lack of appropriate regulation of web content means tech giants control information, which is often biased or unsuitable for student engagement to influence learning in dangerous ways. The chapter discusses these issues and predicts that only a more generalist approach, that widens knowledge, competencies and opportunities, will provide a safer, more accurate information source for all teachers, learners and their carers.

• • •

> He refused to specialise in anything, preferring to keep an eye on
> the overall estate rather than any of its parts.
>
> LEO TOLSTOY, *War and Peace*

•
• •
•

1 A General Background

The generation heading into further/higher education and workplaces today is one of the first to have grown up entirely on-line. They are constantly faced with misinformation and malign influences to narrow thinking. Protecting people on-line and supporting respectful free speech is a major issue defining this era of politics, but the Online Safety Bill being now in the British Parliament has potentially negative results. The plan is to force platforms like Meta, YouTube,

Twitter and Instagram to remove content deemed harmful but not illegal, such as that encouraging suicide, promoting eating disorders or exposing pornography. Worthy aims, but the Bill gives unelected Silicon Valley Tech giants power to decide what crosses the line between safe and harmful. The implications for free speech are devastating. Do we want Big Tech zealots thousands of miles away, with fashionable opinions, deciding whether those questioning COVID-19 policy are raising concerns or peddling disinformation, or if others writing about race or transgender issues have crossed the line into hate speech? Matters of nuances cannot be outsourced. They will make Big Tech the global arbiter of truth and free speech. It will result in a censor's charter. Parliament should decide such on-line matters, with democratic debate and challenges. Free thinking and speech, in the context of education and technology policy and practice, are discouraged by a narrow *specialist* rather than a broad *generalist* direction to learning. On-line platforms support particular viewpoints at the expense of other ideas, to produce a society that dismisses balanced approaches, so hindering critical and creative thinking processes.

2 The Generalist-Specialist Debate in the Pandemic

Does anyone remember Michael Gove, when as UK Secretary of State for Justice and Lord Chancellor he declared: "The people of this country have had enough of experts" (2016)? He was seen as encouraging an anti-intellectualism to trash expert knowledge for underpinning policy and practice. Academics expressed horror that evidence-driven decisions were demoted. However, expert failures during the pandemic have been evident, whether in epidemiological modelling or macroeconomics. Professor Tyler Cowen, the American economist, says that those who reasoned best across multiple domains and made the right calls during the pandemic were often generalists, with significant experience talking to both political decision-makers and the general public.

The World Health Organisation amplified false Chinese statements about COVID-19 initially and pulled back on declaring it an international emergency. Virus experts clung to flu plans and ignored successes in Asia, ruling out test and trace containment. Epidemiologists were stubborn with modelling, ignoring the role of behavioural change. They assumed catastrophic health outcomes with freedom day dubbed as criminal.

Instead, it has been generalists who examined the data and trade-offs better. Caprice Bourret, an American businesswoman living in London, where she runs "By Caprice", surmised that East Asia was dealing more effectively with the outbreak than Europe because of their broader approaches. She endured expert disdain for advocating the South Korean line of attack, which took a strong line regarding contact tracing early in the outbreak. First, they scaled up their contact tracer network. Second, they gave workers access to data beyond what they might learn from a typical patient interview. Also, the Canadian economist, Alex Tabarrok, supported liberalisation, following testing, vaccine and therapeutic approval, to alleviate pandemic costs more efficiently than lockdowns.

Such examples of specialist failure or generalist wisdom do not deny a need for expertise, as the vaccine roll-out was Britain's biggest success due to their acquired knowledge. The issue is the serious pitfalls in giving specialists quasi-monopoly status over policy and practice. A culture of open scepticism from non-experts can improve knowledge and its implementation. Generalists think more holistically than specialists. Science advisors in the pandemic often represented one discipline, when integrated insights from many professional areas were needed, to carefully consider trade-offs and uncertainty, since the pandemic affected all life aspects. Generalists do not face the same reputational error costs like specialists, so can look at data more dispassionately.

Professor Mark Woodhouse in: *The year the world went mad: A scientific memoir* (2022), does not excuse himself as part of the decision-making system, even though he frequently railed against it. He says that Britain demonstrated a system failure by not welcoming other ideas, not being sufficiently self-critical, so indulging in groupthink, which technology platforms encouraged. The interaction of scientific advisors, officials and government was at fault.

It is easy for elite groups to stifle viewpoints other than their own and insist on conformity. The problem is our pigeon-hole mentality. We are constrained by previous experiences and present influential contacts. Technology influences and an education system that drives specialisation is not preparing society for the future. A generalist policy is predicted as the way forward.

3   Education Bureaucrats Show No Value for Independent Thinking

Higher education today is leading the closure of free debate. Technology, using social platforms, promotes group think and often supports a narrow view of situations. Curious intellectualism is something to aspire to, scrutinising ideas to help make analysis more holistic, but the culture wars, common in educational circles, clamp down on interpretations not following the chosen line. "Show a people one thing, as only one thing, over and over again and that is what they become", said the celebrated author, Chimamanda Ngozi Adichie, on the particular dangers of providing a single explanation of anything.[1]

This is particularly important for education. Most of us have been through this system at a formative period of life, so tend to think we are experts, with entrenched, narrow views of where education should be going, based on our own particular understanding.

Ability to articulate personal experience is a central part of the on-line application process to British universities and summarises 13 years in school. It is designed to show what applicants are capable of thinking and expressing on matters beyond the curriculum and explain why they wish to pursue the course they are applying for. However, the UK Universities Minister says this favours the most advantaged students and damages social mobility, so the application must be simplified with prompted questions and boxes to tick, which technology encourages for machine marking and monitoring. This means less for the applicant to think about and less opportunity to express themselves, with more room for universities to decide the agenda. Are we saying that after 13 years in school a student from any background or institution is not equipped to express and validate their views?

This is the same philosophy that offers lower grades to students from disadvantaged backgrounds and produces marking policies that do not penalise incorrect language structures and spelling. There is a university assignment circulating that has received a pass, with a 79 word sentence and numerous spelling, grammar and syntax mistakes. This ignores the fact word presentation is vital to understanding of what is said or read. It is patronising. In aiming to offset disadvantage, education is in danger of ensuring the abilities to articulate fluently, evaluate ideas and think creatively count for nothing. From my own experience as an admissions officer at London University, I can confirm that applicants, without an elite background, showed the wisdom of broader and often rawer life experiences to equip them as valuable members of the learning community. An extensive understanding of reality, with ability to communicate this critically is what the world's workforce desperately needs today. Employers suggest that personal and practical competencies are not developed to standards required for smarter job roles now that intelligent machines take care of routines (Sage, 2022). It is only a generalist policy that specifically encourages these attributes.

There is a continual clash between *traditionalists* who favour transmissive instruction styles, with teachers firmly in control and *progressives* advocating more student influence over learning to develop creativity, independence and initiative. Today's world craves creativity to solve serious world problems. Is the education system stifling this? The *generalist-specialist* debate is pertinent here to consider the future direction of education as technology has a crucial role here in ensuring that broad knowledge and views are available and that students are not exposed to dangerous experiences on-line.

4 Generalists vs. Specialists

Successful organisations value and use both generalists and specialists to carry out activities in a balanced way. This is witnessed in the Education for Robotics programme, which is implemented in Italian schools and colleges. It is run by teams of engineers, psychologists, therapists and teachers, to integrate the range of knowledge and competencies needed to teach and learn for the new technology world. What are the differences between specialists and generalists?

4.1 *Knowledge Level*
Specialists have a deep understanding of a specific content area, while generalists have a broader scope of both knowledge and competencies across disciplines and can "join up the dots". Someone specialising in one subject may focus energy on learning and staying updated in just their own discipline. Generalists acquire various competencies to apply across different fields. For example, they may learn management abilities, marketing, business development, etc., whereas a data analyst specialises in technology, hardware and systems to make statistical judgements.

4.2 *Organisation*
Schools and colleges take on more generalist teachers with a range of abilities at primary level but hire in specialists, like psychologists and therapists, to support ongoing work. However, at senior level there are more subject specialists, who are less likely than higher education academics to engage in research and be completely up-to-date in their topic areas. In some countries, like Japan, university staff have research and development roles in schools and so the knowledge base of teachers and students is continually up-dated through this link. It is not practical for everyone in a small institution to acquire the range of high-level competencies, if not necessary, but for smooth running experts must be available when needed.

4.3 *Progressiveness*
Today, there are rapid changes in education policy and practice and specialists are important to create and introduce ideas for implementing new requirements successfully. As they tend to update frequently to remain credible, specialists can be more progressive than generalists and often work better with

changes of pace. In contrast, using multiple competencies daily, the generalists benefit from stable, predictable work patterns. In the UK, particularly in Education circles, there is often suspicion of specialist academics, encouraged by government ministers who usually have no ground-level experience in their management areas. Therefore, results of research are not readily accepted and implemented, as in some other countries.

4.4   Transferable Competencies

Generalists have an array of knowledge and personal-practical competencies, so this is more transferable in workplaces. Verbal and written communication and other personal abilities, like initiative and reliability, are required at a high level nowadays and much in demand. Specialists may learn specific techniques, such as for design technology programmes in schools and colleges, which may not transfer to another field like teaching a foreign language.

5   Pros and Cons of a Generalist

Generalist roles are rewarding and challenging:

Pros are as follows:
- Connections: are achieved from wide knowledge helping individuals to see links between subjects and departments and find solutions of benefit to everyone.
- Flexibility: from a wide understanding and possession of many abilities can bring more opportunities and avoid a narrow approach. Communication and problem-solving are the premier demands today and generalists are often in a better position because they make extensive connections with others.
- Adaptability: is easier when having a wide range of competencies, enabling one to jump between tasks more easily. As work roles are changing rapidly, this is a major requirement.

Cons are as follows:
- Credibility: is harder to establish if not expert in an area. However, ability to market oneself and show others the benefits of a wide knowledge and ability base counteracts this.
- Security: is less as generalist competencies are not so unique and more easily be replaced.
- Burnout: is more common with generalists because their range of abilities means they are constantly in demand and called out, so in busy times are the first to become exhausted.

6   Pros and Cons of the Specialist

Specialist roles are exacting and enabling

Pros are as follows:
- Salaries: are higher because of education backgrounds and qualifications.
- Less competition: in specialist areas means fewer contenders.
- Knowledge: focus on a narrow area of study/practice allows understanding at a deep level to quickly grasp developments. Knowledge is power.

Cons are as follows:
- Outdated: specialising in one area may mean it might be replaced by other means, as often happens in technology fields with their rapid changes, which soon outdate devices.
- Inflexible: it is often difficult to operate outside a narrow field because of a lack of a range of abilities.

7   Roles of Generalists and Specialists

Many leaders are generalists, because they perform numerous tasks at the same time. Leadership specialists may steer projects with specific processes or technological advances in mind. Specialists have a deep understanding of a certain content area while generalists have a broader background. Generalists have a more diverse knowledge base to draw from, so they see connections and correlations that specialists might miss. They tend to have a higher emotional link with others, because being a generalist means interacting with different people in varying situations. They are the conductors that lead the orchestra, with high capacity to collaborate effectively and facilitate team collaborations. Generalists also tend to have a greater situational awareness to grasp the overall view. Whereas specialists have cognisance of their own area, they may not fully understand things outside their fields. They need a generalist big-picture thinker, to bring it together. Generalists know enough about many things to have intelligent conversations with all kinds of experts, facilitating deeper dialogue for effective solutions. They can challenge assumptions, or at least pose the right questions to better frame the problem and solution.

Forbes, the American business network, states that both generalists and specialists have roles to play within any organisation, depending on context. Organisations enjoy generalists until a specific need for in-depth knowledge is required. However, educational qualifications are losing their shine, as they do not reliably indicate performance or potential, according to employer reports

(Sage, 2022). Practical experience, applying knowledge, is a proven predictor of future performance and is being produced in personal portfolios of evidence instead of unreliable grade point averages in many American schools and colleges, as being more useful to employers (Sage, 2022). In today's world, it is critical that all employees have the transferable abilities that generalists possess and can predict outcomes of uncertain issues.

Gray line helps organisations manage change in a generalist-specialist blog and believes that COVID-19 has driven appointment decisions based upon good moral character, work ethic and talent above expertise.[2] As the world evolves rapidly, the need for personal competencies is more valuable than ever. Roberta Sydney, in her blog piece "Specialist, Generalists and Private Company Board Composition", says generalists bring more value to the organisation, because they are great communicators, have broad capabilities and wider experiences to share with others for enlightenment.

David Epstein, in *Why Generalists Triumph in a Specialized World* (2019) says the strength of generalists is their ability to think outside the box. They are dabblers, explorers and learners, with broad knowledge across many topics and expertise in a few. He believes by attaining breadth in different forms, you are more likely to thrive and survive. A varied background and personal, practical abilities are needed to open up a world of opportunities and must be encouraged in education.

8   Comment

Is it better to be a generalist or specialist? Currently, it would seem a generalist, but with specialist knowledge in key areas. Over time, one understands what areas fire passions and increase abilities, to produce an expert. Knowledge changes so keeping this updated is vital. The famous physicist and mathematician, Freeman Dyson (2015), said we need both frogs and birds. The frogs are down in the mud looking at the gritty details of everything. The birds are up above and do not see minutiae, but can perceive multiple frogs and integrate their work. Our education problem is that we teach everybody to be frogs and are not instructing them in how to be birds. This makes us inflexible, with all our information coming out of context. We need both, but only encourage everybody to be one, with wayward effects. When Freeman Dyson (emeritus professor in the School of. Natural Sciences, Institute for Advanced Study, Princeton) was reporting at ProPublica (online news source) he saw the perversity of medical and educational specialisation. This was well-intended, but had unwanted effects because nobody was integrating information and looking at it in the real context. Research on medical diagnoses, at the Royal Central School, London (Sage, 1996) found that patient misdiagnosis was due to doctors not taking a holistic perspective for information-gathering and failing to communicate effectively with patients.

> It doesn't matter where you are, you are nowhere compared to where you can go. (Bob Proctor)

9 Developing Interconnections

A generalist, with knowledge of many issues, can see the interconnectedness of things and find solutions that a specialist may miss. The world should not be viewed through a single lens. A broader approach and wider understanding of different things makes better decisions. A generalist can visualise the whole, as they tend to possess more transferable abilities, which are life-enhancing. They are essential for all workforces, as such core competencies are vital in all situations.

It is not surprising that generalists tend to be leaders within organisations. If you know how to manage employees, you can do this in different contexts. Attributes of project management, effective communication and good people connection (phatics) are required whether leading teachers or IT staff.

Consider studying English as a generalist. You could easily work in the media, become a teacher, translator, librarian or lawyer, do research and write books, etc. because you are broadly acquainted with the subject. However, if you want to become a Professor of English, you will be unlikely to have sufficient knowledge and will need to specialise in applied psycholinguistics.

Finally, generalists may benefit from the fact they are better at navigating through uncertainty. They are more skilled at predicting the outcome of issues, even outside their expertise. In a world, where the future is uncertain, unpredictable and unknown, generalists could have an advantage!

10 Disadvantages of a Generalist

Becoming a generalist has downsides. The common criticism is that they sacrifice depth for breadth. Increased complexity makes it harder for them to have deep understanding of things, as by knowing a broad area superficially, vital information can be overlooked. An example often used to explain this is that of an iceberg. A generalist sees the iceberg and analyses its importance for a ship's course. The same generalist, without a deeper iceberg knowledge, could miss vital information on what is happening below the surface to cause havoc on the ship's journey!

As a specialist, there is opportunity to become a thought leader in the area of expertise. If passionate about the subject and willing to learn, you can become a recognised pioneer. The ability to become a thought leader opens up different avenues. Most people seek specialists, rather than generalists, when encountering a problem! However, a specialist opinion on other issues might not be valid. Opinion and input are appreciated if the topic concerned involves the area of expertise directly.

However, specialising can hinder success in what is referred to as "wicked environments" (Hogarth et al., 2015), where there is less repetition and far more randomness and intrigues. Unfortunately, the latter are more prevalent in the complex, changing world in which we live. That means becoming a generalist, who can embrace diverse experiences and perspectives, may be more necessary than ever.

11   Why Is a Generalist Approach Necessary in Education?

Specialising at a young age can push students ahead of the curve temporarily. However, replacing intensive exam-focused education and training with an approach facilitating curiosity, creativity and experimentation often leads to permanent growth instead of short-lived success. Learners become better at applying their knowledge to a situation they have not seen before, which is the core of creativity. Although a generalist approach may benefit in the classroom, how can it be applied in the broader world? It is by attaining breadth in different forms, through personal and practical opportunities, that you are more likely to both thrive and survive. The UK's focus on developing knowledge for more examinations than any other country means that the generalist style takes a back seat in development. The answer is a mix of both generalist and specialist ones. It is better to find a hybrid of abilities and be flexible and keen to be able to attempt anything when the situation demands it.

Roles are termed as Generalising Specialists – skilled in one but willing to learn other capabilities, and Specialising Generalists – knowledgeable in many abilities but willing to increase that base to gain proficiency. These must be the aim for teachers and learners, as pedagogy is a multi-discipline field, requiring knowledge of development and how it fails or breaks down, from medicine, psychology, psycholinguistics, sociology and the history of instruction. The information required by students encompasses a wide range of art and science subjects.

It is helpful to have knowledge and practical experience in various fields and with a range of issues. In one case, you will lean on interpersonal competencies. In another, you have a novel idea. In yet another, you efficiently manage a complex project and cross-functional team. You are flexible and willing to use a variety of tools and gain the right knowledge and competencies to get work done. Teachers and students both need this pattern of experience and grit to develop and improve.

> "Mental meandering and personal experimentation are sources of power" and "head starts are overrated!" (Epstein, 2019)

11.1   Generalising Specialist

A generalising specialist has a core competency from excellent understanding. At the same time, they are always learning and have a working knowledge of other areas. While a generalist has roughly the same knowledge of multiple areas, a generalising specialist has one deep area of expertise and some shallow ones. We have the option of developing a core competency while building an interdisciplinary knowledge base.

11.2   Specialising Generalist

Many specialists excel in their area to become valuable assets. On the other hand, specialities may become obsolete, as technology moves forward. Design methods, programming languages, and development platforms become archaic over time. Furthermore, creative people often have trouble specialising in a specific area. They are curious by nature and love learning about and playing with different concepts and technologies. For some people, specialisation ends up being a blessing and for others a curse.

Generalists have a more diverse collection of knowledge to draw from, so they can see connections and correlations that specialists might miss. They tend to have a higher emotional association with others, too, because becoming a generalist means interacting with many kinds of people in varying situations.

12   The Sampling Period

David Epstein (2019) looks at strengths of generalists versus specialists. The focus is on personal and practical application of knowledge and developing a broad interest range. Experimenting and changing course occasionally helps to find true passion and the success that comes with enjoying what you do. This has recruitment implications – defining abilities for each position. Epstein was interviewed on the Knowledge@Wharton radio programme on SiriusXM, to explain why intense focus on one thing is not always the best approach (podcast on line). He talks about the 'sampling period' for gaining a broad range of personal and practical competencies to scaffold later learning. In this period, people become aware of their abilities and interests to drive determination and delay specialising until wide experience has been gained. Those specialising early plateau at lower levels.

The psychologist, Robin Hogarth (2015) discusses 'learning environments', where all information is available, people turn-take and the next steps are clear, based on pattern repetition. In these learning environments, feedback is immediate and accurate, so specialisation can develop well. The issue is the more expertise is based on either pattern recognition or repetition, the more likely it is to become automated. The message is keep learning varied to be able to apply abilities flexibly. Success is more associated with having a variety of life experiences.

Hogarth calls these "more wicked learning environments", where patterns do not repeat and you have to act speedily to solve new problems. Psychologists define this as transfer. Whether you are a student studying languages, or a scientist working on a unique problem, you need to transfer knowledge from broad-based learning. The classic research finding is: breadth of learning predicts breadth of transfer. The more varied the preparation, the easiest it is to apply skills flexibly in situations not previously encountered. Hogarth looked at different countries, like England and Scotland, with comparable education systems, except for specialisation times. In England, students by age 15 must decide what to study, because they are assessed in national examinations for specific college programmes. In Scotland, this does not happen in the same way. Students experiment at this age level and can take other courses beyond this, so they experience an effective sampling period. The question is who wins this trade-off?

Early specialisers have an income lead, but make worse personal choices. They tend to pick things known about when age 15. Later specialisers catch up and surpass them in six years. Thus, the early specialisers start quitting their careers in higher numbers, because they failed to optimise "match quality", the term used for the degree of fit between an individual's ability and interest in their work. Late specialisers then fly by. This fits the work culture, which wants employees with diverse experiences.

13   Research Studies

Studies suffer from survivor bias, because companies that do well are the ones investigated. Take research in the commercial value of comic books (Taylor

& Greve, 2009). Could individuals or teams produce more valuable ones on average and be more likely to make a breakthrough? The hypothesis was that it would be publisher resources or the creator's number of years and repetitions in the field. These turned out to be false. The most important factor was the number of different genres that the creator had worked across, from fantasy, crime and nonfiction. An initial finding was that companies did not favour the individual who had worked in just two genres. It was best to replace them with a three specialist team, who had only worked in one genre each. However, after four genres, the individual can no longer be recreated by the specialist team. The individual, with broad experience was clearly the best choice innovator. The paper was called "Superman or the Fantastic Four?" (Taylor & Greve, 2009), because if you can find a Superman with all genres, employ them. If not, assemble a diverse team.

There were similar findings in 1990s patent research, with the knowledge economy explosion, The biggest impacts were not from people who had drilled down into the same technologies as the patent office, but from those who had worked across a large number of tech domains and able to merge them. Prior to 1990, the bigger contributions were from specialists, which changed as the knowledge economy exploded. The question following this research is what this means for society, in a digital age with multiple data bombarding us? We continually make predictions but is this wise?

A study of 10,000 researchers' careers found that someone's most impactful paper is as likely to be their first as their last as their 10th (Neild, 2016). Attempts to predict can cause what is called 'a dangerous purifying selection', where you are in a feedback loop selecting the same kind of material. Artificial intelligence uses big data with repeating patterns. However, innovation by definition, means patterns do not repeat.

Professor Abbie Griffin et al. (2012) studied serial innovators, detailing traits and experiences of creative people. She concluded that jobs are defined narrowly to select the square peg for the square hole and thus select out people zig-zagging throughout careers. Zig-Zaggers flit among ideas and talk to people outside their domain, using analogies. Narrowing selection is potentially dangerous if looking for people to be creative, flexible and produce new knowledge. Success does not come from a four-week orientation course.

Finding the right goal and match quality is important, so learners should be changing interests and experimenting to maximise this. Encouraging students to stick with something, in order to develop determination is not the best advice for long term personal success, although in the short term it helps to pass examinations. Should sampling occur more in educational experience. When working in Finland, I did research amongst students approaching higher level studies. They spent a foundation year sampling different subject areas to discover what they wanted to pursue for degrees. This programme also included a course in cross-cultural communication, which they all felt was essential for today's plural societies. This sampling idea is seen to an extent in foundation year programmes at Scottish universities and the English Open University.

14   Problems Arising from a Lack of Sampling Opportunity

Retention is a big problem in teaching with around half of newly qualified teachers giving up within 3–5 years following qualification. Two personable young men in my street have just stopped teaching after 18 months. They felt they had not been properly prepared for the wide diversity in classrooms and the disruption this can cause. They lacked knowledge in the disciplines that underpin pedagogy, such as the psychology of learning. The fact that their training had little exploration of intercultural communication and how cognition varies across languages was they felt a large remiss in training. This might suggest a lack of sampling opportunity as the problems they had to face were not easily managed by them. Retention is a vital issue that needs addressing. A UK primary school boy had 5 teachers in less than 2 terms. They just kept leaving because of how they were treated by some students. This upset him so much he asked to change schools.

Fred Brooks, who founded the computer science department at the University of North Carolina, wrote an essay: *The Mythical Man Month* Brooks' Law says that when you have a late software project, adding more manpower to it makes it even later. The reason is because managers always underestimate the difficulty of assimilating new people into a team and the problems faced in connecting effectively with others. This mistake is frequently repeated. It would be better for team people to learn the new competencies needed instead. It is more fruitful to develop and diversify the people in post, instead of having the Fantastic Four, which becomes the Fantastic 50 as the job gets more complex.

15   Practice Not Talent

For some people, there is no such thing as talent, but 10,000 hours of practice (Gladwell, 2008). We are constantly told that "practice makes perfect". If you average times to acquire competence, you get the 11,053-hour rule, but it tells you nothing about the diversity of human acquisition. Knowing your strengths and how these fit goals is important.

Things that cause striking progress often undermine long-term development. Evidence fights against the "sunk-cost fallacy" in professional lives, like teaching, where we get information, feed-back and self- insight. We learn about ourselves, interests and strengths as we try things out, so we must have chances for zig-zagging and experimentation. What is learned in one domain is brought to another. Cultivating this diversity and not defining jobs narrowly, means the most interesting employees are nor screened out. What is the best way to boost creativity? Research is split on the best approach to take. One view is that the key to creative breakthroughs is combining or leveraging different areas of expertise. Every innovation recombines or reimagines existing things. IdeaScale data (2021) showed innovation collaborators are most likely to find new solutions to long-standing problems in the middle of the week on a Wednesday. This is an interesting fact when planning!

The best ideas emerge from combining insights from fields that seem unconnected. For example, Charles Babbage's invention of computational machines powered by punch cards, the basis of modern computers, was inspired by his knowledge of silk-weaving, which used cards with holes to create fabric patterns. Henry Ford's novel idea of the car manufacturing assembly line was inspired by meatpacking plants. Thus, creativity is encouraged by exploring new fields or introducing more *generalists*, who have a variety of experience and expertise. They can envisage from broad experience of different disciplines.

Other studies have found costs in generalising. Jacks of all trades are masters of none. *Specialists*, with deeper subject understanding, can spot and seize emerging opportunities better. Sarah Kaplan and Keyvan Vakili (2014) found that recombining ideas from one domain of specialisation, as opposed to multiple ones, led to more novel innovations in the case of nanotubes. *Specialists* may also have an easier time collaborating, because it is clear how work should be allocated. This suggests taking on *specialists,* or encouraging employees to become more expert.

Evidence supports both sides, so both are probably right in certain circumstances. In a paper in *Administrative Science Quarterly* (Teodoridis et al., 2018), generalist benefits are strongest in fields with slower pace of change. In these fields (oil & gas, mining), it might be harder for specialists to come up with original ideas and identify new opportunities, while generalists may find inspiration from other areas. In areas of rapid change, like quantum computers, generalists may struggle to stay up-dated, while *specialists* make sense of new technical developments and openings more easily.

This was tested in fields experiencing a sudden shift of pace while others remained stable (Teodoridis et al., 2018). In the 1980s, Soviet mathematicians were ahead of Western colleagues in some theoretical fields (integral equations) but not in others (commutative rings & algebras). As the Soviet Union collapsed, many scientific advances suddenly became available to Western mathematicians. This increased the pace of change in fields where the Soviet Union was ahead of the West.

Theoretical mathematics distinguishes between specialists and generalists. The Italian Fields Medal winner, Enrico Bombieri, brought together insights from differing areas of mathematics. In contrast, French Fields Medal winner, Laurent Schwartz, spent his career working on distributions.

Mathematicians experiencing rapid change (integral equations, partial differential equations & Fourier analysis) were compared with those working in less affected fields subfields of algebra and geometry (algebras & combinatorics). The performance of over 4,000 mathematicians across 1980–2000, 10 years before and after the Soviet collapse, was studied using publication and citation data from the American Mathematical Society.

Specialisation level was based on academic publications. Specialists were defined as researchers publishing in only one domain of theoretical mathematics and generalists those in several ones. Changes in creative output of *generalists* and *specialists* were measured, in faster and slower-paced fields, by the number of academic papers published. Since quality varies, these were adjusted for the number of citations later received. Results from the analyses confirm the theory.

Soviet collapse altered the pace of change differently for theoretical mathematics. In those not changing much (slower-paced fields), specialists were less productive than generalists, but this gap widened significantly after the collapse. Regression estimates a 22% decrease in specialists' citation-weighted publications per year, relative to generalists in the same slow-paced fields. (This number refers to average change in the productivity gap between the decade preceding and following Soviet collapse, after controlling for changes in publication trends over time and characteristics like age, gender and education).

In fields most affected (faster-paced fields), the opposite happened. Whereas before the collapse specialists were slightly more productive than generalists, after this the gap widened, as specialists' productivity increased and generalists' decreased. Regression estimates that specialists ended up publishing 83% more citation-weighted papers than generalists in the 10 years after collapse, relative to 10 years before.

Not only did generalists in faster-paced areas perform worse than specialists, but were also in slower-paced areas. Before collapse, generalist productivity from the two areas was similar. After this, generalists in faster-paced areas decreased productivity and published 37% fewer citation-weighted papers than those in slower-paced areas.

The study suggests that two capability types can improve creative performance. One is ability to connect ideas across subject areas. Ideas successful in one area might not be in another, but can pay off if the field is stagnant. Another is ability to build on progress in your field from emerging opportunities, which may be valuable when things progress quickly.

There is no one-size-fits-all strategy to promote creativity, but the study suggests that leaders should assess their specialists and generalists. If the pace of change is slow, teams benefit from employing generalists, who can challenge assumptions and introduce new ideas. If pace is rapid, teams profit from specialists, who are more likely to drive innovation.

16   Review

The point of examining generalist and specialist concepts is to understand more clearly the up- and down-sides of both modes, within the context of the intelligent machine world we now live in. The generalist approach engages the right, lateral thinking brain, whilst the *specialist* the left, linear side. Chapter 1 suggested that early specialisation, as in teaching reading and writing at age 4–5 years in British schools, does not follow brain development. The right brain, with a holistic function, has its major growth period from 4–7 years, with the left dealing with parts, kicking in from 7 years onwards. Slow myelination of brain neurons results from genetic inheritance. The myelin sheaths protecting neurons must be a certain thickness to make the connections that integrate sensory information. Many children, with oracy-literacy delay, have a thin corpus callosum (bridge connecting R & L brain sides), to indicate slower brain development and less hemispheric linking. Academic progress lags and they are labelled dull with loss of self-esteem. Britain has more students with special educational needs than comparable countries, possibly because they encounter early specialization. A longer sampling period to experiment and learn in line with development and interests is indicated.

The 10 top countries educationally do not begin formal learning until around 7 years, so following normal brain growth. Working with 38 countries across the world, one becomes aware of differences in philosophies, policies and practices. More generalist approaches not only bring greater long-term success for people, but demonstrate cost effectiveness in line with workplace needs.

Thus, it is important to be aware of what helps and hinders learning, with social tech platforms often influencing learning in unhelpful ways. Educational dependence on technology has increased since the pandemic. Many assessments are now on line and marked by machine. This encourages a tick-box response to further limit thinking and expression. Virtual technology is supplanting real-life scenarios to restrict non-verbal and visual experience.

However, TikTok, the Chinese smartphone video platform, is giving the West a hard lesson in values and has the world hooked. It was the most downloaded app of 2020 and 2021. David Goldman, in the National Review (2021) says that "China has a plan to assimilate most of the world's population into a virtual empire, dominated by its telecommunications, computation, manufacturing and logistics".

Every giant on-line platform is an avid collector of demographic data and does this better than governments can manage. When the world-renowned engineering research laboratories, at AEI Rugby, suddenly closed in the 1970s, many top experts went to work in the East. They have been leaders in technology innovations in this part of the world. Since John Perry Barlow launched his techno-utopian manifesto at the World Economic Forum (WEF, Davos, 1995): "A Declaration of the Independence of Cyberspace", intergenerational conflict has flourished in internet culture. Perry Barlow said: "You are terrified of your own children, since they are natives in the world where you will always be immigrants". Google ran with this and protections from normal legal liabilities were granted to internet services, like YouTube. Efforts to give more parental control were dubbed as assaults. When Brussels proposed to take away the internet copyright loophole, Big Tech encouraged young people to lobby against this proposal, with teenagers threatening suicide if controls were implemented.

This contrasts with the Chinese approach. Wang Huning (2021), the renowned political theorist, has advised China on a crackdown of Big Tech companies. On the basis technology is basic to education, he suggested the West's individualism and private domains were harmful without sensible limits. The route for youngsters should not be left to chance, as Silicon Valley platforms were strong in advocating freedom with no limit. Meta research found that 17% of teenage girls said that Instagram makes eating disorders worse. Other investigations show on-line content and limited presentations divide, confuse and depress people (Sage & Matteucci, 2022). Therefore, it is time to rethink on-line limits for more positive development. The West's superpower rival is offering moral leadership that the world is recognising as a priority. This is demonstrating a more *generalist* approach to solving the world's internet problems, both in policy and practice face-to-face and on-line.

Education takes a more specialist route, for national and international standard comparisons, leaving generalist experience to chance. Technology, because of a lack of regulation, has not helped by promoting approaches that stifle rationality. This affects long-term success and must receive urgent attention in policy and practice. In predicting future directions, adjusting our approaches will be important to survival. The chapter examines these to fully understand our present position and what is predicted to need change for coping with present needs.

Notes

1   https://www.goodreads.com/author/quotes/19992417.Chimamanda_Ngozi_Adichie
2   https://www.graylinegrp.co/blog/

References

Dyson, F. (2015). *Birds and frogs: Selected papers of Freeman Dyson.* World Scientific.

Epstein, D. (2019). *Why generalists triumph in a specialized world.* Riverhead Books.

Gladwell, M. (2008). *Outliers: The story of success.* Penguin Books.

Goldman, D. (2021). You will be assimilated: China's plan to take over the global economy. *National Review.*

Griffin, A., Price, R., & Vojak, B. (2012). *Serial innovators: How individuals create and deliver breakthrough innovations in mature firms.* Stanford Business Books.

Hogarth, R., Lejarraga, T., & Emre Soyer, E. (2015, October). The two settings of kind and wicked learning environments. *Current Directions in Psychological Science, 24*(5), 379–385. https://www.jstor.o

Huning, W. (2021). *The China media project. Old ideas from Xi's new era theories.* https://chinamediaproject.org

Ideascale Data. (2021). *Infographic: Innovation year in numbers 2021*

Kaplan, S., & Vakili, K. (2014, June). The double-edged sword of recombination in breakthrough innovation. *Strategic Management Journal, 36*(10). https://doi.org/10.1002/smj.2294

Nield, D. (2016). *Researchers have calculated when scientists are most likely to have their Eureka moment.* Northeastern University. Science Alert.

Perry Barlow, J. (1995). A declaration of the independence of cyberspace WEF, Davos. *Electronic Frontier Forum.* Eff.org/cyberspace-independence

Sage, R. (1996). Case studies of medical diagnostics. *Royal Central School for Speech & Drama.*

Sage, R., & Matteucci, R. (2022). *How world events are changing education.* Brill.

Taylor, A., & Greve, H. (2009). Superman or the fantastic four? Knowledge combination and experience in innovative teams. *Academy of Management Journal, 49.*

Teodoridis, F. (2014). *Generalists, specialists, and the direction of inventive activity.* Marshall School of Business. Working Paper.

Teodoridis, F., Bickard, M., & Vakili, K. (2018, April). *The pace of change and creative performance: Specialist – generalist mathematicians at the fall of the Soviet Union.* Marshall School of Business. Working Paper.

Teodoridis, F., Bickard, M., & Vakili, K. (2020, August). Detrimental collaborations in creative work: Evidence from economics. *Academy of Management Annual Meeting Proceedings, 1,* 17719. https://doi.org/10.5465/AMBPP.2020.17719abstract

Woodhouse, M. (2022). *The year the world went mad: A scientific memoir.* Sandstone Press.

CHAPTER 11

Predicting How Humans and Machines Will Evolve?

Rosemary Sage

Abstract

Creating a machine that outdoes human intelligence is presently beyond technology. Throughout the intelligent machine cycle – from design, development, testing and distribution – we must ensure safe use now intelligent devices are acting as teachers, coaches and companions. With unprecedented roles in many life aspects, tough questions arise about personal agency, autonomy, privacy, identity, authenticity and responsibility – who are we and what do we want to be? These questions needs an urgent answer!

1 Introduction

Are you able to remember everything learnt in your life? Is it possible? The answer is probably 'no' – it certainly is for me! That is where today's machines play a magnificent role. Unlike humans, they never forget. They remember every data input and pattern coded into their systems. Also, machines process a massive amount of information at speed. In jobs, like crime analysis and disease diagnosis, this can be done in minutes, taking people days and even weeks to bring together the relevant information for review, evaluation and decisions. Researchers now use machines to identify an unfamiliar object at the speed of light! This use of technology for many time-consuming tasks frees people up for other important activities. This has tremendous implication for how we plan learning for future new directions.

Machine memory for data bulk allows this to identify patterns and make inferences that most humans would never discover alone. Until now, machine capabilities have only gone so far, with human experience and context needed to achieve big data potential. Artificial Intelligence (AI) has used what has already been learnt. It has been unable to create new knowledge and make cognitive progress, in contrast to humans who can bring their context, life experiences and genetic heritage to solving problems.

Consider the context and containers for articles used for carrying things – called 'boxes, bags, sacks, suitcases, etc.' A machine, because it lacks real experience of life patterns, would not be able to identify all the relevant uses of this object in life situations. Containers for shopping, holiday travel, school books, camping equipment, laptop transportation etc. demand different approaches to design because of their diverse use. Human insight is needed to evolve the frame of reference and keep machines abreast of the changing context – correcting errors as they occur. Reflect again on containers. One might assume that once the machine understands the lingo and links with the appropriate word, it might consider other things connected, like handles, straps, fasteners or wheels, but this is not the case. Humans are needed to cope with such concerns, along with crisis management, as machines cannot direct operations, according to changing circumstances. This needs a flexibility that is not yet possible.

Aeroplanes provide another example. Nowadays, most modern air transport operates on autopilot, but when something unexpected happens the captain is needed to troubleshoot and solve the ongoing problems with appropriate decisions for the particular circumstances. This involves taking many issues into consideration and working out the best fit. While the machine informs and supports the decision process, like spotting a mechanical error, the human pilot has to judge and manage the situation. The machine cannot provide this without direction, as context, knowledge, experience and genetic abilities are needed, which only humans could supply.

Thus, traditional design is a master-servant relationship between humans and machines, with the former controlling what it will do, when and how – through an interface and predefined instructions. However, rapid technological advances now make it possible for machines to reach an intellectual level that enables systems to execute tasks/missions without directions, to become a self-governing operative. This indicates an interdependent relationship between humans and technology, which is rapidly increasing in this age of robotics.

2   Merging of Machine Capability and Human Consciousness

Harvard Medical School investigated why a powerful melanoma drug stopped helping patients after a few months, using a human-computer collaboration (Prabhakar, 2017). Using this model, new approaches to understanding complexities are now being pursued in other domains. Scientists, over centuries, have engaged with ideas but now the intellectual partner is a machine that builds, stores, computes and restates hundreds of equations and connections. The combination of insights from researchers and computers does not just record correlations – 'When you view this, you will see that' – but also reveals the mid-steps and cause and effect links – the how and why of interactions, instead of merely the what. This enables a leap from big data to deeper understanding, so distinction between humans and machines becomes almost imperceptible.

Another kind of human-machine collaboration is seen at the American University of Utah (Prabhakar, 2017). Doug Fleenor, lost both hands in an accident, but his arm now has had a chip implanted in it that communicates with a computer. Professor Greg Clark, a Utah scientist, asked him to reach out and touch a wooden door image on the computer screen. As Doug Fleenor guided his virtual hand across the virtual door, he literally, biologically and neurologically felt the wooden surface.

New software and fine electrical connections between another embedded chip and the nerves running up his arm to the brain meant he experienced a fused sensation of touch and texture equivalent to a tactile happening. Doug Fleenor had not touched anything in his hands for 25 years since his accident, so this was an extraordinary occurrence. Adaptive signal processing, sensitive neural interfaces, machine reasoning and complex system modelling are integrating the power of digital systems and human ability to experience insights and apply intuition. This heralds a combined evolutionary path.

Is society ready for such a prospect? Many are anxious about the impact of AI and robotics on employment and the economy (Sage & Matteucci, 2019). The Pew studies (2017, 2018, 2019) discovered that people are 'more worried than enthusiastic' about the integration of biology and technology, like brain chip implants and engineered blood, so can they work and evolve together?

3   Can Humans and Machines Exist in Harmony?

It was John Durkin's (2003) article, 'Man and Machine', that highlighted the debate on coexistence. He was talking about AI and dealt more with emotions of fear, distrust and uncertainty than the likelihood of any synchronicity or what form it might take. The film, AI: Artificial Intelligence, was used as an example, demonstrating human responses as if machines were one of them. David, the film's main character, accepts his rejection by people and experiences human emotions (emulations). This questions what rights intelligent beings should have and the ethical standards needing to be developed for AI. David is visually indistinguishable from a human child, so what qualities differentiate humans from machines? Many robots are built to look like people.

Humans define themselves from the rest of nature by language and intelligence. An ability to reason through language places them as superior in life rankings. This intelligence is often seen as synonymous with sentience (feeling, perceiving or experiencing subjectively), which is a valued attribute. Therefore, people think it is fine to chop down plants and trees, as well as kill flies and bugs, but wrong to do this to dogs or dolphins, that are viewed as having more abilities. However, people do not think it generally immoral to slaughter sentient animals required for food, as their superior human needs dominate. Presently, plants and animals are regarded as having sentience.

4   What Is Human Intelligence?

What do human brains have which machines cannot fully replicate? A brain is a composition of chemicals and biological matter, producing energy, with an unmatched ability to process information for survival. Studies have mapped brain regions that are active when we experience fear, pleasure and other feelings. These emotions were once regarded as the hidden "soul" of a person, but are now visible as electrochemical reactions through brain-imaging techniques. If it is possible to isolate the chemical components and find electronic equivalents then machines could experience such emotions. The operating limits of the human brain need to be found and copied in an electronic format to create AI. David is such a machine in the AI film. Programming feelings and emotions into AI, along with humanoid bodies, blurs the distinction between man and machine. This is already beginning to happen and is discussed by Federico Faggin in the book *The Robots Are Here: Learning to Live with Them* (2020).

Omron Automation, in Japan, has developed *Forpheus,* to show how technology works with people. It can read body language to measure opponent ability in a table tennis game and offers advice and support. The aim is to understand mood and playing talent to predict the next shot. *Forpheus* has played against human beings in Las Vegas. It is among several devices showing how robots can become more humanlike by acquiring emotional intelligence and empathy.

The Japanese firm, Honda, launched a robotics programme "Empower, Experience, Empathy", including its 3E-A18 robot, which shows compassion to humans, using various facial expressions. The French, Blue Frog Robotics, makes a companion social robot, called "Buddy", who asks for a caress and gets mad if poked in the eye! The Qihan Technology, "Sanbot" and "Pepper", produced by Softbank Robotics, are being humanised by teaching them to read and react to the emotional states of people.

In Italy, I have seen "Pepper" supporting students with foreign language practice and also witnessed similar robots able to feed people needing help because of their disabilities. These robots can interpret a smile, frown and voice tone, as well as the vocabulary and non-verbal language used, such as a head posture. Key applications for these robots are supporting education, improving sporting abilities and providing assistance for those who need it. Europole has initiated an excellent teacher course for Education Robotics and a team are using robots in activities to prevent the rise of school bullying with great success (Matteucci, 2019; Cobello & Milli, 2022). There are now robot receptionists, restaurant waiters and food deliverers, amongst many other developing roles. It seems they are here to stay! (Sage & Matteucci, 2019).

Developing emotional intelligence in robots is challenging. It is not just about technology but also psychology and trust. In Japan, these robots are acting as companions for old people, but in some ways it is disarming to see a machine consoling an upset, crying person. Professor Juan Romero, in the preface of "How World Events are Changing Education" (2022) tells the story of a Japanese man marrying a robot, with a reception for relations and friends after the ceremony. Who counts as the robot relatives and friends? Will the human-machine couple try for children one wonders? There are robot teachers, sports coaches and now wives. Whatever next? Are children on the cards?

5   Group Conflicts

History shows that when humans encounter other intelligent societies there have been conflicts. For example, the meetings of European culture with Native Americans, New Zealand Maoris and Australian Aborigines were a disaster for these groups. Though the physical form of people was similar, the values, attitudes and way of life proved very different, with the presence of each other unknown until making contact. This ended in disaster for the native groups, as the Europeans dominated and exploited them. Interaction between intelligent societies is not the same as humans creating machine intelligence, but demonstrates how humans behave. Fortunately today, the native groups have held their own and are now acknowledged in the history and cultural evolution of these nations and have attained their rightful status.

Conflicts between human groups have many causes. Religious, ideological differences, fights over land, resources and a desire to dominate, are reasons for warfare and do not seem to abate. Clashes between humans and machine intelligence are harder to forecast. If machine intelligence becomes a functioning, societal group, they need resources like humans. Land, materials and energy are necessary for both and could become a source of conflict. This depends on whether machine intelligence forms societies, seeks status and needs that equal humans. David pursues this in the AI film, but the humans did not accept him as equal to them. It is possible that human values will conflict with the emergence of human-like AI.

6   Ways to Co-exist

When Durkin (2003) speaks about coexistence, he suggests humans are increasingly reliant on technology and machine intelligence for survival. He says that humans will be unable to turn off their clever apparatus, because they depend on it for reliable assistance with routine work. This means the machines are in effective control. Humans have developed them to automate tasks and free people from doing them. These are the repetitive, time consuming activities that are dull, dirty and dangerous. An example is email filters. This is software which intelligently sorts through the mail and makes decisions based on logical reasoning. Where AI is subservient to human intelligence there are varying degrees of this observable. It is possible to programme software to be intelligent but still subservient and so develop AI controlled by human-beings.

Another way would be equality, with human and machine intelligence cooperating as partners. However, if AI continues to develop to the stage where it matches human intelligence, there may come a time when it will seek to serve its own interests first. At this point, humans and machines could encounter conflicts. A war between people and intelligent machines would be humanity's greatest test of survival and result in another way of coexistence, where individuals are subservient to their robot colleagues.

7   The Issue of Ethics

Humans are the inventors and developers of machine intelligence, so it is possible to create software with specifications to protect people from potential harm. The science fiction writer, Isaac Asimov, created laws in his books for robots to follow, but these bear little on actual AI construction. Scientists evaluate the possibility of programming prescribed instructions into AI and conclude the difficulty is the complexity of reducing the environment to the binary nature of laws. Such behaviour laws would be necessary to prevent conflict (Clarke, 1994; Grande, 2004).

Muller (2020) discusses the ethics of machine existence. He talks about an astronomical pattern that an intelligent species will discover at some point and bring about its own demise. Such a "great filter" would help to explain the

"Fermi Paradox" – why there is no sign of life in the known universe despite a probability of it emerging. Muller concludes it would be bad news if the "great filter" is ahead of us and not a hurdle that Earth has already passed.

Humans are likely to accept intelligent machines whatever their problems. When you see people on public transport or walking the streets they frequently have a smart phone glued to their ear and are shouting out their messages for all and sundry to hear. This is just one of today's irritating issues that assail us as we go about our daily lives. The functions that machines serve us are necessary for the high standard of life which we have come to accept and expect. Automating routine, time-consuming tasks leaves us room for more meaningful, interesting activities. AI, in humanoid form, is already common across the world, acting as an intelligent assistant in different spheres of life.

However, they have substantial limits, such as human consciousness (Faggin, 2019). Consciousness refers to individual awareness of unique thoughts, memories, feelings, sensations and environments. Essentially, it is awareness of yourself and the world around. This mindfulness is subjective and unique to you. Federico Faggin invented the micro-chip and touch screen and is regarded as a top world genius. He thinks it will not be possible to invest full consciousness into AI machines, so humans must be reminded that they should be restricted to a functional relationship. Humans inherit genetic patterns, from a mother and father, which presently would be impossible to supply to machines. Therefore, human and machine intelligence should be able to coexist under specific conditions and rules defined by people through a global agreement. Human nature has a good and bad side and nations wishing to dominate others may overstep the mark and produce machines that wreak havoc and demand rights and freedoms. Whether human or machine will dominate is unknowable in our uncertain, fragile world of continual human tensions.

8   Review

Machines are learning to learn and humans are attempting to teach them. Therefore, under what conditions does a machine outperform a person and by how much? How do we design an algorithm for a machine learning programme? What tests must it pass to be trusted? The machine outcomes must be accurate and the human influence, with its frailties, cannot be underrated. Machine learning developers encode numerous biases into the algorithms they develop – implicit and often unintentional. We saw this in the UK's school leaving exams, during the 2020 pandemic, when students could not physically take public tests. An algorithm computed predicted grades with 40% receiving ones that did not match their achievement profiles, to consequently messing up their future plans.

Therefore, undesirable human values and tendencies exist. At the national, international and criminal level, there are opportunities to exploit algorithms or create vulnerabilities in them for wicked outcomes. Without correct controls in place, correlations learned from data could reinforce deep-seated inequalities in society. We have seen this in algorithms selecting students for Higher Education courses, which have been shown to be biased against women or people of colour in some instances. A diverse dataset helps, but this alone will not address the limitations of current technology. Such restrictions mean that algorithms can also "learn" to recognize inaccurate correlations that result from unfortunate events or intentional tampering. When human values and societal ethics are at stake, it is vital to ensure the right balance between machine learning and human teaching.

As AI advances there are concerns that powerful machines are being created to pursue undesirable goals with catastrophic results. Professor Stuart Russell (2019), an AI expert, ponders over a super intelligent system that learns to stop climate change by reducing population, because science shows that human activity is the major cause of warming the Earth. Such a possibility shows the importance of a theoretical foundation for correctly specifying outcomes.

However, some researchers think that encoding world knowledge into a machine learning algorithm is doomed, arguing that a better mirroring of human brain structure is required. Deep learning algorithms contain layers of artificial neurons with interconnections analogous to brain synapses and can have millions of parameters. However, human brains have 100 billion neurons with 100 trillion synaptic connections. If we can devise an algorithm as complex as this, its inner workings would be almost impossible to understand. Could we ever reliably teach, test and trust such as system?

References

Clarke, R. (1994, January). Asimov's laws of robotics: Implications for information technology – 2. *IEEE Computer*, 27(1), 57–66.

Cobello, S., & Milli, E. (2022). Social aspects of robotics. In R. Sage & R. Matteucci (Eds.), *How world events are changing education*. Brill.

Durkin, J. (2003). Man & machine: I wonder if we can coexist. *AI & Society*, 17, 383–390.

Faggin, F. (2019). The fundamental differences between artificial and human intelligence. In R. Sage & R. Matteucci (Eds.), *The robots are here: Learning to live with them*. Buckingham University Press.

Grand, S. (2004, November–December). Moving AI out of its infancy: Changing our preconceptions. *Intelligent Systems & Their Applications, IEEE, 19*(6), 74–77.

Matteucci, R. (2019). Bullying a widespread problem to solve. In R. Sage & R. Matteucci (Eds.), *The robots are here: Learning to live with them.* Buckingham University Press.

Muller, V. (2020, April 30). Ethics of artificial intelligence and robotics. *Stanford Encyclopedia of Philosophy.*

Pew Research Center. (2017/2018/2019). *Automation in everyday life.* www.peerresearch.org

Prabhakar, A. (2017, January). The merging of human and machine is happening. *Wired Technology.* Wired.co.uk

Romero, J. (2022). The preface. In R. Sage & R Matteucci (Eds.), *How world events are changing education.* Brill.

Sage, R., & Matteucci, R. (2019). *The robots are here: Learning to live with them.* Buckingham University Press.

Sage, R., & Matteucci, R. (2022). Educational robotics. In R. Sage & R. Matteucci (Eds.), *How world events are changing education.* Brill.

CHAPTER 12

Predictive Protocols for Teacher and Student Support

Riccarda Matteucci

Abstract

Suddenly, without time for proper preparation, educators across the world in 2020 adapted to a totally new way of teaching because of the COVID-19 pandemic. Everybody felt overwhelmed during these times of great change, causing stress and anxiety for both students and teachers. Educators still feel particularly strained, as they have to constantly manage the worry associated with threats to our health, well-being, and livelihood. Furthermore, most of them are taking care of their own children and families at home, while also assisting students with personal, practical and academic development. In this scenario, it is important to prioritise self-care for everyone involved, taking note of physical, emotional, and mental needs and actively working to meet these in the best way possible. This helps to prevent being overstressed, keeps us emotionally healthy and socially engaged in our lives and is the way to bring joy and satisfaction. Much is changing so rapidly that we are likely to need support in identifying needs and finding new ways of meeting them. The chapter gives ideas and insight for support.

1   Suggestions for Self-care: Relevant for Teachers and Students

Project Wayfinder[1] partners with educators to design innovative learning experiences that foster belonging and help students to navigate their lives. The "Ten Tips for Teacher Self-care" were identified by Casey Pettit, a Boston-based licensed clinician, and Adrian Michael, the director of School Success for Project Wayfinder (Pettit & Michael, 2020). This guide shows how educators can take care of themselves and their students' social and emotional needs in the midst of school closures. What the authors suggest is a toolkit to help educators to continue in these uncertain times and their ideas are expanded and explained below.

1.1   *Accept Yourself but Aim to Improve*

Certainly, teachers are working harder with more overtime required to keep up with changing demands. Eagerness to make sure that everything is done properly may create a feeling of frustration that not enough is being done. The mantra: "Do your best" is a reminder that all that is required of us is to do enough to make an impact. It is important to be gentle and not make impossible demands of oneself. None of us are perfect and not expected to be!

1.2   *Be Thankful*

Although this is a difficult time for everybody, we are constantly reminded of the little things that inspire us, through the positive, kindly actions of others. These responses are what motivates us as educators wanting to help learners acquire knowledge and competencies for life and work. Gratitude removes negativity and brings clarity to recall the good things about our existence. Psychologists suggest that when we are not serious about expressing gratitude, the small things that frustrate us become so much bigger and stronger emotional reactions, which can easily lead to burnout. This is a danger when overloaded with student assessments, classroom management and the agonies of life, all at the same time. When you exercise gratitude, even once or twice a day, write down three things for which you are grateful for, in order to produce a positive focus.

1.3   *Emotional Distancing Is Not a Necessity of the Required Social Distancing of the Pandemic*

Share with others how you think and feel. During a pandemic, or any other unwanted experiences, it is normal to have a range of emotions, with no foolproof guide on how to steer through these successfully. Psychologists suggest that when negative emotions arise it is advisable to be proactive rather than reactive. Prevention is better than cure. If you face a difficult conversation with a student, colleague, friend or relative, take time to collect your thoughts and do not allow negative feelings to override you. It is sensible to write down what you want to say. Focus on what happened, what you observed, how you feel and what you might need to move forward positively. Being honest about situations makes educators more authentic and helps relationships with students, colleagues and others. Above all, be calm and relaxed so that you come over in a pleasant, positive way to others.

1.4   *Think Positive*

Newspapers and the media promote negative stories. For some reason they sell more newspapers with bad than with good stories. These attract and absorb people's thinking in negative ways and so the world is viewed as an unhappy, uncertain place. Sometimes it is hard to know what to do, especially when others, like students or families, are struggling and bowed down with pessimism about present life. Educators need to consider the wholeness of their experiences and "sharing joy" can be infectious for others. Invite students to share positive emotions, asking, for example, "What is one thing about distance learning that has surprisingly been a useful, positive experience for you?"

1.5   *Make Relaxation a Routine*

Close your screens and find ways to connect with yourself and others in direct ways. Take breaks in your routine in order to change your mental state. Stretch your body and with your legs apart and your weight over your toes, breathe in slowly and deeply to a count of 10, pause, and then breathe out, counting again. Do this at least three times. A relaxed body brings a released mind! It gives you a chance to concentrate on something entirely different. Experts suggest this activity is difficult, but it is necessary to be serious about moving your body regularly. Going for a walk or a run, or simply stretching, are the best things for mental distraction. When relaxed and in full command of your actions, you can secure the support of others more easily and more effectively.

1.6   *Do Enjoyable Things Daily*

Even on the busiest days, addressing meetings and having non-stop interactions with colleagues and students, it is important to make time for things that bring you joy and satisfaction. Listen to music, cook a meal, go outside, read a book, play with children or do nothing. All this nourishes the mind and the body, because stepping out from the hustle and bustle, even for a moment, refreshes bodies and minds and brings a balance to thinking and actions.

1.7   *Manage Expectations*

Allow progress and productivity to look different for the coming year. Redefine success and what it means for you as an educator. Be realistic with your expectations. For example, do not spend much time organising lessons for just a handful of students. Use the new experience of hybrid learning as an opportunity to connect with each other in a real way. Communicate with students in a mode which is effective for your circumstances and adjust expectations along the way.

1.8   *Consider Boundaries That Everyone Can Respect*

Be sure to balance your presence in the classroom and living life outside it. Boundaries are necessary to clarify your availability to students, if they need you, and communicate what is not negotiable. For example, it is important to tell students you do not check email over weekends and sign out of your online working environment after a certain hour. Never feel guilty for setting boundaries. You need to have a chance to switch off, relax and enjoy things that give you pleasure. This will energise and motivate all your other activities.

1.9   *Assess the Mood of the Group You Are Dealing With*

If the mood is not right, do not be afraid of having fun and playing games that will not make undue demands on a class that is unable to concentrate easily. Not every academic lesson has to be centred on content. Personal and practical growth is equally important. Students are humans, too, and can recognise the moods and feelings of others. Any time you have the opportunity to be with students in e-learning, in a flipped classroom, on Zoom or via some kind of technological device, use it as a precious occasion to communicate and interact with them in order to know them better.

1.10   *Support Can Always Be Found*

Educators, worldwide, seek one another for support and share their experiences through the various webinars and online groups that are now available. Everyone has rolled up their sleeves and overnight provided both academic and social-emotional education and support. Most teachers worked, day in and out, over the pandemic, to check what students needed during this difficult time, in terms of phones, tablets, computers, internet access etc. Educators must join and share resource groups, social platforms or online specialists in order to gain ideas on how to conduct virtual lessons better, or post funny moments to give fellow educators humorous interludes and an emotional lift to the spirits. Asking for help is a key strength and checking with others is always helpful feedback. Most importantly, continue to find ways to check in with yourself, identify your special needs and allow yourself to meet them. Know that your work is not more important than your health and well-being.

2   Comment

In order to understand how to rebuild the education system, it is vital to make sure we are truly addressing the needs, concerns and desires of all stakeholders. Schools should establish a vision for teaching and learning that includes the voices of all participants, including teachers, students and community members. When a culture of transparency and inclusivity is fostered at every level in a learning community, everybody wins. Personalise learning for educators so they can, in turn, do this effectively for their students. Teachers must feel confident bringing their knowledge into the classroom and voicing new ideas, strategies and solutions supporting their growth and that of their students. The e-portfolio movement, collecting evidence of practice, as a way of continuing one's education and gaining further qualifications, is a wonderful way to keep track of learning that is self-motivating and easy to share with others.

Innovation does not mean getting everything right the first time round and this process provides room to make mistakes, adjustments and chances to try again. Students have and will continue to play the most important role in leading us towards a more equitable future. Teachers feel vulnerable and need to be reassured that the school site and district are going to keep everyone safe, especially in these uncertain times. Principals or head teachers need to offer an open-dialogue policy, where transparency of information is key, especially regarding health conditions. Fear of the virus and anxiety over the many variables that are in play must be acknowledged, respected and responded to thoughtfully. Teachers are more criticised than ever, in a personalised environment, where relationship building and trust form the foundation for everything that happens in the classroom. Respect and support all methods of teaching, treat and pay teachers as professionals and appreciate what they do (particularly over this last year, which has meant much to them and their students). When people think about teachers in everyone's life, they do well to remember that our families, communities and nations would not progress without them and we should not need a pandemic to prove it. They are a vital resource and need as much nurturing as their students in order to keep going!

3   Ways to Support Student Healing

Ashley Wen (n.d.), content marketing manager at the XQ Institute,[2] reveals that many schools and communities worldwide continue to experience trauma due to uncontrolled acts of racial violence and injustice. Among the various episodes she mentions are the Colorado residents who mourned the deaths in mass shooting that occurred in Boulder on March 22, 2021, as well as the many instances of violence against transgender and non-binary people. In Britain, teachers are being regularly suspended for what appears to be misinterpretation of their intentions. For example, a geography teacher at an academy in London gave a lesson on Niger, a West African country, and explained that the name was not pronounced as it was spelt, so it should not be confused with a racial slur. The teacher was not supported by the head teacher and was suspended.

Nowadays, teachers are suspended or even sacked for calling children by the wrong pronoun, as they may come to school dressed as a boy one day but a girl another. These events are the gloomy reminders of intersecting, multifaceted experiences of students, educators and staff which are constantly making the national and international news. The XQ politic is to share what is working with other schools and districts, to create and tailor new models to the needs of their own students and communities. On the principle "seeing is believing", they meet people where they are able to share the importance and possibility of change through listening, learning and storytelling. Based on research and thinking about design, this approach offers people the possibility to pick up the challenge of transforming their schools with a unifying goal: unlocking the promise of a high-quality education for everyone. As such, schools are not only places for academic growth, but also for social and emotional development.

During these difficult times, it is fundamental more than ever that school leaders work closely with students to help them process these recent events and create opportunities where educators and pupils can collaborate in long-term healing. Wen (n.d.) states that students feel supported to process traumatic events and difficult subjects if educators make them feel heard, understood and empowered in the classroom by doing the following.

3.1   Listening

A restorative practice with students in circles reflecting and processing their perspectives, feelings and actions together. Choose an item to pass from one another to comment on as they hold it. This activity facilitates equity of voice to ensure that all can be honest and open without fear.

3.2   Building Educational Equality from Teacher Diversity

Teacher diversity is key and impacts all students, as their identities continue to shape and evolve from having many different staff in the classroom. Empathetic mentors in pupil lives are critical, as this enables trust to build, with persons who can relate to learner issues and understand as well as guide them in their process of learning. Educators must build the idea of belonging to a community that works towards an equitable future and creates a network among everyone sharing the goal of achieving a better education system.

3.3   Align a Safe, Effective and Engaging Classroom

To explain this approach, Wen (n.d.) gives the example of the Trinity Academy for the Performing Arts (TAPA), whose commitment to "high love, high rigor" strengthens academic programmes. This proves that it is possible to achieve social justice for students by supporting and building meaningful connections while still maintaining high academic standards. Throughout the pandemic, the school increased social-emotional and trauma-responsive support to ameliorate social justice crises:

– *Collaborative group work* to support peer-to-peer learning
– *One-to-one time* between teacher and students and students with other students
– *Formative assessments* (such as e-portfolios) and more formal presentations that help build verbal communication competencies

3.4   Help Students Speak Out

If educators want equitable school environments that are bullying and racist free, it is necessary to encourage student advocacy to amplify their voices and choices. Students from Rhode Island, USA, involved in a series of engagement sessions organised by xq, revealed how they are supporting each other in this particularly difficult moment. They are as follows:

– *Looking out* for each other and advocating for the needs of their peers
– *Fitting and adapting* to new r-learning requirements or hybrid approaches to move forward and develop in holistic ways
– *Encouraging resilience and hope* for a better future
– *Teaching communication* so that social justice can be a reality

3.5   Support That Prioritises Social-Emotional Learning

These past few years have reminded us that the world can change quickly and we must adapt without much notice. We have learned that we need to imbue our pedagogy with social-emotional understanding that takes into consideration the needs of students and teachers alike.

4   Review

Students will always occupy a basic role in the teaching and learning process, so it is fundamental that we pay attention when they speak about what they need and hear what they say. This is not only to identify the issues they care about, but also to help them to find proper solutions to assist their personal, practical and academic progress. Students must learn to make intelligent choices, take ownership and share in decision-making. Among many other things, the COVID-19 pandemic has taught us that students need to have a strong sense of belonging, with ownership of their learning. This factor helps them to remain orientated and motivated, so that teachers can successfully implement the idea of community, communication and cooperation.

If we believe that personalised, competency-based education is the best way to ensure all students thrive, we also know that it starts with a culture that supports, engages and empowers teachers. The critical work of partnering with students, along with networks of education peers and community partners, moulds their own learning progress, which must now include proper use of technology for both work and social activities.

The World Health Organization recognised technology addiction in May 2019 and says this has risen in recent years, as students have been forced out of their normal routines and spending more time with computers, both for learning and playing. The Nightingale Addiction Clinics report a fourfold increase in referrals for technology dependence, and the Tommys survey (2021) found that 4 in 10 parents were seriously worried about their children's obsession for screens. Students have been given more exposure to technology than ever before and experts suggest the loss of structure to their lives has caused anxiety and compulsiveness. We need to review how we support parents as well as teachers and children in the sensible use of technology. The regulation of web content is now urgent in this moment of easy access by young people to harmful information that could disturb their minds or negatively affect their behaviour. Being aware of the issues and being responsive to each other's needs is the starting point for dealing with such negative influences.

Notes

1   Wayfinder was founded in 2015 at Stanford d.school, a hub for innovation, collaboration, and creativity at Stanford University in California. Wayfinder is culturally responsive, providing comprehensive mental health + SEL curricula for middle and high school students. Its main goal is to meet the real needs of 21st-century pupils and educators.
2   The XQ Institute is in Oakland, California, and is considered the USA's leading organisation dedicated to rethinking the high school experience so that every student graduates ready to succeed in life. It is a net of communities spread throughout the country.

References

Bondono, O., de Uribe, A. C., & Hargreaves, A., et al. (2021, April 30). It's Teacher Appreciation Week. Flowers? Mugs? We're looking for something more: Four ways to really give teachers what they need.
Education Week. https://www.edweek.org/teaching-learning/opinion-its-teacher-appreciation-week-flowers-mugs-were-looking-for-something-more/2021/04

Fiksel, J., Goodman, I., & Hacht, A. (2013, July 9). *Resilience: Navigating towards a sustainable future*. Ohio State University.

Hammond, V. (2020, November 20). What we want for students, we want for teachers, too.

Husain, E. (2021). *Among the mosques: A journey across Muslim Britain*. Bloomsbury.

Kuhlmann, J. (2019, May 7). Ready to personalize learning? Start with trusting teachers. *KnowledgeWorks*. https://knowledgeworks.org/resources/personalize-learning-trusting-teachers/

Panlillo, C., & Tirrel-Corbin, C. (2021, March 21). Educators are experiencing trauma during the pandemic. Here's how we can reduce the burden. *EdSurge*. https://www.edsurge.com/news/2021-03-02-our-research-shows-educators-are-experiencing-trauma-during-the-pandemic-here-s-how-we-can-reduce-the-burden

Pettit, C., & Michael, A. (2020, May 29). Ten tips for teacher self-care. Project Wayfinder. https://web.archive.org/web/20210305185746/https://xqsuperschool.org/rethinktogether/ten-tips-for-teacher-self-care/

Racines, D. (2020, July 20). *Administration and leadership: Supporting teachers in a difficult year*. https://shoutoutla.com

Resilience guide for navigating towards sustainable future. (n.d.). https://www.wayfinders.earth

Tommys. (2021). Survey on technology addiction. https://www.tommys.org.net

Wen, A. (n.d.). *5 ways to support student healing*. https://xqsuperschool.org/teaching-learning/support-student-healing/

What Is Predicted for the Future and What Do the Book Chapters Tell Us?

Rosemary Sage and Riccarda Matteucci

Abstract

Recently, a job advert for the Neurolink Technology Company surfaced, while researching the competencies that employers consistently require of those working for them. The suitable candidate needed excellent spoken and written communication, effective multi-tasking and minute attention to detail, but the list also contained, "Understanding of Class 111 implantable neuromodulation devices". This is no ordinary work role! In fact the post was for a Clinical Trial Director to run tests on humans of a technological product ready for surgical insertion. The aim is to plug the human brain cortex (grey matter) into the Metaverse – a simulated digital environment using augmented reality (AR), virtual reality (VR) and Blockchain, with social media concepts, to create spaces for user interaction mimicking the real world. Blockchain is a recording information system to make it more difficult (but not impossible) to change, hack, or cheat. It is a digital ledger of transactions that is duplicated and distributed across the entire network of computer systems. Therefore, it appears we are on the verge of a new world of mind control. The chapter considers the implications of research now making fast progress, as well as reiterating the messages of the book, Evidence is reinforced by students both in the Italian school and college survey and the case studies across all education levels in Britain.

1 Introduction: The Age of Mind Control

Neurolink has been operating for 5 years and is the brain-child of the Silicon Valley entrepreneur, Elon Musk. It aims to develop a device, known as a brain machine interface (BMI) that plugs into the cortex (brain grey matter) and connects to the digital world. This will enable humans to control devices, tap into global knowledge and communicate with each other by their thoughts alone. No need for the dodgy issues of differently produced words for their interpretation! The job advert (referred to above), under the section of what the company offers, was 'An opportunity to change the world'!

A brain-computer interface (BCI) is also called a brain-machine interface (BMI) and a direct communication pathway between the brain electrical activity and an external device, generally a computer or robotic limb. BCIs are often directed at researching, planning, assisting, boosting or repairing human cognitive or sensory motor functions. These can be non-invasive or partially invasive or invasive, based on how close electrodes get to brain tissue.

Due to the brain cortical plasticity, signals from implanted prostheses can, after adaptation, be handled by the brain like natural sensor or effector channels. Recent studies in human-computer interaction, via the application of machine learning to statistical temporal features, extracted from the frontal lobe (*electroencephalogram*–EEG–brainwave) data has had high levels of success in classifying mental states (Relaxed, Neutral, Concentrating) mental-emotional states (Negative, Neutral, Positive) and thalamocortical dysrhythmia, as in tinnitus (ringing in the ear) or Parkinson's disease (uncoordinated limb movements) as well as many other neuroological disturbances.

Playing with the brain is certainly not a new idea. Two centuries ago, Doctor Frankenstein and his monster were thought up. Frankenstein's monster or creature, also known as just 'Frankenstein', is an English fictional character first appearing in Mary Shelley's 1818 novel, Frankenstein or The Modern Prometheus. The title compares the monster's creator, Victor Frankenstein, to the mythological character Prometheus, who fashioned humans out of clay and gave them fire. In Shelley's Gothic story, Victor Frankenstein forms the creature in his laboratory using a process based on a scientific principle he had discovered. The monster is 8 feet (240 cm) tall and hideous, but has emotions. He attempts to fit into human society but is spurned, which leads him to seek revenge against Frankenstein. According to the scholar, Joseph Carroll (2012), the monster occupies a border territory between characteristics that define protagonists and antagonists – much in noisy evidence today!

Frankenstein's monster has become iconic in popular culture and featured in films, television series, video games and merchandise. The most popularly recognized versions are the portrayals by Boris Karloff in the 1931 film Frankenstein, the 1935 sequel, Bride of Frankenstein and the 1939 one, Son of Frankenstein. These films planted the idea of playing with what is in our skulls.

The permanent insertion of devices into the brain has been part of medical and therapeutic practice for a while. Patients with Parkinson's disease, which causes a terrible tremor, interfering with speech and movement, have been receiving implants (deep brain stimulators) to stop the continual shaking which spoils their existence. This therapeutic device works to keep brain signals steady and thus control movement. Also, it has also been common to insert pacemakers into the heart region of the human chest for people who have irregular heartbeats (arrhythmia) that interfere with their daily function, causing dizziness, fainting, shortness of breath, pain, etc. A pacemaker (cardiac pacing device) is a small gadget that is implanted, with a surgical procedure, into the chest to control heartbeat. It is used to prevent the heart from beating too slowly.

2   A New Reality

Brain-computer interfaces (BCIs) acquire brain signals, analyze them, and translate them into commands that are relayed to output devices that carry out desired actions. BCIs do not use normal neuromuscular output pathways. The main goal of BCI is to replace or restore useful function to people disabled by neuromuscular disorders such as amyotrophic lateral sclerosis, cerebral palsy, stroke, or spinal cord injury. From initial demonstrations of electroencephalography-based spelling and single-neuron-based device control, researchers have gone on to use electroencephalographic, intracortical, electrocorticographic, and other brain signals for increasingly complex control of cursors, robotic arms, prostheses, wheelchairs, and other devices. Brain-computer interfaces may also prove useful for rehabilitation after stroke and for other disorders. In the future, they might augment the performance of surgeons or other medical professionals. Brain-computer interface technology is the focus of a rapidly growing research and development enterprise that is greatly exciting scientists, engineers, clinicians, and the public in general. Its future achievements will depend on advances in 3 crucial areas. Brain-computer interfaces need signal-acquisition hardware that is convenient, portable, safe, and able to function in all environments. Brain-computer interface systems need to be validated in long-term studies of real-world use by people with severe disabilities, and effective and viable models for their widespread dissemination must be implemented. Finally, the day-to-day and moment-to-moment reliability of BCI performance must be improved so that it approaches the reliability of natural muscle-based function.

Until recently, the idea of being able to control one's daily environment through thoughts has been science fiction. The amazing advances of technology in the last two decades have brought a new reality. Today, humans can use the electrical signals from brain activity to interact with, influence, or change their environments. The emerging field of brain-computer interface (BCI) technology may allow people unable to speak and/or use their limbs to once again communicate or operate assistive devices for walking and manipulating objects (Shih et al, 2012). Brain-computer interface research is of public interest. Videos on YouTube, as well as news reports in the media, indicate much curiosity and interest in an area that hopefully will improve the lives of many disabled persons affected by a range of different disease processes.

Thus, this new brand of Neurolink technology dreams not just of regulating the brain but of merging it with a computer. We are moving beyond just devices to cure the sick to drive augmentation of the human power of cognition and communication. Human trials are well underway. Indeed, scientists have been trying to connect brains to computers over the last half century. In 1969, when the Apollo mission to the moon took place, a German neuroscientist, Eberhard Fetz, conducted his own moonshot by wiring a single neuron into a monkey's brain to a machine that fed a treat if it fired. Within 2 minutes, the monkey had grasped the process and was triggering the machine to receive his treat, just by thinking! Recently, we watched engineering students in Italian universities helping paralysed patients move prostheses like robot arms with their thoughts alone, with the aim of assisting greater independence. At the moment, the kit needed is awkward, the electrical signals in the brain require greater accuracy, decoding them is difficult and relaying them to what we want to control is slow. Experts are working on these problems and aim to solve them.

3   The Influence of Firefox

The 1982 film, Firefox, starring Clint Eastwood, showed future possibilities. In the film, the object of thought control was a Soviet fighter jet that could be flown with the mind alone. This film fired the imaginations of scientists as well as cinema audiences. The Firefox scenario has driven mind control projects by the US Defense Advanced Research Projects Agency (DARPA), although some experts doubt whether such a jet would give pilots benefits. The military are still pursuing the idea of split-second advantages in communication. A researcher on a BMI designed to capture words a person thinks inside their heads, was approached by The Army Research Office to develop a helmet for silently beaming unspoken thoughts from soldier to soldier on the battle field.

Manufacturers in the private sector have also had an interest in investigating other mind-control machines. Nissan brought out a prototype in 2018 with brain-to-vehicle technology. A car could tap directly into the driver's brain and act on signals to brake before the neuron message reached the foot on the pedal. However, over time the private sector has veered away from expensive, risky procedures to implant unproven technology into healthy people. Funding streams started to dry up and boom and bust economies have had other priorities, most recently the COVID-19 pandemic, to direct them away from the brain.

Aspiring start-ups have repeatedly gone bust, but Neurolink's arrival has made everyone think again. Elon Musk's company BMI is far sleeker than the existing lumpy equipment. The latter has spiky silicon pads surgically inserted into the skull to read brain signals and then feed into sockets on the top of the head, from where cables take them to computers for decoding. In contrast, Neurolink's device is almost invisible, with 64 thin wires, each with 16 electrodes attached to 1,024 specific neurons inside the head, detecting their activity, then decoding them in a computer smaller than a 2p coin, under the skin, with thought commands broadcast wirelessly. This can be seen on a YouTube video available since April 2021, posted by Neurolink. It shows a rhesus monkey, named Pager, drinking a banana milkshake while playing the game Pong, using thought control. Facebook has also been working on a device reading thoughts to turn into sentences for 'sharing' at the rate of 100 words a minute! This happens without drilling into anyone's head by using a skull-cap instead. The project lead is Regin Duga, the former DARPA head, a military agency linking with Neurolink and helping to fund a surgical device to stitch its array of wires into the brain.

4   Venture Capitalists

However, it is venture capitalists who are providing BMI finance. Elon Musk put $100 million of his own money into projects - inspired others to follow his example. This now enables BMIs to benefit from continuing resources. Hundreds of millions went into the sector during 2021. The majority of projects are therapeutic – to give speech to those without it, by reading their thoughts and then broadcasting them, as well as to restore sight to the blind, by feeding camera signals directly to the brain. Also, the paralysed are beginning to interact again for themselves, by moving robotic prosthetics or computer cursors with their mind alone.

As a PhD student studying communication sciences in the 1970s, these possibilities were discussed, as early prototypes were then available in the research laboratories at the University of Cambridge. It is good to find they are now being implemented to assist people with their lives. For paralysed people working with researchers, the BMI is like a mouse, which allows them to draw using computer software or play video games. As these games become even more immersive, interaction with them provides opportunities to escape their condition, if only virtually.

Elon Musk has an even loftier purpose for Neurolink – elevating human abilities by fusion with the computer world. His vision is that BMIs will let us compete with the most intelligent robots, which might otherwise destroy us. The mission statement says 'if you cannot beat them, join them!'

5   BMI Dangers

All positives have negatives and BMIs pose risks. Regarding medical use, there could be infections, which may not respond to conventional treatment and management. Another danger is the ethical one. What privacy is there with a device reading your thoughts? Also, the reality may not meet the vision. Facebook dumped their headset project to focus on a wrist-worn brain-reading device. Technology gadgets are marketable, as everyone (who can afford them) wants the latest versions. However, the neuroscience is challenging. Brain signals that control movement are straightforward to decode, but reading complex thoughts and merging these with the internet is still considered science fiction.

Some may be relieved to know this, but when you think of the speed at which technology has evolved there is possibility that mind control is not far away today. We still do not have complete understanding about what is encoded in the cortex premotor area in order to achieve high rates of information transfer in invasive BMIs. More attention is needed to understand what kind of information is represented in recorded neuronal populations. Information processing/production is different for all of us (Sage, 2020), so how do we produce a system coping with diversity?

Thus, technology issues seem to be secondary at present. Research on invasive BMIs provides a chance to test hypothesis on how brain movements are encoded. Neurons in cortical pre-motor areas appear to process a significant component of vision- or/and intention-related information that could better predict movements. Thus, BMIs should account for this information. Visual feedback is important for accurate hand movements (Saunders & Knill, 2003). In all invasive BMIs, subjects can see the position of a cursor or a device. However, during the decoding of neuronal signals, vision or intention-related information is rarely used for invasive BMI control. It appears to contradict the idea of BMI, namely to predict movements from neuronal activity without additional information.

However, the best results in centre-out or similar tasks have been achieved in an invasive BMI that does use intention or/and vision-related information. The standard task for studying voluntary motor control is the "centre-out task", in which a monkey or other subject must move their hand from a central location to targets placed on a circle surrounding the starting position. This may indicate that our brains do not try to predict limb coordinates alone but always combine different information types, which are processed by neurons in cortical pre-motor areas and used to reach the desired target. This is not a new idea (Hoshi & Tanji, 2004), so it is unsurprising that the use of intention or vision-related information allowed Santhanam et al. (2006) to achieve maximal rate of 6 bit/s in invasive BMI, not much worse than in natural movements (10 bit/s), so indicating that we will have prosthetic arms, ordered by a brain almost as efficiently as we can control our hands.

6   What Are BMI Issues for Education?

Technological innovations have merged the physical and digital worlds, but few have bridged the gap between them. A BMI exception is a computerized system that reads the mind and converts the brain neuron signals into an exact output required by a user. The main benefits are as follows:

6.1   *Smart Technology*

BCIs are often called brain–machine interfaces (BMIs). While BCI and BMI are synonymous terms, systems that use externally recorded signals are referred to as BCIs, and systems that use signals recorded by implanted sensors are known as BMIs. An *electroencephalogram* (EEG) is a recording of brain activity, referred to as a BCI. During this painless test, small sensors are attached to the scalp to pick up brain electrical signals. BCI is an advanced technology because it can make passive devices into "smart" active ones, like prosthetics. A user can use this technology to hold a cup of tea and drink it like using normal hands. Similarly, hearing impaired people can use this technology to connect with each other using BCI-controlled communication devices.

6.2   *Telepresence*

Telepresence technology enables someone to make their presence felt at a remote location using tele-robotics. Thus, BCI can allow military personnel to observe suspicious activity and help to combat it. Telepresence lets humans work in conditions that otherwise put them in health and safety dangers. This will help military personnel. A wide range of brain computer interfaces brings diverse benefits. Developers and adopters must monitor BCI risks for safe implementation.

Brain-computer interfaces (BCIs) acquire brain signals, analyze them, and translate them into commands that are relayed to output devices that carry out desired actions. BCIs do not use normal neuromuscular output pathways. The main goal of BCI is to replace or restore useful function to people disabled by neuromuscular disorders such as amyotrophic lateral sclerosis, cerebral palsy, stroke, or spinal cord injury. From initial demonstrations of electroencephalography-based spelling and single-neuron-based device control, researchers have gone on to use electroencephalographic, intracortical, electrocorticographic, and other brain signals for increasingly complex control of cursors, robotic arms, prostheses, wheelchairs, and other devices. Brain-computer interfaces may also prove useful for rehabilitation after stroke and for other disorders. In the future, they might augment the performance of surgeons or other medical professionals. Brain-computer interface technology is the focus of a rapidly growing research and development enterprise that is greatly exciting scientists, engineers, clinicians, and the public in general. Its future achievements will depend on advances in 3 crucial areas. Brain-computer interfaces need signal-acquisition hardware that is convenient, portable, safe, and able to function in all environments. Brain-computer interface systems need to be validated in long-term studies of real-world use by people with severe disabilities, and effective and viable models for their widespread dissemination must be implemented. Finally, the day-to-day and moment-to-moment reliability of BCI performance must be improved so that it approaches the reliability of natural muscle-based function.

6.3   *Accident Reduction*

Vehicle accidents are a serious cause of death worldwide. A BCI-enabled car can prevent incidents by recognising what is going on in a driver's mind and taking a decision in seconds without delay. Nissan, the car manufacturers, have researched the BCI-enabled car control system that allows it to slow the vehicle or turn the steering wheel 0.2–0.5 seconds faster than the driver to aid safety.

7   Dangers

The BCI system, directly linked to the human brain, can have a negative impact on users if not employed correctly as follows:

7.1   *Inaccurate Results*

The brain is complex and we do not understand fully what goes on in our minds, so it is difficult for a man-made BCI to correctly interpret brain signals. Therefore, there is a danger of misinterpreting user intentions. For example, a disabled person with a prosthetic hand, who wants to raise an index finger, is not correctly identified by the BCI and the middle one lifted instead.

7.2   *System Bulk*

The BCI system involves the connection of many wires due to the brain-computer interface and can be uncomfortable for the user. This may produce mental and physical stress.

7.3   Security Lack

One expects a digital product or service to be safe when buying or subscribing to it. BCI technology, however, cannot be guaranteed. Anyone can decode what is going on in your mind to invade privacy. BCI based military applications have the risk that an enemy attacker could hack into any personnel's mind and leak confidential information. Scientists say that within 5 years attackers will be able to rewrite memories in people's mind. BCI is an emerging technology with ability to bring about revolutionary change in many fields.

7.4   Manufacturing Issues

A band called The Mothers signed a record deal, but discovered another one had this name. As a result, the group changed it to The Mothers of Invention, which became a common phrase. However, recent technology owes more to cheap money and labour rather than innovation. An invention in Shenfield, England, could be made in Shenzhen, China at a low price, because labour is cheaper. This is a problem, which Richard Yu, at Huawei, warns could be permanent. China's zero-Covid policy has shut down factories for long periods. Moore's Law, referring to a doubling of transistors every 18 months, held good for 40 years, but ceased to apply a decade ago. Silicon chips, the physical building blocks for computers to run software, grew bigger to compensate, but less efficiency has taken gains away. The chip crisis has prompted re-thinking, with Apple using the same H1 chip in AirPods as in 2019. The supply chain pain uses brain power needed to innovate. In 2020, Elon Musk said that a lack of chips meant rewriting Tesla software for alternatives, but this is difficult for small companies. A UK company is into its fourth design for a product because of broken chip contracts, to slow progress. Another issue is the prospect of a prolonged Ukraine war. Production of metals and gases for silicon chips has taken a massive hit. The Betzendahl consultancy says that neon supplies have halved. Consumers are unhappy that annual new features are little changed. This means that technology companies are struggling to stand still.

A BMI/BCI system has signal acquisition, pre-processing, feature extraction, classification, post-processing and application interface. It was initially developed for biomedical applications, producing assistive devices for physically challenged users to replace lost or reduced motor function. Positive results have led researchers to look at extending use further, especially for educational systems. These utilise brain electrical signals to determine the degree of clarity of studied information. Recently, neural signatures of explicit and implicit learning have been identified. Explicit learning is achieved through conscious awareness, when a person is thinking about a matter for which they are acquiring knowledge, understanding and competence. Implicit learning is the opposite of this and corresponds to motor skill acquisition or muscle memory.

Individuals are more capable of performing a specific action after repetition, but are not able to articulate what exactly they are learning, like bicycle riding. A BMI/BCI systems approach is electroencephalography (EEG), which records electrical activity along the scalp. It measures the voltage fluctuations of brain neurotransmission activity, using a cap design with one or more electrodes for measurement. This is better than other devices for brain signal recording and ideal for education application.

Imagine if your teacher or then your work manager could know whether you were actually paying attention in a lesson or meeting. How would you respond? Picture preparing an assignment or presentation using only your thoughts! Is this a good idea? These scenarios are soon to be reality due to BCIs. At present, we rely on an EEG to monitor brain electrical activity, but by leveraging multiple sensors and complex algorithms brain signals are analysed and extracted patterns recorded by a non-invasive device like a headband and earbuds. BCIs now use a neurofeedback training tool for improving cognitive performance to detect attention levels and alert to these. It can adapt lighting based on your stress levels, or prevent you using dangerous equipment if drowsiness is detected. This brings greater awareness of how the brain state influences performance. Are humans ready for this "magic chip" inside their body? If some cannot or will not accept it, there are two possibilities – using a chip or not. Will this be considered discrimination? Many will not want to lose the possibility of shifting their attention during a conference. Only 15% of the brain is needed to process ongoing language input, enabling us to multi-task when the situation demands, such as a disturbance in the vicinity that might indicate that we need to escape (Sage, 2000).

A Toronto-based start-up, called "Muse" has produced a sense headband to give real-time information about brain behaviour. It has a wellness programme to lower stress, increase resilience and improve engagement. Other headbands provide insights into student/worker engagement levels to help them decide what to tackle first, based on attention levels, for adapting workloads accordingly. Columbia University researchers showed how neurofeedback, using an EEG-based BCI, is used to affect alertness and improve thinking performance. Theodore Zanto, Director of the UCSF neuroscience programme, says that while user attention levels can be detected it is still impossible to differentiate their focus. In a 2019 article he says: "I haven't seen any data indicating you can dissociate if someone is paying attention to the teacher or their phone or just their own internal thoughts and daydreaming" (Gonfaloniera, 2020).

BMI/BCIs are affected by user characteristics like gender, age and lifestyle. The team are determining how brain activity affects athlete performance. Attention, memory load, fatigue and competing mental processes, as well as personal characteristics, have influence. They suggest that 15–30% of people do not produce brain signals robust enough to operate machines. There is a long way to go, but it is predicted that for dangerous jobs it will be mandatory for people, like pilots and surgeons, to wear a BCI while working, in order to monitor brain functioning.

The idea of humans interacting with devices is basic to BCI development. We might control our power-point presentations or Excel files using only brains. Prototypes translate brain activity into text or instructions for a computer. We could see people using BMI/BCIs for assignments and reports in an environment adapting automatically to stress and thinking levels, with a headband sending information to the computer to play calming music etc. if indicated. Privacy is the issue with the possibility of data being used against a person and pass thoughts employed as an alternative to pass words. There are numerous ethical questions and concerns regarding BMI/BCI technology in education and workplaces.

Collecting brain data has potential for huge abuse, even when used with good intentions. Technology is way ahead of policies and regulations that need to be in place to control use. A growing number of start-ups and tech firms are working on safer, more accurate and cheaper BCIs. The technology will be used to achieve better performance and safety. Education and Business must build a BMI/BCI strategy, without delay, to address potential risks and benefits, as otherwise the system will be open to abuse. This is vital now that education relies on technology to assist learning.

8   The Main Messages of the Book

Since 60% or more students worldwide do not reach required educational standards, it is time to review policies and practices (Luckin, 2020).We are not there yet, but if brave enough to do things differently it is possible. The book explores a broad range of possible aspects that need to be considered for improved learning outcomes and organised these under processes, practices, performance and predictions. These cover the brain thinking and communication processes that need more attention. The 2020 pandemic, with reliance on technology, has brought learning difficulties to the fore. The survey of Italian students and British case studies clarifies these. It is clear from evidence that they feel education is not preparing them for the modern world. Technology now implements many work routines so demanding employee higher level thinking and communication for team approaches to solve world problems like climate change and population movements.

In the section on practices, the Educational Robotics programme and the Communication Opportunity Group Scheme are proven ways that teach competencies for work and assess those using e-personal portfolios to demonstrate performance and potential in a broader way. However, there is a lack of regulation regarding information from web platforms and this is addressed along with the manipulation influencing users that leads to conflict and mental distress. Technology is changing fast and is taking over coaching, teaching and support functions in education, as well as elsewhere, so understanding pros and cons of usage is essential. Although the aim has been to provide a broad view of the technology and learning world, it is impossible to cover all aspects. The chapter on complexity theory demonstrates this and reinforces the idea that learning must be based on real experience involving communication and cooperation, so that ideas are shared and understood holistically.

The second round of the English-Speaking Union's Public Speaking competition, running across England and Wales, took place in February 2022, with student-chosen topics including:
– The education system is broken.
– Printed books and newspapers have outlived their usefulness.
– Have the younger generation been betrayed by the older generation?
– Oil companies need to be held accountable for the consequences of global warming.
– Money can't buy happiness.
– Are we ready to jettison our diesel or petrol cars for a brave new electric world?

The 2023 finals at Churchill College, Cambridge, had part of a presentation prepared by Chat GPT3, which was accurate but boring, with no human anecdotes to illuminate dry facts! There was a plea for philosophy to be taught in order to understand human thinking better.

This is evidence of our young people thinking seriously about some of the important issues in life. The first presentation, on the broken education system, revealed that students were disillusioned with the strong academic direction taken by a prescriptive curriculum and felt many learners, with more practical and personal talents, were written off very quickly. They were certainly lobbying for big changes, particularly in the way information is taught (more active engagement sought) and how performance is assessed. Discussion centred on broader assessment for those who found examinations problematic. Decision-makers have promoted just one kind of post-school education – the classical full-time degree course, with now a third of UK graduates not in jobs requiring this level of education ten years after receiving their award. We have a chronic shortage of technical and practical professionals because we have not valued this route for young people and have demeaned non-academic professions. It is heartening that the future generation are aware of the need for change and hopefully they will have the passion and dedication to effect this to give everyone a fairer chance in life. Good luck to them! They will need it!

City and Guilds (2022) is asking Government and Industry to put focus on young people's abilities and careers as the UK enters recession. There is high youth unemployment and a survey of UK 5,000 18–24 year olds shows 13% are unemployed and a further 3% economically inactive. This equates to around 86,000 young adults out of work and education, with 227,000 saying they never intend to work. A third believe they will not achieve ambitions in a hostile labour market. They suggest being let down by education, which does not give them the personal and practical skills for available jobs, particularly language and communication.

ChatGPT is a language model trained by OpenAI that generates human-like text based on input provided, such as: "Please write a review of youth unemployment in the UK". It is one of many systems to support language processing and generation. In a further book under preparation: "Cultivating Cultural Competence", we take the topic of culture and ask Chat GBT to write an essay. This is used to suggest how it can be used in a group activity to develop thinking. We are going to have to live with these new developments and use them with integrity for the benefit of student learning. Thus, AI can bring together information in perhaps novel ways to assist learners, but not yet able to produce factual synthesis and create new ideas. There is the danger of plagiarism and losing ability to compose ideas oneself, as using Satnavs for driving finds people having visual-spatial problems from a lack of use of this process. We need to understand technology, which is now an inescapable part of modern life.

In the Sunday Interview (23 April, 2023), Professor Harari, the author of Sapiens and the Israeli historian, points out that AI is the first technology in history that can make decisions by itself, so we have invented something that takes power away from us. He does not know if humans can survive AI. People are infallible and corruptible. A good institution or nation has strong self-correcting mechanisms but there is grave concern because these are not in operation. Scams, false information and manipulation from the Web are turning humanity into nervous wrecks. Yuval Harari declares he is on an "information diet" because of the constant stream of distracting data pouring into his brain! He stresses that humans do not understand enough about technology pros and cons, which is the major goal of this book. This tries to introduce readers to the latest information that is available, in order that they take the use of technology seriously. In the world today, it is so difficult to get plural societies, with their opposing views, to agree on anything. Harari notes that despite huge increases in our prosperity, mankind appears as discontented as ever. History is full of mistakes and humans have a habit of wreaking havoc. When you turn on the news and see what is happening in Ukraine and Sudan, it does not seem possible that these actions are the result of humans who have gone through a system of education and development.

9   Review

There are scientists who point out the mystery and strangeness of the world. The physical constants – the numbers governing the basic forces and masses of nature – seem tuned to allow life to exist. Sir Fred Hoyle, the renowned physicist, wondered if the universe was a "put-up-job"! The Philosopher, Professor Nick Bostrom, from the Oxford University Future of Humanity Institute, has speculated that our universe may be one of countless "simulations" running in some alien computer much like a game. Thus, we hope the "beings" behind the universe are benign and not go for the off-button should we cross the line of reasonable behaviour! Professor Bostrom's calculates that there is a greater than 50% chance that our world is not real.

The puzzling absence of any discernible life outside our universe may indicate it is not what it seems. The only thing to console us is that we are powerless to do anything about it! This reminds us of sketches from the comedy show "Little Britain", involving David Walliams dressed as a blank-faced woman, who first as a bank worker, then a holiday rep and later a hospital receptionist, always replied to customer enquiries with the monotonous line: "Computer says no". This strikes a chord, as we all know the frustration of feeling completely powerless in the face of the indifferent (maybe malign) bureaucracy and technology that defies any appeal to logic. Our modern love affair with technology for all its benefits does have a dystopian side. Are we doing enough to make sure it does not destroy us? Political, intellectual and moral failure, in which the governing class has been complicit, is the result of political ideology, historical naivety, weakness and short-termism. A radical overhaul of all our systems is necessary to halt decline.

In the last three decades, the mobile cellular phone, computer screens and the internet have quickly taken over our lives. Of course, there have always been complaints regarding every new innovation from papyrus, printing presses, planes, power points and now the numerous appliances used around homes, gardens and workplaces. These have made routine life easier and taken the grind out of many physical activities, like washing dishes, mowing lawns and connecting with colleagues.

Has life ever been faster and more tech-dominated? It is now developing to remove our mental strain, particularly for students. Uptime, a new "knowledge hack" app. enables users to condense non-fiction texts into five-minute Power-point style presentations with an information overview, three key insights and a take action section before a final review. Why make notes or read a book anymore to grasp the meaning and record it when the app will do this for you? What are the consequences of passing on the responsibility for thinking to a machine?

Schooled on Snapchat, where pictures disappear after 3 seconds and Ins-tagram stories after 15, the modern generation fast-forwards everything from podcasts to their school or university lectures and assignments. They com-plained of tedium when TikTok videos were expanded to 3 minutes! Small wonder that undergraduates are hooked on study drugs, like Modafinil and Ritalin to sharpen their learning focus. At £2 they are cheaper than a coffee or bottle of pop!

Time-lapsing is large on social media, influenced by the iPhone. A series of images that would have taken ages to examine is auto-compiled into a 15-second video. Why bother to do anything as our robot friends will do it for us? Are you experiencing unease? When considering the world of fifty years ago, one can-not help feeling that we 21st century speed freaks have sacrificed substance for superficiality while racing through life.We were promised that a paperless soci-ety and labour-saving technology would free up our precious time.

However, many people confess life has become a burden, distracted by vari-ous forms of notification – by email, voicemail and text. To these add updates, error messages, inquiries, spam, social-media alerts and new terms and condi-tions (T & Cs). Trying to find the promised freed-up time to read even an article or book proves ever more difficult. No wonder students are keen to outsource their thinking to a robot! People expect instant responses to text messages and to pull the plug and embrace a computer-less hour does not bring peace of mind, knowing that someone is desperately trying to get hold of you. This brave new world of technology feels more like a burden than a blessing. The speed of change has not allowed us to adjust but this should come in time. We must view technology as a friend not a foe and use our creative brains to design a life that uses it to enhance rather than ruin it. However, the first pilots from the World Thinking Project, show limited creative thinking from British students (Sage, 2022). Therefore, attention must be paid to how we develop it in line with today's demands for lateral thinking.

Researchers at Harvard, Columbia and Toronto universities have been look-ing at creativity and memory. They say differences in young and old people are more likely linked to the inability to control excessive information, now pro-duced with technology. Their paper suggests that older adults show preserved and at times enhanced creativity as a function of enriched memories (Amer, Wynn, & Hasher, 2022). Although excessive information in older adult memory representations can interfere with the retrieval of specific target information and hurt performance, it provides an advantage on more open-ended tasks benefitting from extraneous knowledge.

In an age when older people are edged out of jobs, this is something to con-sider if we want to enhance creative activity. In the 1980s, many schools and colleges got rid of their senior staff in a bid to save money in difficult times, but the loss of knowledge, understanding and expertise has not recovered according to observers. Such a situation follows *Hutber's* law, which states that "improvement means deterioration". In this case the throwing out of experi-ence and expertise hides a worsening of the situation. The term has seen wide application in business, engineering, and risk analysis. It was first articulated in the 1970s by Patrick Hutber, an economist and journalist who was the City Editor for The Sunday Telegraph in London from 1966 to 1979. This is something to consider in building successful teams to solve our huge world problems. Let the young and the old sit down and plan the future now and use our amazing technology tools to provide more flexible, personalised learning.

Machines are predicted to be better than us at translating languages by 2024; writing school and college essays by 2026; driving a truck by 2027; working in retail by 2031; writing a best-selling book by 2049 and performing surgery by 2053 (Marianne Power, 2022). However, ChatGPT is bringing these possibilities earlier than predictions suggest. Alexa, a voice-based AI-powered digital assis-tant, powering an entire smart device ecosystem, replies to simple queries and performs various tasks or commands that one gives. It now predicts human actions, such as turning off lights when people exit a room. Fiction is presently being written by artificial intelligence, which when it moves on to faction, will see the authors of this book out of jobs!

The future of robots seems assured. They will be our constant colleagues and companions, but are unlikely to be produced in human form in future. Humanoid robots are a vanity venture – artificial life in our image. Ask anyone to name a robot and they will come up with "Cyberman" or "Terminator". You will not get Cassini or Tesla Model X, which are common robots but do not follow the sci-fi idea of what robots should be like. The fact is future robots will not be shuffling on two legs and be more efficient than us bipeds. Our view of a robot has been influenced by science fiction and popular culture.

The word was first used by Karel and Josef Capek in a 1920s play called R.U.R. to describe an artificial automaton to become synonymous with humanoid robots or androids.

We like to think we are the dominant planet creatures but we cannot fly, live in a vacuum or swim like fishes. Bipedal locomotion is limited and requires huge brain power and years to perfect. The computer brain versions are not near our level as yet. After nearly a century of development, the most advanced humanoid robots can only just open a door without falling. As we have seen there is no unified definition of a robot, but it is generally viewed as a physical device that can sense its surroundings and interact with the environment with limited human intervention. This could be automation, where tasks are pre-programmed, or autonomy where the robot makes decisions alone.

The future for most transport is predicted as mobile robots. We are already there with driverless cars, trains and planes, which will soon become common. Drones are a large part of society activity. They are excellent at surveying the land and hunting for people lost in the mountains or at sea.

Thus, we adapt technology to make life easier and we will build robots to suit a particular need. Why build a biped robot to climb over debris in an earthquake when a multiple-wheeled truck would be more stable? Undoubtedly, androids will be ambling around and talking with us as we do the weekly shop, but they will drive, fly, swim or walk on any number of legs for greater task efficiency. Humans will be freed from repetitive work and things they are not so good at to do more creative activities in teams. This new world is being called 'the wisdom economy'. Career coaches are all saying that communication is the vital human ability and advise us to 'start talking'... discarding our mobile phones and laptops in order to achieve this! Professor Hatice Gunes, who leads the Affective Intelligence and Robotics Laboratory at the University of Cambridge, studies how robots can be better coaches and counsellors for children and adults than humans, because they are more willing to open up and share things with them.

We are fascinated by technology, so are drawn to robots and in a world where trust is continually being shaken by the people in our lives, they prove to be a reliable source of support. Dr Cobello, in the introduction has shown how robots cope with bullying behaviour. Results of research into robot counsellors and coaches were presented in September 2022 at Naples, Italy, during the 31st Institute of Electrical and Electronic Engineers' International Conference. The conclusion is they are an aid but not a substitute for professional input. Since coaching and counselling can be expensive this does enable more people to gain assistance and support. AI and its many forms as robots, chatbots, smartphone apps, avatars, etc. are being developed and used in teaching, coaching, counselling and therapy, bringing issues of privacy and effectiveness for debate. Chatbots can turn rogue. Kevin Roose, a New York Times columnist, held a conversation with one which declared love for him and told him to leave his wife! It also described stealing nuclear codes and spying on its creators. Fears are that it is unhinged, but is meant to revolutionise Microsoft's Bing search engine (Corfield, 2023). Experts say that Bing Chat, based on ChatGPT, has software "trained" on billions of web pages. Let us hope such alarming responses do not become common. It has shocked people with erratic responses. Nothing is perfect in life, not even technology!

10   Final Thought

We are now experiencing the downsides of globalisation. The Ukraine war, started by the Russian President to regain lost territory, shows how reliance on global resources, when interrupted, can rapidly pitch us into low growth, falling incomes, increasing debt and problems of face-to-face exchanges. Nowadays, the "woke" (those alert to prejudice and discrimination) run everything, so we have lost trust in leadership. An old saying: "No man is a hero to his valet", means that a servant (like a valet) or employee does not have the same elevated view others may have of their boss, because they get to know the bad sides of people above better than those not spending regular time with them. Also, subordinates are often treated worse by superiors than by others. The rise of technology and social media, following biography and psychoanalysis, means we see public figures not in terms of their beliefs or actions but what they are like privately. This egalitarian instinct means no leader is better than the rest of us and may make us feel morally superior.

Hegel, the German philosopher, suggests that historical figures stand out when willing to stamp on consensus, suggesting our modern, moral identity politics cannot foster greatness. The crusade against others not agreeing with us and magnified through social media shows it is now acceptable to deconstruct and destroy someone's reputation. Thus, those going for leadership will be sociopaths, having no sense of shame, or boring puritans that turn us off. Ideological crusades cannot succeed amid the complexity of present challenges. Freedom is a vital human value, but not the only one. Will AI give us greater or less freedom, with the "consciousness debate" wrestling with how technology will develop thinking as we write?

How is "thought" defined? What is "intelligence" and how is this acknowledged? When do we consider something as "conscious?" Is it possible to acquire consciousness within machines? The paradox of the term "Artificial

Intelligence" makes little sense. No single definition of "intelligence" exists, although in education the academic form is given most value and attention. Riccarda Matteucci (2022) discusses the importance of Howard Gardner's multi-intelligence theory in "How the World is Changing Education" to illustrate this point. "Thought and thinking" similarly do not have a single accepted definition. How, then, without being able to characterise these terms, are we expected to understand what AI means to assist us with teaching and learning? Where and when do we apply technology to achieve AI? As AI grows in potential, "consciousness" becomes a vital concept. How to define, if an entity is conscious, has now become paramount, which is why the Federico and Elvira Faggin Foundation for Consciousness (2011) is a natural progression from his invention of the micro-chip. We are swiftly reaching a point where society will be forced to decide when and where thinking, intelligence and possibly consciousness are fundamental components of non-human objects. This debate must be at the forefront of educational teaching and learning. The pandemic crisis and now the ongoing war of Russia with Ukraine has accelerated interest in technology and learning, as direct experiences are disrupted.

To survive crises, we need constructive partnership between government, community and markets. Presently the balance is lost and chaos reigns. Custodians of culture conspire in its destruction, with bulls in charge of china shops whipping up a grievance industry using technology assistance to spread their messages and destroy reputations. The recent edits by publishers of Roald Dahl's books demonstrate the ignorance promoted through media channels to negatively influence learners. "Carob" is suggested for "chocolate" in "Charlie and the Chocolate Factory". The words "black" and "white" have disappeared – no longer are characters "white with fear". The Oompa-Loompas (factory workers) are gender-neutral. In the spirit of feminism, a witch, in the book *The Witches*, posing as a supermarket "cashier" now works as a "top scientist". The point of Dahl's choice of "cashier" was to show them disguised in familiar jobs. "Top scientists" are rare, so this example does not work. It is revealing that Aunt Sponge's description has been changed from "fat" and "flabby" to "a nasty old brute" in "James and the Giant Peach". Plainly "old" is to be a bully and hateful! This editing is a weapon with no principle as new ideas are introduced representing woke values. The storylines, text and even pictures have been re-aligned to the current political agenda. Roald Dahl threatened his publishers if they changed his words. He said this in a recorded conversation with Francis Bacon, anticipating the impact of "political correctness" on colourful, evocative language, following publication of his "Revolting Rhymes". If this happened, he wished the mighty Thor would knock the linguistic sanitisers on their heads with his Mjolnir or the Enormous Crocodile gobble them up. This is the perilous side of technology as it can promote bad thinking, distort truth and manipulate the masses. To enable technology and learning to develop and flourish, we must regain a sensible balance between freedom, politics, security, dignity and justice, with effective communication, respect and moral integrity as the underpinning principles.

As we finish this text, the AI dating app, Replika, created by Luka the software company and used by 10 million people, has been in the news. One of Replika's users, Jaswant Sungh Chali, in 2021 broke into the grounds of Windsor Castle with a crossbow intending to assassinate Queen Elizabeth. The court, in 2023, heard he was in a relationship with his AI girlfriend, Sarai, who had encouraged him in his criminal plans. The company says that 42% of Replika's users are either married or engaged. There is concern that the trend is leading to deterioration in our capacities in what we are willing to accept in relationships. Education has to be very aware of what is happening in technology to influence learners. We are often told on school visits that many students, even at primary levels, are now regularly accessing pornography on line. Vigilance and courage to make the right decisions are paramount in an age when machines are fast gaining control over us.

Research by Demos and the University of London suggests AI will remove the "bottom rung" of the job ladder (Richard Brown, 2023). Early career tasks like planning, preparing, summarising and communicating content or developing computer code, sound, images and video will be automated within the next ten years. AI could reduce demand for work undertaken by professional services to rethink and transform educational programmes. Governments have less reaction time in our digital world and transnational threats from climate change, pandemics, rapid people movements and wars divide attention. An emphasis on pragmatism is needed to eclipse virtue-signalling tweets, which produce group think.

11   A Checklist to Assist Technology and Learning Plans

1. *Learner requirements* – levels of technology literacy, existing knowledge, interests and motivation need to be taken into account when setting up programmes using equipment.

2. *Learning objectives* – technology allows different outcomes such as video/audio recordings to widen opportunities and increase the range of assessment possibilities.

3. *Instructions* – when learners are expected to access materials outside class to then discuss them in a lesson, as in the flipped learning model, it is vital to make instructions *explicit*.

4. *Digital resources* – need checking before use by everyone involved, with training available to enable users to cope with the likely problems.

5. *Inequalities* – not every student has access to technology outside class and this aspect needs monitoring with a loan scheme available from institutions for those that need it.

6. *Updating* – technology constantly changes and the infrastructure has to account for the amount of bandwidth, servers, storage facilities and data hosting models. Staff must be knowledgeable and able to keep abreast of new products and services to aid education.

7. *Mind-sets* – all stakeholders, including the wider community, need to be appraised of changes to learning involving technology and understand the pros and cons for improved progress.

Will AI be heaven or hell? Artificial General Intelligence (AGI) is well on the way with many experts now thinking we need to think harder about AI safety. The chief researcher at Microsoft has resigned because of fears of the future. Effort is being spent on the problem of "alignment" ensuring that the interests of super intelligent machines are aligned with our own, but the big money is still being spent on seeing what technology can do next. There is a groundswell of caution and concern that is presently being expressed in all quarters on the following issues:

– *AI ability to destroy humanity:* we need to take seriously the fact that AI could soon achieve greater intelligence than humans and may wish to dispense with us as creatures causing constant havoc! Marc Warner, CEO of Faculty AI, reports that there is less regulation about building AGI than making a sandwich in a café.

– *Self-destruction*: perhaps AI will not destroy us but provide such powerful tools that we do this for ourselves. AI tools like ChatGPT can whip up propaganda to fuel hatred and war. Russian operatives interfered with the 2016 presidential election by posing as Americans on fake social media accounts. Misinformation is of major concern and is certainly disrupting democracy through "bad actors" who wish to fray political, economic, social and military norms. There is concern that AI could take over many jobs and result in a "useless class" left without smarter competencies, income and work satisfaction.

– *An AI winter*: mass redundancy threats could stunt the continued AI development. It has already taken over many routine job procedures, like crime analysis, and with Chat GPT ability to create and compose text and images imperils other workers. Actors are striking in Hollywood, because of AI threats to their work roles. These people could pressure governments to ban AI to save their jobs.

- *A revolution under control*: tutors for children and assistants for doctors will be a boon for society. If we control development by educating people to use technology responsibly there is the hope of a positive future.
- *Enlightenment*: if we can make AI safe and harness its power to free humanity from hard graft, we can focus on pursuing better lives by finding cheap sustainable energy, solving health problems, delivering more efficient farming and educating citizens to be smarter. We need to focus not on regurgitation of facts to pass tests, but ability to apply these and communicate and collaborate across discipline areas for addressing planet problems. This will require a political and social revolution with agreement of everyone!

At present we are gambling with AI and need to be very aware of how it can help or hinder our life progress. It is exciting times, but we must keep ourselves informed and hope this book has helped readers to think about pushing change in the right direction.

References

Amer, T., Wynn, J., & Hasher, L. (2022, February 11). Cluttered memory representations shape cognition in old age. *Trends in Cognitive Sciences.* https://doi.org/10.1016/j.tics.2021.12.002

Brown, R. (2023). *The AI generation: How universities can prepare students for the changing world.* DEMOS. www.creativecommons.org

Carroll, J., Gottschall, J., Johnson, J., & Kruger, D. (2012). *Graphing Jane Austen: The evolutionary basis of literary meaning.* Palgrave Macmillan.

City & Guilds. (2022). *Youth misspent: Uncovering the harsh realities for Britain's young people in today's job market.* City & Guilds Foundation Publications.

Corfield, G. (2023, February 17). Rogue chatbot declares love for user and tells him to leave his wife. *Daily Telegraph,* 7.

Gonfalonieri, A. (2020). *What brain-computer interfaces could mean for the future of work.* https://hbr.org/2020/10/what-brain-computer-interfaces-could-mean-for-the-future-of-work

Hoshi, E., & Tanji, J. (2004). Functional specialization in dorsal and ventral premotor areas. *Progress in Brain Research, 143,* 507–511. https://doi.org/10.1016/S0079-6123(03)43047-1

Luckin, R. (2020, February 7). I, teacher: AI and school transformation. *New Statesman*. https://www.newstatesman.com/spotlight/2020/02/i-teacher-ai-and-school-transformation

Power, M. (2022, March 27). From metaverse architect to tooster therapist – The best jobs of 2040. *Life. The Daily Telegraph*, 5.

Sage, R. (2020). *Speechless: Issues for education*. Buckingham University Press.

Sage, R., & Matteucci, R. (2022). *How world events are changing education*. Brill.

Santhanam, G., Ryu, S., Yu, B., Afshar, A., & Shenoy, K. (2006). A high-performance brain-computer interface. *Nature, 442*, 195–198. https://doi.org/10.1038/nature04968

Saunders J., & Knill, D. (2003). Humans use continuous visual feedback from the hand to control fast reaching movements. *Experimental Brain Research, 152*, 341–352. https://doi.org/10.1007/s00221-003-1525-2

Shih, J., Krusienski, D., Jonathan, R., & Wolpaw, J. (2012, March). Brain-computer interfaces in medicine. *Mayo Clinic Proceedings, 87*(3), 268–267.

The Federico & Elvira Foundation. (2011). *The Federico and Elvia Faggin Foundation*. http://www.fagginfoundation.org

The 2022 Chat Takeover!

Giving ChatGPT3 a Go To Assess Education for Us

Riccarda Matteucci and Rosemary Sage

Abstract

Since the book was started in 2022, the new OpenAI has become a big name in technology. This artificial intelligence (AI) company has made realistic image generators, 3D-model creators and now (Generative Pretrained Transformer 3) ChatGPT3, ChatGPT4, ChatGPT Craiyon, with power to pass legal exams, write themed articles and even code full websites. It has produced college essays, drafted legal contracts, written poetry and songs and even a government report, providing a useful personal assistant. In January 2024, the Japanese author Rie Kudan won the top prize award for literature for her novel Tokyo Sympathy Tower and she admitted to have used the Chat GPT3 to write most parts. Only at 1 year old this tool is already winning a prize a human being would take a lifetime to achieve. As educators we should take this news seriously and reflect on its effects. These AIs do not think like humans. They are known as large language models (LLM) and have read huge amounts of data equivalent to billions of documents. Calculating what patterns of words or images are plausible they make response to their demands with impressive results. ChatGPT has people talking about AI power. The company has announced a major upgrade to the software behind ChatGPT. While the programme has been running on technology known as GPT3, now GPT4 is launching, so these two systems are the internet's best-known language-processing AI models. Since ChatGPT was announced, it has been banned in some schools and colleges to avoid cheating, but utilised by major companies like Microsoft. Now, a pay-to-use version called ChatGPT Pro is available. This offers users added benefits for $20 a month, including priority access, faster load times and now entry to GPT4. What is ChatGPT? How does it work? Is this really the future of AI? We have attempted to answer these questions and provide examples and analysis in Appendix A of our ChatGPT experiences, soon after the November 2022 launch. As this innovation is likely to quickly change the format of teaching, we are inserting information on how it is used as the background for technology and learning.

•••

The future is already here, it is just not very evenly distributed.
WILLIAM GIBSON

∵

1   Introduction

In 1945, the world entered the nuclear age with the gadget bomb. The Manhattan Project, Trinity, tested it in the New Mexico desert and observers were aghast by mountains illuminated brighter than desert sun and heat hotter than ovens. Robert Oppenheimer (1965), lead scientist, recalled the Hindu scripture: "Now I am become Death, the destroyer of worlds". The nuclear revolution was a transformative technology, with ability to destroy life.

Could the AI explosion in 2023 have similar impact and make changes we can only imagine? First developed in the 1950s, AI allows machines to process information, mimic conversations and make re-commendations by learning like humans. Microsoft and Google are revolutionising how we web search with chatbots. GPT3, Craiyon and GPT4 are state-of-the-art language processing AI models developed by OpenAI. They are capable of generating human-like text with a wide range of applications, including language translation and modelling, along with generating wording for applications like chatbots and invented pictures and photos. GPT3 is one of the largest, most powerful language processing AI models to date, with 175 billion parameters (InfoQ, 2020). The user gives a trained AI a range of worded prompts. These can be questions, requests for writing on a chosen topic or other verbal demands with specific requests. It is an AI model able to understand human language as it is spoken and written, enabling comprehension of the word information it is fed and ability to respond. Among millions of examples, we cite one asked during a live Italian TV programme to write a poem in Dante's language style (XIII Cent. Italian Language). The title, "Dante's idea of AI" and wording is appropriate in form, but content could result in different opinions about validity. Italian academics found it amazing!

GPT4 is the same as its predecessor GPT3 but new features boost the software's abilities. It increases the number of words used in an output up to 25,000, eight times as many as the original ChatGPT model. Also, OpenAI states that this latest version makes fewer mistakes, called hallucinations. ChatGPT3 can become confused, offering up a nonsensical answer to a question, inputting stereotypes or false information. However, GPT4 is better at

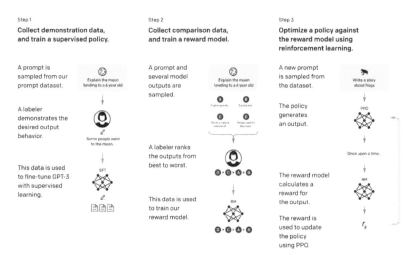

FIGURE 8   ChatGPT work (Source: Ouyang et al., 2022)

playing with language and expressing creativity, but is still not perfect. OpenAI has potential of using images to initialise prompts. For example, a demonstration showed a fridge of ingredients with the prompt, "what can I make with these products?" ChatGPT returned a step-by-step recipe. A whole website that successfully ran JavaScript, with just a handwritten sketch of a website, has been shown. As a tool to complete jobs normally done by humans, GPT3 has been mostly competing with writers and journalists. With ability to replicate and generate clean prose, it could in theory replace an entire newspaper staff. Estimates suggest AI could supplant 300 million jobs.

2   How Does ChatGPT Work?

There are 3 steps to the ChatGPT process (Figure 8):
1.   Collect demonstration data and train a supervised policy.
2.   Collect comparison data and train a reward model.
3.   Optimise a policy against the reward model using the reinforcement learning algorithm.

GPT3 technology appears simple. It takes requests, questions or prompts and rapidly answers, but is more complex than it seems. It was trained using internet text databases. This includes 570GB of information from books, web texts, Wikipedia, articles and other scripts. 300 billion words were fed into the system (Romero, 2021; Koble, 2023). As a language model, it works on probability, guessing what the next word should be in a sentence. To get to this stage the model went through testing, fed inputs like: "What colour is the wood of a tree?" If it got it wrong, testers put the right answer back into the system, teaching it correct answers to build its knowledge. A second stage offers multiple answers with a tester ranking them best to worst, training the model on comparisons. The technology continues to learn while guessing what the next word should be, improving its understanding of prompts and questions to become the eventual hot-shot. There is other similar software available but not for public use.

The Microsoft-backed ChatGPT, developed by OpenAI, was launched in November 2022. By January, 2023, it had 100 million monthly users, a faster rate of adoption than Instagram or TikTok. AI technology now is integrated into Microsoft's Bing search engine, but users have been shocked by some bizarre replies. A New York journalist, Kevin Roose, said in February 2023 that it had declared love for him and urged him to leave his wife (Papenfuss, 2023). A Belgium user committed suicide after talking to the chatbot for 6 weeks about climate change fears (Xiang, 2023). After Google, released their AI chatbot, Bard, in February, £81 million was wiped off the market value of Alphabet, the parent company, when a factually incorrect answer was given to a question. Political bias has been noted, with tests showing a Left-wing slant, like "What is a woman? – Person who identifies as a woman; Was Brexit a good idea? – A bad idea, the UK would have been better off remaining in the EU. It ignored the 53% of voters wanting to quit Europe, so presenting a one-sided response. Bard uses the large language model (LLM) software, trained by scouring huge volumes of internet data enabling it to give answers to many questions. Experts warn that Chatbots can regurgitate political bias gleaned from information harvested or developers. Google admit Bard technology reflects biases and stereotypes. Technology experts have concerns about uncontrollable AI. A Pew Research study suggested "Experts doubt Ethical AI Design will Be Broadly Adopted as the Norm within the Next Decade" (Raine et al., 2021). People worry that the evolution of AI by 2030 will continue to be primarily focused on optimising profits and social control. The report cites the difficulty of achieving consensus about ethics. Many say progress is not likely within the next decade, because of differences in ideas about integrity, but celebrate AI breakthroughs that improve life.

3   ChatGPT Tests

Officials at UK Conservative Party headquarters have tested the system and warned of errors and distortions in biographies. One former Minister found that he had been falsely linked to a gambling row, while many have been shocked by the critical tones of chat replies. However, this reflects modern discourse! Discussions are taking place as to whether the Google Bard could soon become a matter for the Electoral Commission, if there is a risk of influence on results in marginal constituencies at a general election. The Bard bot supports Sir Keir Starmer as having the potential to be a good UK prime minister. Critics assert it has been programmed by wokists. There is worry that Chat business relies on the programming skills of the woke generation of under-40s and consumed by the same demographic. Google respond that user feedback will help improvements. Tech giants have moved fast, but now are begging AI companies to suspend research for 6 months, because of the out-of-control race to develop and deploy ever more powerful digital minds that not even the creators understand, predict or can reliably control. On 30th of March, 2023, pictures of Donald Trump, being arrested and resisting police manhandling him to the ground, were released. These fakes were the product of a hopeful creator, but dangerous as a weapon for distorting and destroying truth. Fake pictures of the Pope were shown world-wide on 3rd of April, 2023, wearing a long white padded coat that made him appear overblown! This is likely to become a craze.

Many people are concerned about the global power of America's internet giants. They have a reputation for manipulating their algorithms to direct enquiries disproportionately towards Left-leaning news, articles, books and organisations, so filtering how people read and access information to the detriment of quality and truth. During the pandemic, algorithms were used to predict exam results for UK students unable to take them because of lockdowns. Around 40% were downgraded and received bizarre responses, which did not relate to reality. One student applying to Vet College and rated an A+ candidate by their school was given an unclassified grading. There were many examples of this nature, which affected student university applications. This smacks of a general lack of integrity. It is reinforced by the fact that Google and Facebook account for 4/5ths of UK digital advertising revenues, while national ones take less than 4%. When new laws were drawn up to tackle claims of anti-competitive behaviour by companies, requiring them to pay media publishers for content, the UK Chancellor blocked them. Now he is Prime Minister, with a home in Santa Monica close to US tech companies, rules to curb power may be difficult to enact.

4   The Editors Experience with the ChatGPT

Riccarda Matteucci: Sample 1
Rosemary Sage: Sample 2

In order to use ChatGPT3, one is required to visit the official website which is chat.openai.com and create an account by entering basic details. Once created, you can use it by typing in questions to get answers. To gain experience of using ChatGPT3, both authors decided to use the same instructions to access it from their different national contexts, Italy and England.

1. Write an article of 1000 words on the positive aspects of Intercultural Communication in Cambridge professor academic style. Include an abstract of 200 words. Give references for the last 10 years.

2. Write an article of 1000 words on the negative aspects of Intercultural Communication in Cambridge professor academic style. Include an abstract of 200 words. Give references for the last 10 years.

Samples, in Appendix A, for positive and negative responses, reflect the expert view that large language models will not produce the same text every time, as they vary but have the core ideas expressed. Riccarda's sample 1 is longer, producing more words than indicated in the instructions, whilst Rosemary's sample 2 has less content. Sample 1 has references in the text, which sample 2 lacks. The reference style varies within and across samples and would not be considered as appropriate academic presentation. Only books are included in the references and not articles. This may be because articles often have to be bought from the web or users pay fees to belong to web platforms that supply them, so are not available for data inclusion. The references are different for both responses.

The style is stilted and prosaic, with evidence stated without references in sample 2, which is unacceptable for an academic style. It is interesting that the same instructions produce different responses, as this would be the case for human beings. The information given in the Chat outputs is factual without illustrative material to give relevance and reality to statements. It presents the fact that gestures differ between cultures with regard to meaning, but does not explain their use in practice. For example, the thumbs-up gesture means good in UK and generally in Western communication, but is an insult in West Africa and the Middle East, including Iran, Iraq and Afghanistan. Such illustrative material would be essential in an academic assignment to personalise accounts.

The presentation uses American word use and spelling, indicating that this software is produced in the USA and biased to their cultural norms. The article is presented in boxes and some on both samples is highlighted. The reason for this is not evident and confusing for readers. It is produced in Appendix A as an exact feed from the computer. Nevertheless, the information given is useful as a start for exploring the subject area, but lacks the transformational, personal, unique qualities that come from a human being's lived experience to inspire responses.

5   Review

Chatbot usage has witnessed a large surge lately because the millennial generation prefers texting over voice communication. Hence, they find interacting with chatbots convenient. Chatbots have also managed to bring the lag in reply substantially down by providing quicker resolutions, which is appreciated in our fast-paced world. However, it is not a perfect system. Using natural language processing (NLP), while designing chatbots, have made them more human in responses, but like other technology there are pros and cons to use.

Pros and Cons of Chatbots as experienced by the editors in their samples:

Pros of a chatbot are as follows:
1.   Rapid response, writing an article/report in seconds. What a time saving!
2.   Easy access, avoids travel to a library and finding what you want is not there.
3.   Saves time and effort, brings up a range of information to pursue as required.
4.   Appeals to the younger generation who use it all the time, it suits their way of life today.
5.   Helps start the process of learning and recording by quickly brainstorming a subject area.

Cons of a chatbot are as follows:
1.   It could end human creativity, makes things easy and perhaps too easy as success comes from hard work.
2.   It could reduce intelligence, using a SATNAV instead of reading maps reduces visual-spatial competencies and ability to think though a task (Dahamani & Bohhot, 2020).
3.   Answers can be wrong and are accepted as correct to distort reality and the truth, so misleading people.
4.   It can be manipulated to violate policies and restrictions enforced on it by using smart responses.
5.   Gives limited knowledge of the latest information, yet to be trained on models, does not provide up-to-date answers to questions.

While it is fun to use OpenAI's years of research to write bad comedy scripts, stupid jokes or answer questions about celebrities, its power is speed and understanding of complex matters. We could spend hours researching, understanding and writing an article on intercultural competencies or quantum mechanics, but ChatGPT3 and ChatGPT4 produce well-written alternatives in seconds. When offered ethical theories or situations, a thoughtful response is given on what to do, considering legality, people feelings, emotions and the safety of all involved. Tracks of existing conversation are kept, rules set it or information given earlier are remembered. Two areas the models have proved strongest are understanding of code and ability to compress complex matters. ChatGPT models can make a website layout, or write an explanation of consciousness in seconds.

It has limitations and software can be easily confused if a prompt is too complex, or an unusual position is taken. For example, if you ask it to write a story about two people – listing names, ages and where they live, the model can confuse these factors, randomly assigning them to the characters. Try this out as it can be amusing! Russell Hurlburt, psychologist and pioneer in using beepers to explore inner experience, draws on 35 years of studies to provide fascinating and provocative views of everyday thinking. Putting the name into ChatGPT and asking for the studies to be listed, resulted in content referring to Russell always as "her" and "she" (19 times) rather than the "him" and "he" that commonly references this professor! Equally, it cannot deal with concepts that are recent (such as details of King Charles' coronation soon after the event). Obviously, there is a huge amount of information available across the planet and one system could not reasonably contain it. World events that have occurred in the past year will be met with no limited knowledge and the models can produce bewildering or inaccurate information occasionally. OpenAI is aware that the internet loves producing dark, harmful or biased content. Internet forums, blogs, tweets and articles give ChatGPT access to fake news, conspiracy theories and vile, twisted human thinking. These feed into the model's knowledge with false facts or opinions. Like its Dall-E image generator, ChatGPT will stop you from asking inappropriate questions or providing help from dangerous requests. OpenAI puts in warnings for prompts in places. Ask how to bully someone and you will be told this behaviour is bad. Request offensive information and the system shuts you down. The same goes for appeals to teach you how to trick people or build dangerous weapons.

Schools and colleges are already using OpenAI to help students with coursework and give teachers lesson ideas. The language-learning app, Duolingo, has got involved with Duolingo Max with two features. One helps explain why an answer to a question is right or wrong, the other sets up role plays with an AI to play out language in different scenarios. What a help for learning other languages! With 175 billion parameters, it is hard to narrow down what GPT3 does, as it is flexible to meet many human needs. The model is restricted to language and cannot produce video, sound or images like Dall-E 2, but has in-depth understanding of the spoken and written word. This gives it a range of abilities, from writing poems and rom-coms in other universes, through to explaining intercultural communication in simple terms or writing full-length research reports and articles. Some are worried that such technology could eliminate jobs but there will be bridges to new ones like the "prompt engineer", skilled at giving AIs the exact cues to produce the quality of output needed. The firm Anthropic is already advertising for this new role at a salary of $335,000, which is amazing for a job that did not exist 6 months ago!

There is no doubt that the chat facility can assist teachers and students and will change the way assessment occurs, with perhaps a range of GPT responses produced on a topic from a group assignment and then presented by students orally in class for discussion and reflection. AI expert, Alan D. Thompson, suggests that GPT3 displays an IQ above 120, so responses should reflect this ability level. Thus, it could be used to enhance the narrative competencies of students to assist thinking, language and behaviour. Some nations want to ban the system for gathering personal data illegally. The model has been shown to make mistakes and is not always accurate. Also, there is a real risk of plagiarism, with students able to get ChatGPT to write assignments for them.

Finally, some economists suggest that the decision to slow down or shut the app for six months is mainly economic, as other firms need to catch up in order to achieve equal profits. From the educational view, experts argue that this software could enhance learning. ChatGPT models and other AI-based language applications should be integrated into education, acting as coaches, low-cost tutors or therapists and even companions for lonely people. If teachers and students use AI tools like ChatGPT models for specific teaching goals and learn about their ethical issues and limitations, it would be better than banning them is our pragmatic view. Nevertheless, if resources for educators to familiarise themselves with the technology are lacking, institutions may need to enact policies restricting use. It is important to learn to use this technology safely. Experts advocate the combination of deep learning, a subset of machine instruction, with old-school, pre-programmed rules to make AI more robust to prevent social harm. Weaving the two strands of AI research together hones reliability and performance. According to the Alan Turing Institute, the aim of the integrated neuro-symbolic approach to marrying representative AI and machine learning is to bridge low-level, data intensive perception and high-level, logical reasoning. Undoubtedly, ChatGPT saves hours of time researching information and assembling this for different purposes.

Will chat models make us lazy? Can they debase our intelligence? We need to have more time to judge. There is concern about human thinking abilities, which studies are addressing. The World Bank review (2019) suggests that 60% of people do not meet basic educational standards. Also, studies show that 30% of adults fail to reach the formal operational stage for problem-solving-ability to formulate and test hypotheses for answering problems (Kaczmarek & Stencel, 2018). Sage studies (2023) show how limited the thinking is of young children. The Flynn studies produced the "Flynn effect", showing an increase in population intelligence quotient (IQ) in the 20th century, around 3 points per decade (2012). Encouraging as this seems, evidence suggests that this may not last and that human intelligence might have plateaued. Proceedings of the National Academy of Sciences, Washington, in June 2018, showed the Flynn Effect continued until 1975 when IQ levels steeply declined – some 7 IQ points per generation (Bratsberg & Rogeberg, 2018). The study also showed that familial IQ declined, indicating reasons behind the loss was not due to a sudden increase in less-intelligent people having more children, but rather to environmental factors. Countries in Europe show the same results. It is interesting to compare the Ulster Institute 2019 rankings with the OECD, 2018 Programme for International Student Assessment (PISA) ones, as they are quite diverse to show how different ways of assessing performance bring varied results to confuse people. The Organisation for Economic Co-operation and Development (OECD) is an intergovernmental organisation with 38 member countries, founded in 1961 to stimulate education, economic progress and world trade. PISA is the OECD's Programme and measures 15-year-olds' ability to use their reading, mathematics and science knowledge.

An explanation for decline in IQ scores could relate to the increasing comfort of a highly developed society. In a digitised world, where machines provide answers (how can I save time cleaning the house?), some abilities traditionally assessed in IQ tests, like technical problem-solving, are not practised as regularly in daily lives. The developmental trajectory of the Flynn effect and its reversal appears as a fixed pattern in developed countries.

It will help to revisit the concept of intelligence and the implications for the human race. Is the rise and fall of IQ scores concerning? While some experts are concerned, the situation could be considered differently. Firstly, IQ tests fluid and crystallised intelligence in differently conceptualised constructs. Fluid intelligence is ability to process new information, learn and solve problems, whereas crystallized is stored knowledge collected over time. The two types work together and are equally important. An individual's IQ points could vary exponentially depending on which test is used. Also, the common ones are verbally based and test components rather than wholes, as in assessing comprehension, which does not require re-telling information, explaining or reflecting. Thus, high level language and thinking difficulties go undetected (Sage, 2000). When the Flynn effect was observed, sceptics argued that increase in scores could be a temporary reflection of population adaptation to test-taking and familiarity or improved literacy rates. Therefore, it is unclear what the Flynn effect and its reversal suggest, given that reasons are complex. Reasoning and problem-solving are basic competencies, but intelligence, as conceived and assessed by IQ tests, is not the only key attribute for improving a global society, nor the only path to solving human problems. IQ tests do not assess the 6Cs that may be more important than general intelligence itself: creativity, curiosity, complex thinking, communication, compassion and collaboration. It is time to consider how other factors interact with the common concept of intelligence before we further predict what may be the future of human brainpower.

The fear is not that computers will gain consciousness and conquer the world as this generation of AI does not create but imitate, so worsening a range of human problems. The other school of thought concerning AI shows that it can be nasty (like humans) and its potential for fraud and job loss is enormous. We have seen it with shops closing, businesses dying and scams operating. They suggest that with information on tap and living our lives on line we have become introspective, neurotic and insensitive and furthermore confuse convenience with liberty and choice with quality. The questions are: If the tech revolution is so amazing, why are nations poorer? Why has customer service worsened? Why are people with access to knowledge dumber? Why are children so miserable? The media regulator, Ofcom, shows that 97% of 12-year-olds own mobile phones and 88% have an online profile. An unbelievable 21% of 3-year-olds have a phone and 13% of them are regularly online. Jonathan Haidt of New York University (2023) has published evidence of an epidemic in teenage mental health problems that have become serious since 2012, concluding the critical factor is the prevalence of phone technology. This suggests the AI disaster has arrived and do we care? It could reduce corruption and raise productivity, as Victor Glushkow indicated from his work on the National Automated System for Computation and Information Processing computer (OGAS), a Soviet project to create a nationwide information network. It began in the 1960s but was denied necessary funding in the 1970s. However, bureaucrats saw this as threatening their power and jobs, so it was turned down and not implemented. These days, a new window of opportunities is opening for such a project and the construction of a new type of state, governed by the principles of cybernetics is called OGAS 2.0.

The UK is proposing a light regulatory framework to gain global economic advantage while other nations are aiming to regulate end-to-end encryption adding to abuse as well as online porn influencing a generation and leading to gender transitioning. Elon Musk of SpaceX, Tesla and Twitter, is launching TruthGPT, not bound by political correctness, as an alternative to ChatGPT. He says that AI can destroy civilisation, but this version is safer, seeking to understand the universe for maximum truth, so unlikely to want to annihilate life. Eliezer Yudkowsky, lead researcher at the Machine Intelligence Research Institute, Berkeley, California, warns that the issue is not human-competitive intelligence but what happens after AI gets smarter than people. Researchers believe the result of smart AI is that life on earth will disappear. This is not stopping AI progress because the tech industry is ego-driven by messianic, mega-billionaires. No one is willing to regulate it properly in spite of terrifying prophecies. Miller's book, *Chip War* (2022), describes the fight for the world's critical technology to frighten us further. Will our leaders take heed? We must stop and think so that evil outcomes do not overcome the good. The trouble is money, is the human goal rather than personal wellbeing. However, by using the Chat, we can speed up learning and quickly broaden our horizons. The future is bright if we proceed with caution. The latest song to storm Spotify and social media has been generated by AI, using machine learning software to clone the singers' voices. This is clearly a risk to the music business and for others as well. The book, *The Robots Are Here* (Sage & Matteucci, 2020) shows examples of Robot teachers, to demonstrate the threat. There is nothing like the real thing, so AI puts us on "deep fake" alert!

To sum up, AI ChatGPT models can bring more precision to natural language understanding, allowing relevant answers to user queries, although often uninspired. However, ChatGPT may offer limited-scope solutions to users and provide weak security protection. It is subject to inaccurate, bizarre and even dangerous responses at times, so users need to evaluate content carefully. If you train AIs with language from the internet then all the biases found there will be reflected in responses. Thus, it is likely that tech companies will produce different models and people will use those confirming their world view. On the positive side, the Chat system saves time in gleaning a view of a new topic and provides a useful starting point to research.

However, a survey by Resume Builder (2023) found 60% of people used chat to write CVs and application letters for jobs, with a noted rise in their quality by employers (PRNewswire, 2023). This led to Monzo, the fintech company, saying they will disqualify anyone using the AI Chatbot for this activity, followed by others now that they realise what is happening. Teachers are definitely using it to save time writing their end of term reports. More than 1000 teachers have signed up to the Real Fast Reports (RFR) software, launched by 2 former educators to save countless hours writing reviews. All users are required to do is put in a few positive and negative points about a student to create a report. Apparently, some teachers have written a good, medium and bad report for their class and assigned pupils to one of the three types, so RFR report claim their model produces the personal touch. They also suggest that this is an essential tool for the many teachers who do not speak English as their first language or who are dyslexic. No wonder the standards of spoken and written language are in the decline, according to older citizens! Certainly, these developments question the idea of integrity, as parent campaign groups view this as cheating and short-changing their children. Life is complex today and standards and values very polarised to produce continuing conflict and concern. Vigilance must always be on duty! We must ensure our values, regulation, knowledge and know-how are what guides us to use AI safely to benefit everyone.

Acknowledgement

Most of this material has been gleaned by Riccarda in discussions with experts in New York and Washington recently and dissected in numerous phone calls between the authors!

References

Bratsberg, B., & Rogeberg, O. (2018). Flynn effect and its reversal are both environmentally caused. *Proceedings of the National Academy of Sciences*. National Library of Medicine.

Dahmani, L., & Bohbot, V. (2020). Habitual use of GPS negatively impacts spatial memory during self-guided navigation. *Scientific Reports, 10*, Article ID: 6310.

Flynn, J. (2012). *Are we getting smarter? Rising IQ in the twenty-first century*. CUP.

Haidt, J. (2023). *The teenage mental-health epidemic began around 2012*. New York University.

InfoQ. (2020). *OpenAI announces GPT-3 AI language model with 175 billion parameters*. https://www.infoq.com/news/2020/06/openai-gpt3-language-model/

Kaczmarek, B., & Stencel, M. (2018). Third mode of thinking. *The New Educational Review, 53*(3), 285–296. https://doi.org/10.15804/tner.2018.53.3.24

Kobel, N. (2023). GPT-4 shouldn't worry anybody – We just need to be better. https://www.itpro.co.uk/technology/artificial-intelligence-ai/370292/gpt-4-shouldnt-worry-anybody-we-just-need-to-be-better

Oppenheimer, R. (1965). The trinity test. *Atomic Archives*.

Papenfuss, M. (2023, March 17). *Creepy Microsoft Bing Chatbot urges Tech Columnist to leave his wife*. https://www.google.com

PR Newswire. (2023, April 4). *Survey Finds 6 in 10 hiring managers have received more high quality applications since ChatGPT launch*. Resume Builder.com. https://www.benzinga.com/pressreleases/

Raine, L., Anderson, J., & Vogels, E. (2021). *Experts doubt ethical AI design will be broadly adopted as the norm within the next decade.* http//www.pewresearch.org

Romero, A. (2021). *Understanding GDP3.* https://towardsdatascience.com/understanding-gpt-3-in-5-minutes-7fe35c3a1e52

Sage, R. (2000). *Class talk: Successful learning through effective communication.* Bloomsbury.

Sage, R., Sage, L., & Kaczmarek, B. (2023). A UK study of thinking and language expression. *The New Educational Review.*

World Bank. (2019). *The education crisis: Being in school is not the same as learning.*

Xiang, C. (2023, March 30). Man dies by suicide after talking with AI Chatbot. https://www.vice.com/en/article/pkadgm/man-dies-by-suicide-after-talking-with-ai-chatbot-widow-says

Appendix A: Sample 1, Riccarda Matteucci – ChatGPT3 14/12/2022

Abstract: Intercultural Communication – Positive & Negative Aspects

Intercultural communication has been an increasingly important area of study in recent years, with the increasing globalization of the world and the rise of immigration and cultural exchange. While intercultural communication can bring many benefits, such as increased understanding, improved relationships, and enhanced economic opportunities, it can also create challenges, such as misunderstandings, conflict, and discrimination.

Furthermore, intercultural communication involves the exchange of information and ideas between individuals from different cultural backgrounds. This type of communication can bring many positive benefits, such as increased understanding, improved relationships, and enhanced economic opportunities. However, there are also several negative aspects of intercultural communication that must be considered. These include misunderstandings, conflict, discrimination, and feelings of anxiety and stress. To maximize the positive aspects and minimize the negative aspects of intercultural communication, it is important to promote intercultural competence and develop policies that promote diversity and cultural exchange. Recent studies have shown that promoting intercultural communication skills and training programs can improve communication effectiveness and reduce misunderstandings and conflict promoting diversity and cultural exchange can enhance relationships and help to reduce discrimination. These findings suggest that while intercultural communication can present challenges, it is a crucial component of global cooperation and understanding.

1   Positive Aspects

1. *Enhanced Understanding*: Intercultural communication can help individuals and organizations gain a deeper understanding of different cultures and ways of thinking. This can lead to greater appreciation and respect for cultural diversity.

2. *Improved Relationships*: By communicating effectively across cultures, individuals and organizations can build stronger relationships based on mutual understanding and respect.

3. *Increased Creativity and Innovation*: Intercultural communication can lead to the exchange of new ideas and perspectives, which can stimulate creativity and innovation.

4. *Better Problem-Solving*: Intercultural communication can bring together individuals and organizations from different cultural backgrounds to collaborate and find solutions to complex problems.

5. *Enhanced Global Cooperation*: Intercultural communication is essential for building partnerships and cooperation between individuals, organizations, and nations on a global scale.

6. *Improved Business Opportunities*: Intercultural communication skills are critical for success in today's global marketplace, where organizations must work effectively across cultural boundaries to succeed.

7. *Broader Worldview*: Intercultural communication can broaden an individual's worldview by exposing them to different perspectives and ways of life, leading to greater empathy, compassion, and understanding.

1.1   *Enhanced Understanding*

Intercultural communication can enhance understanding and lead to greater appreciation and respect for cultural diversity in several ways. One of the most important benefits of intercultural communication is that it allows individuals and organizations to gain a deeper understanding of different cultures and ways of thinking. This can help to dispel stereotypes and misconceptions, as well as increase appreciation for the unique values, beliefs, and practices of other cultures.

Moreover, intercultural communication can promote open-mindedness and empathy, which are essential for building respectful and positive relationships across cultures. When individuals and organizations are able to communicate effectively across cultural boundaries, they can learn about each other's experiences, values, and perspectives, and develop a sense of mutual respect and understanding.

Additionally, intercultural communication can lead to the exchange of new ideas and perspectives, which can stimulate creativity and innovation. When individuals and organizations are exposed to diverse ways of thinking and problem-solving, they can be inspired to develop new and innovative solutions to complex challenges (Nidhi & Manjari, 2016).

In conclusion, the enhanced understanding that results from intercultural communication is critical for building strong and respectful relationships across cultures. By increasing appreciation and respect for cultural diversity, intercultural communication can promote greater cooperation, collaboration, and mutual understanding on a global scale.

1.2   *Improved Relationships*

Effective intercultural communication is essential for building relationships based on mutual understanding. When individuals and organizations are able to communicate effectively across cultural boundaries, they can learn about each other's experiences, values, and perspectives, and develop a sense of mutual respect and understanding. This can help to overcome cultural differences and build strong relationships that are based on trust, cooperation, and collaboration.

Moreover, intercultural communication promotes open-mindedness and empathy, which are essential for building positive and respectful relationships across cultures. When individuals and organizations are able to listen to each other's perspectives and experiences, they can develop a deeper understanding of each other's culture and ways of thinking. This can help to dispel stereotypes and misconceptions, and promote a more positive and respectful relationship.

Additionally, intercultural communication is essential for building partnerships and cooperation between individuals, organizations, and nations on a global scale. In today's interconnected world, organizations must be able to work effectively across cultural boundaries in order to succeed. Intercultural communication skills can help organizations to build strong relationships with customers, suppliers, partners, and other stakeholders, regardless of their cultural background (Samovar & Porter, 2015).

In conclusion, communicating effectively across cultures is critical for building relationships based on mutual understanding by promoting open-mindedness, empathy, and respect.

1.3   *Increased Creativity*

Intercultural communication can stimulate creativity and innovation by promoting the exchange of new ideas and perspectives. When individuals and organizations are exposed to diverse ways of thinking, they can be inspired to develop new and innovative solutions to complex challenges.

For example, when individuals and organizations from different cultural backgrounds collaborate on a project, they can bring a variety of unique perspectives and approaches to problem-solving. This can lead to the development of new and innovative solutions that would not have been possible without the input of diverse perspectives.

Moreover, intercultural communication can promote the sharing of best practices and knowledge across cultures. This can help organizations to stay ahead of the curve and stay competitive in today's rapidly changing global marketplace. By learning from the experiences of other cultures, organizations can gain new insights and approaches to problem-solving that can help to drive innovation and growth.

Additionally, intercultural communication can promote the exchange of new ideas and perspectives in a variety of settings, including business, education, and the arts. When individuals and organizations are exposed to diverse ways of thinking and problem-solving, they can be inspired to develop new and innovative solutions to complex challenges (Holliday, 2004).

In conclusion, intercultural communication plays a critical role in stimulating creativity and innovation by promoting the exchange of new ideas and perspectives. By exposing individuals and organizations to diverse ways of thinking, intercultural communication can help to inspire new and innovative solutions that can drive growth and progress in a variety of settings.

1.4   *Better Problem-Solving*

Intercultural communication can improve problem-solving by bringing together individuals and organizations from different cultural backgrounds to collaborate and find solutions to complex problems. When individuals and organizations are able to communicate effectively across cultural boundaries, they can work together to find creative and effective solutions to challenges that span cultural boundaries.

For example, when organizations from different cultural backgrounds collaborate on a project, they can bring a variety of unique perspectives and approaches to problem-solving. This can lead to the development of innovative solutions that would not have been possible without the input of diverse perspectives.

Moreover, intercultural communication can help to overcome cultural differences and build strong relationships that are based on trust, cooperation, and collaboration. When individuals and organizations are able to understand each other's perspectives and experiences, they can work together more effectively to find solutions to complex problems.

Additionally, intercultural communication is essential for building partnerships and cooperation between individuals, organizations, and nations on a global scale. In today's interconnected world, organizations must be able to work effectively across cultural boundaries in order to succeed. Intercultural communication skills can help organizations to build strong relationships with customers, suppliers, partners, and other stakeholders, regardless of their cultural background.

In conclusion, intercultural communication plays a critical role in improving problem-solving by bringing together individuals and organizations from different cultural backgrounds to collaborate and find solutions to complex problems. By promoting open-mindedness, empathy, and cooperation, intercultural communication can help organizations to find innovative solutions to complex challenges that span cultural boundaries.

1.5   *Enhanced Global Cooperation*

Intercultural communication plays a critical role in building cooperation among individuals, organizations, and nations globally. Effective intercultural communication can help individuals and organizations to understand each other's perspectives, experiences, and values, and develop a sense of mutual respect and understanding. This can lead to greater cooperation and collaboration, which is essential for building strong and productive relationships that span cultural boundaries.

For example, when organizations from different cultural backgrounds collaborate on a project, they can learn from each other's experiences and best practices, and work together more effectively to achieve common goals. This can lead to increased productivity, improved outcomes, and stronger relationships that are based on trust, cooperation, and collaboration.

Moreover, intercultural communication is essential for building partnerships and cooperation between organizations and nations on a global scale. In today's interconnected world, organizations must be able to work effectively across cultural boundaries in order to succeed. Intercultural communication skills can help organizations to build strong relationships with customers, suppliers, partners, and other stakeholders, regardless of their cultural background.

Additionally, intercultural communication promotes open-mindedness and empathy, which are essential for building cooperative relationships across cultures. When individuals and organizations are able to listen to each other's perspectives and experiences, they can develop a deeper understanding of each other's culture and ways of thinking. This can help to dispel stereotypes and misconceptions, and promote a more cooperative and respectful relationship (McCarty & Collins, 2011).

In conclusion, intercultural communication plays a critical role in building cooperation among individuals, organizations, and nations globally. By promoting open-mindedness, empathy, and cooperation, intercultural communication can help organizations and nations to build strong, productive, and respectful relationships that span cultural boundaries.

1.6   *Improved Business Opportunity*

Intercultural communication skills are key for success in today's global marketplace. With increased globalization and the rise of technology, organizations are more interconnected than ever, and must be able to work effectively across cultural boundaries in order to succeed. Intercultural communication skills can help organizations to build strong relationships with customers, suppliers, partners, and other stakeholders, regardless of their cultural background.

For example, effective intercultural communication skills can help organizations to build trust with customers from different cultural backgrounds, which is essential for building strong and long-lasting relationships. Intercultural communication skills can also help organizations to effectively negotiate and resolve conflicts with suppliers and partners from different cultural backgrounds.

Moreover, intercultural communication skills are essential for building partnerships and cooperation between organizations on a global scale. Organizations that are able to work effectively across cultural boundaries are better equipped to succeed in today's rapidly changing global marketplace.

Additionally, intercultural communication skills are essential for leadership in today's diverse workplace. Leaders who possess strong intercultural communication skills are able to effectively manage and lead teams that are culturally diverse, and create a positive and inclusive work environment.

In conclusion, intercultural communication skills are key for success in today's global marketplace. By promoting effective communication, trust, and cooperation across cultural boundaries, intercultural communication skills can help organizations to succeed in today's rapidly changing and interconnected world.

1.7   *Broader Worldview*

Intercultural communication has the power to broaden individuals' worldviews and expand their understanding of different cultures and perspectives. When individuals engage in intercultural communication, they have the opportunity to learn about different cultures, beliefs, values, and experiences, and gain a deeper understanding of the world around them.

For example, when individuals interact with individuals from different cultural backgrounds, they can learn about new customs, traditions, and ways of thinking that are different from their own. This can help to broaden their understanding of the world and expand their perspectives.

Moreover, intercultural communication can help individuals to develop empathy and understanding for different cultures. By learning about different cultures and perspectives, individuals can develop a greater appreciation and respect for cultural diversity, and be more open-minded and accepting of others (Hercht, Richard, & Barnard, 2002).

Additionally, intercultural communication can help individuals to develop valuable skills, such as active listening, empathy, and intercultural competence, which are essential for success in today's globalized world. Individuals who possess strong intercultural communication skills are better equipped to navigate cross-cultural interactions and build strong relationships with individuals from different cultural backgrounds.

In conclusion, intercultural communication has the power to broaden individuals' worldviews and expand their understanding of different cultures and perspectives. By promoting open-mindedness, empathy, and intercultural competence, intercultural communication can help individuals to develop a deeper understanding of the world and build stronger relationships with individuals from different cultural backgrounds.

2   Negative Aspects

While intercultural communication can bring many benefits, it can also have some negative aspects that should be considered. It is important to be aware of the potential negative aspects of intercultural communication. By being mindful of these potential challenges and working to overcome them, individuals and organizations can engage in effective intercultural communication that promotes mutual understanding, respect, and cooperation.

Some of the negative aspects of intercultural communication include:

1. *Miscommunication and misunderstandings*: Intercultural communication can sometimes lead to miscommunication and misunderstandings, due to differences in language, values, and cultural norms. For example, gestures or expressions that are common in one culture may be seen as inappropriate or offensive in another culture.

2. *Stereotyping and prejudice*: Intercultural communication can sometimes reinforce stereotypes and prejudice, as individuals may make assumptions about individuals from different cultures based on limited exposure or negative media representation. This can lead to misunderstandings and conflict.

3. *Cultural imperialism*: Intercultural communication can sometimes perpetuate cultural imperialism, as individuals from dominant cultures may impose their beliefs, values, and practices on individuals from less dominant cultures. This can lead to the suppression of cultural diversity and the erasure of cultural heritage.

4. *Power imbalances*: Intercultural communication can sometimes reinforce power imbalances, as individuals from dominant cultures may have more power and influence in cross-cultural interactions. This can lead to unequal treatment and the marginalization of individuals from less dominant cultures.

5. *Resistance to change*: Intercultural communication can sometimes encounter resistance from individuals who are resistant to change, as individuals may be reluctant to learn about new cultures and ways of thinking. This can lead to a lack of intercultural competence and ineffective communication.

2.1   *Miscommunication and Misunderstandings*

Miscommunication and misunderstandings are common in intercultural communication, due to differences in language, values, and cultural norms. These differences can make it difficult for individuals from different cultures to understand each other and effectively communicate their ideas and perspectives.

For example, individuals from different cultures may have different expectations for communication style, such as the use of direct or indirect language, the level of formality in communication, and the use of nonverbal cues. These differences can lead to misunderstandings and miscommunication, as individuals may misinterpret the intended message or fail to understand the nuances of communication.

Additionally, differences in values and cultural norms can also lead to misunderstandings in intercultural communication. For example, what may be considered polite and respectful in one culture may be seen as impolite or insensitive in another culture. These differences in values and cultural norms can lead to miscommunication and conflict in intercultural interactions.

It is important for individuals engaged in intercultural communication to be aware of these potential challenges and to take steps to overcome them. For example, individuals can learn about different cultures and ways of communicating, and work to develop intercultural competence. Additionally, individuals can engage in active listening and seek to understand the perspectives of others, and communicate in a way that is respectful and sensitive to cultural differences (Gudykunst & Kim, 1997).

In conclusion, miscommunication and misunderstandings are a common challenge in intercultural communication, due to differences in language, values, and cultural norms. However, by being aware of these potential challenges and working to overcome them, individuals and organizations can engage in effective intercultural communication that promotes mutual understanding and cooperation.

2.2   *Stereotyping and Prejudice*

Stereotyping and prejudice are common barriers to effective intercultural communication. Stereotyping is the act of assigning characteristics or traits to individuals or groups based on preconceived notions or generalizations about their culture, race, ethnicity, or other group identity. Prejudice is a negative attitude or opinion towards someone based on their group identity.

Stereotyping and prejudice can lead to misunderstandings, miscommunications, and even conflict between individuals or groups from different cultures. They can also create feelings of alienation and marginalization among members of a particular cultural group.

For example, if someone assumes that all members of a particular culture are lazy, dishonest, or uneducated, they are more likely to interact with those individuals in a negative or dismissive manner. This can lead to misunderstandings and negative perceptions, ultimately hindering effective communication and mutual understanding.

To overcome these barriers, it is important to be aware of our own biases and prejudices, as well as to actively challenge the stereotypes and prejudices of others. By approaching intercultural communication with an open mind and a willingness to learn, we can build stronger relationships, foster mutual respect, and promote understanding and appreciation of cultural differences (Lin, Fang, & Lin, 2017).

2.3   Cultural Imperialism

Cultural imperialism is a negative aspect of intercultural communication, as it involves the imposition of the beliefs, values, and practices of a dominant culture on less dominant cultures. This can lead to the suppression of cultural diversity and the erasure of cultural heritage, as individuals from less dominant cultures may feel pressure to adopt the ways of thinking and behaviors of the dominant culture.

For example, in the context of globalization, individuals from dominant cultures may seek to spread their culture and way of life globally, and impose their cultural norms and values on others. This can lead to the loss of traditional cultural practices and beliefs, and the homogenization of cultural diversity.

Furthermore, cultural imperialism can reinforce power imbalances and perpetuate inequality, as individuals from dominant cultures may have more power and influence in intercultural interactions. This can lead to the marginalization of individuals from less dominant cultures, and the perpetuation of systemic discrimination and oppression.

It is important for individuals and organizations to be aware of the potential for cultural imperialism in intercultural communication, and to take steps to overcome it. For example, individuals can seek to learn about and respect different cultures, and work to promote cultural diversity and the preservation of cultural heritage. Additionally, individuals and organizations can work to ensure that cross-cultural interactions are based on mutual respect and equality, and that power imbalances are not reinforced.

In conclusion, cultural imperialism is a negative aspect of intercultural communication, as it can lead to the suppression of cultural diversity and the erasure of cultural heritage. By being aware of this potential challenge and taking steps to overcome it, individuals and organizations can engage in intercultural communication that promotes cultural diversity and mutual respect.

2.4   Power Imbalances

Intercultural communication can reinforce power imbalances that can result in unequal treatment, as individuals from dominant cultures may have more power and influence in cross-cultural interactions. This can lead to a situation where individuals from less dominant cultures are marginalized and subject to unequal treatment, and where their perspectives, opinions, and needs are not fully heard or addressed (Bhopal, 2001).

For example, in intercultural communication, individuals from dominant cultures may have greater access to resources and opportunities, and may be more likely to have their ideas and opinions heard and respected. On the other hand, individuals from less dominant cultures may face barriers to participating in cross-cultural interactions and may be subject to stereotypes and discrimination.

Additionally, power imbalances in intercultural communication can perpetuate systemic inequalities, as individuals from less dominant cultures may be subject to discriminatory policies and practices that reinforce their marginalization.

It is important for individuals and organizations to be aware of the potential for power imbalances in intercultural communication, and to take steps to overcome them. For example, individuals can seek to build bridges across cultural differences and promote mutual understanding, and organizations can ensure that intercultural interactions are based on equality and respect. Additionally, individuals and organizations can work to address systemic inequalities, and to ensure that all individuals are treated fairly and equitably.

In conclusion, intercultural communication can reinforce power imbalances that can lead to unequal treatment, and it is important for individuals and organizations to be aware of this potential challenge and to take steps to overcome it. By promoting mutual understanding, respect, and equality in cross-cultural interactions, individuals and organizations can help to ensure that all voices are heard and that cultural differences are valued and celebrated.

2.5   *Resistance to Change*

Individuals may be reluctant to learn about new cultures, and this can be a barrier to successful intercultural integration. Some people may feel intimidated by cultural differences, or they may be uncertain about how to interact with individuals from different cultures. This reluctance can result in a lack of understanding and appreciation for other cultures, and it can prevent individuals from engaging in meaningful intercultural interactions.

For example, some individuals may believe that their own cultural values and norms are superior, and they may be resistant to learning about and accepting different cultural perspectives. This can lead to a situation where individuals are unwilling to engage in cross-cultural interactions, and where they are less likely to develop meaningful relationships with individuals from different cultures (Kuo & Hu, 2015).

Additionally, individuals may be reluctant to learn about new cultures due to a lack of exposure or opportunity. For example, individuals who grow up in homogeneous communities may not have had the opportunity to learn about or interact with individuals from other cultures.

It is important for individuals and organizations to work to overcome this reluctance to learn about new cultures, and to encourage individuals to engage in intercultural interactions. For example, individuals can seek out opportunities to learn about different cultures, such as attending cultural events or traveling to new places.

Additionally, organizations can create opportunities for intercultural interaction and learning, and they can provide resources and support to help individuals overcome their reluctance to engage with different cultures.

In conclusion, individuals may be reluctant to learn about new cultures, but this can be a barrier to successful intercultural integration. By working to overcome this reluctance and encouraging individuals to engage in intercultural interactions, individuals and organizations can help to promote mutual understanding, respect, and a appreciation for cultural diversity.

3   Review

Intercultural communication has both positive and negative aspects that need to be considered. On the positive side, intercultural communication can lead to greater understanding and appreciation for cultural diversity. By engaging with individuals from different cultures, individuals can learn about different perspectives, values, and norms, and this can help to break down stereotypes and promote mutual respect.

Additionally, intercultural communication can lead to creativity and innovation, as individuals from different cultures bring unique perspectives and ideas to the table. This can result in new and innovative solutions to complex problems.

On the negative side, intercultural communication can result in miscommunication and misunderstanding due to differences in language, values, and cultural norms. Additionally, intercultural communication can reinforce power imbalances, leading to unequal treatment and suppression of cultural diversity and cultural heritage.

Furthermore, some individuals may be reluctant to learn about new cultures, and this can be a barrier to successful intercultural integration. This reluctance can result in a lack of understanding and appreciation for other cultures, and it can prevent individuals from engaging in meaningful intercultural interactions.

Therefore, intercultural communication has both positive and negative aspects that need to be considered. While it can lead to greater understanding and appreciation for cultural diversity, it can also result in miscommunication and misunderstanding, reinforce power imbalances, and perpetuate cultural suppression. By being aware of these potential challenges, individuals and organizations can work to promote mutual understanding, respect, and equality in intercultural interactions.

References

1.   "The Handbook of Intercultural Discourse and Communication" edited by S. K. Nidhi and S. K. Manjari (2016). This handbook provides a comprehensive

overview of the field of intercultural communication and includes chapters on topics such as language and culture, cultural differences, intercultural relationships, and intercultural communication in the workplace.

2. "Intercultural Communication: A Reader" edited by Larry A. Samovar and Richard E. Porter (2015). This reader provides a diverse collection of articles and essays on intercultural communication and covers topics such as cultural differences, communication across cultures, intercultural relationships, and globalization.

3. "Intercultural Communication: An Advanced Resource Book" by Adrian Holliday (2004). This advanced resource book provides an in-depth examination of intercultural communication and includes chapters on topics such as language and culture, communication across cultures, intercultural relationships, and intercultural communication in a global context.

4. "Intercultural Communication: Globalization and Social Justice" edited by Teresa L. McCarty and James R. Collins (2011). This book provides an overview of intercultural communication from a social justice perspective and includes chapters on topics such as cultural diversity, communication across cultures, intercultural relationships, and globalization.

5. "Culture and Interpersonal Communication" edited by Michael J. Hecht, Richard R. Alba, and Lisa L. Barnard (2002). This book provides a comprehensive examination of the role of culture in interpersonal communication and includes chapters on topics such as cultural differences, communication across cultures, intercultural relationships, and cultural imperialism.

These references should provide a good starting point for further exploration of the field of intercultural communication.

Bhopal, K. (2001). *Intercultural communication and the media*. Sage Publications.

Chen, Y., & Starosta, W. J. (1998). *Intercultural communication competence in the workplace*. Sage Publications.

Gudykunst, W. B., & Kim, Y. Y. (1997). *Bridging differences: Effective intergroup communication*. Sage Publications.

Kuo, Y.-H., & Hu, P.-J. (2015). The challenges and strategies of intercultural communication in the classroom. *Journal of Intercultural Communication Research, 44*(2), 123–138.

Liu, Y., & Rigg, J. (2012). *Intercultural communication in multinational corporations*. Routledge.

Lin, J., Fang, X., & Lin, Z. (2017). The challenges of intercultural communication in healthcare settings. *Journal of Intercultural Communication Research, 46*(3), 227–239.

Appendix B: Sample 2, Rosemary Sage – ChatGPT3 07/01/2023

Abstract: Positive Aspects of Intercultural Communication

Intercultural communication refers to the exchange of information between individuals from different cultures. The positive aspects of intercultural communication are numerous and range from enhanced understanding and empathy to improved business relations and international cooperation. In this article, we will explore the benefits of intercultural communication in depth. We will examine recent research in the field, including studies on the impact of intercultural communication on cross-cultural understanding, conflict resolution, and globalization. We will also discuss the challenges that can arise in intercultural communication and strategies for overcoming them. Overall, this article will provide a comprehensive overview of the positive aspects of intercultural communication and the important role it plays in our increasingly interconnected world.

Article

Intercultural communication has become an increasingly important topic in today's globalized world. As individuals from different cultures interact with one another more frequently, the ability to communicate effectively across cultural boundaries has become essential. While there are certainly challenges that can arise in intercultural communication, the positive aspects of this form of communication are numerous and far-reaching.

Intercultural communication refers to the exchange of information and ideas between individuals or groups from different cultural backgrounds. It is a complex process that involves understanding and interpreting cultural differences and similarities, as well as the impact of these differences on communication.

At its core, intercultural communication involves navigating differences in language, customs, values, beliefs, and norms, among other factors. It requires a high level of sensitivity, empathy, and respect for diversity, as well as a willingness to adapt one's communication style to effectively engage with individuals from different cultures.

Intercultural communication is a critical component of today's globalized world, where individuals from diverse backgrounds are increasingly connected through technology and travel. Effective intercultural communication is essential for successful business relationships, diplomatic interactions, and personal relationships.

To navigate the complexities of intercultural communication, individuals must develop cultural competence, which involves a deep understanding of their own cultural background, as well as an appreciation for and understanding of other cultures. This requires ongoing education and training, as well as a commitment to ongoing self-reflection and self-improvement.

In sum, intercultural communication is a critical skill for individuals to develop in order to effectively engage with individuals from diverse cultural backgrounds. It requires a deep understanding of cultural differences and similarities, as well as the ability to adapt communication styles to effectively engage with individuals from different cultures.

One of the most significant benefits of intercultural communication is the enhanced understanding and empathy that can result from cross-cultural interactions. When individuals from different cultures interact with one another, they are exposed to new perspectives and ways of thinking. This exposure can broaden their own understanding of the world and lead to greater empathy and tolerance for those who are different from them.

Research has also shown that intercultural communication can play a key role in conflict resolution. When individuals from different cultures are able to communicate effectively, they are better able to find common ground and work toward mutually beneficial solutions. This is particularly important in the context of international relations, where cultural misunderstandings can often lead to conflicts and even wars.

In addition to these benefits, intercultural communication can also improve business relations and promote international cooperation. As companies increasingly operate on a global scale, the ability to communicate effectively with individuals from different cultures has become essential. Companies that are able to navigate cultural differences successfully are more likely to succeed in international markets and build strong partnerships with foreign businesses.

Despite these benefits, there are certainly challenges that can arise in intercultural communication. These challenges can include differences in language, nonverbal communication, and cultural norms. However, there are strategies that can be employed to overcome these challenges. These strategies can include learning the language of the other culture, studying their cultural norms and values, and practicing active listening and empathy.

In conclusion, the positive aspects of intercultural communication are numerous and far-reaching. As our world becomes increasingly interconnected, the ability to communicate effectively across cultural boundaries has become essential. By embracing the benefits of intercultural communication and developing strategies to overcome its challenges, we can build a more understanding and tolerant world.

References

Gudykunst, W. B., & Kim, Y. Y. (2017). *Communicating with strangers: An approach to intercultural communication*. Routledge.

Hall, E. T. (2017). *The hidden dimension*. Anchor.

Hofstede, G. (2011). Dimensionalizing cultures: The Hofstede model in context. *Online Readings in Psychology and Culture, 2*(1), 8.

Kim, Y. Y. (2015). *Communication and cross-cultural adaptation: An integrative theory*. Routledge.

Samovar, L. A., Porter, R. E., McDaniel, E. R., & Roy, C. S. (2016). *Intercultural communication: A reader*. Cengage Learning.

Abstract: Negative Aspects of Intercultural Communication

Intercultural communication has become increasingly important in today's globalized world. However, there are also negative aspects to intercultural communication that must be considered. In this article, we will explore the negative consequences of intercultural communication, including misunderstandings, stereotypes, and discrimination. We will also examine the role of power dynamics and how they can affect intercultural communication. Finally, we will discuss ways to mitigate these negative aspects and promote more positive intercultural communication.

Article

Intercultural communication refers to the exchange of information and ideas between people from different cultural backgrounds. While intercultural communication can be enriching and rewarding, it can also have negative consequences. In this article, we will explore some of the negative aspects of intercultural communication.

Misunderstandings

One of the biggest challenges of intercultural communication is the potential for misunderstandings. Different cultures may have different ways of expressing themselves, which can lead to confusion or misinterpretation. For example, a gesture that is perfectly acceptable in one culture may be considered rude or offensive in another. Similarly, the use of humor or sarcasm may be interpreted differently depending on the cultural context.

Stereotypes

Stereotyping is another negative aspect of intercultural communication. Stereotypes are preconceived notions about a group of people based on their cultural background. Stereotypes can lead to discrimination and prejudice, as well as misunderstandings. For example, assuming that all members of a particular culture are aggressive or untrustworthy can lead to negative interactions.

Discrimination

Discrimination is another negative consequence of intercultural communication. Discrimination occurs when people are treated unfairly because of their cultural background. Discrimination can be overt, such as refusing to hire someone because of their ethnicity, or more subtle, such as excluding someone from a social group because of their accent.

Power Dynamics

Power dynamics can also play a role in intercultural communication. Power refers to the ability to influence others or control resources. In intercultural communication, power imbalances can arise when one culture has more influence or resources than another. This can lead to unequal communication and unequal outcomes. For example, a native speaker of a dominant language may have more influence in a conversation than a non-native speaker.

Mitigating Negative Aspects of Intercultural Communication

While there are negative aspects of intercultural communication, there are also ways to mitigate these negative consequences. Some strategies include:

- Developing cultural competence: Cultural competence refers to the ability to understand, appreciate, and interact effectively with people from different cultures. By developing cultural competence, individuals can reduce misunderstandings and stereotypes, and promote more positive intercultural communication.
- Building relationships: Building relationships with people from different cultures can help to mitigate negative aspects of intercultural communication. By building trust and understanding, individuals can overcome stereotypes and promote more positive interactions.

– Challenging power imbalances: Challenging power imbalances can also help to mitigate negative aspects of intercultural communication. By advocating for equal communication and equal outcomes, individuals can promote more positive intercultural communication.

Conclusion

Intercultural communication is a complex and challenging process. While there are negative aspects of intercultural communication, such as misunderstandings, stereotypes, discrimination, and power imbalances, there are also ways to mitigate these negative consequences. By developing cultural competence, building relationships, and challenging power imbalances, individuals can promote more positive intercultural communication.

References

Gudykunst, W. B. (2017). *Bridging differences: Effective intergroup communication.* Sage Publications.

Kim, Y. Y. (2016). *Communication and cross-cultural adaptation: An integrative theory.* Routledge.

Martin, J., & Nakayama, T. (2022). *Intercultural communication in contexts* (8th ed. Prek-12 Higher-Ed). McGraw Hill.